Eight Fundamentals
of the
Christian Faith

Dr. Charles R. Vogan Jr.

1 2

ISBN 978-0-6151-3862-6

Ravenbrook Publishers

A subsidiary of
Shenandoah Bible Ministries

www.shenbible.org

Copyright © 1997 Charles R. Vogan Jr.
All rights reserved

Scripture taken from the HOLY BIBLE, NEW INTERNATIONAL VERSION, Copyright © 1973, 1978, 1984 International Bible Society. Used by permission of Zondervan Bible Publishers.

Contents

Introduction	1
The Importance of Knowledge	10
The Knowledge of God	49
The Fear of the Lord	87
Faith in Christ	128
The Christian and the Law	176
Led by the Spirit	213
The Church	273
Judgment Day	315
Conclusion	360

Introduction

People in the Church have come from different backgrounds. Some people grew up in the Church, and their families were active in Church functions. They learned a lot about the Bible from their youth, like young Timothy:

> But as for you, continue in what you have learned and have become convinced of, because you know those from whom you learned it, and how from infancy you have known the holy Scriptures, which are able to make you wise for salvation through faith in Christ Jesus. (2 Timothy 3:14-15)

Other people have had very little experience in the Church before they were converted; they knew almost nothing about the Bible, and everything they learned from that point on would be entirely new to them. Still others have had a lot of "unlearning" to do, because before they were converted they spent a lot of time in the enemy's camp. All they knew were lies and half-truths. They were experts in the "vain philosophies" of this world.

So at our conversion to Christianity we may already know a lot or just a little bit about what's going on. The Bible may either be a familiar book to us already, or a perfectly strange book to us. Thankfully, conversion itself doesn't depend on how familiar we were with God in our past. The moment that Christ personally confronts us and deals with our souls, all he is working on for the moment is the *root* problem: the fact that we are dead

Introduction

to God, dead in sin, and without hope for eternal life. Conversion is literally a spiritual resurrection from the dead, so that now we walk in the light (1 John 1:7) and can see and know God. Once he gets us to that point of spiritual life, he can start working on other issues.

And one of the things he's going to start working on after conversion is helping us with knowledge about God's spiritual world. He wants to lay the necessary groundwork for the things in the future that he has planned for us. It's like training a soldier for battle: the soldier has to go through drill camp, and specialized training, in order to be ready for combat. God has a lot of work for us to do, and he has high expectations of us. When troubles, temptations and trials come, will we know what to do in order to honor him? When he sends people to us who are in desperate need, will we know what to do to help them? When the enemy launches a furious attack, will we know how to stop him and push him back?

All these future circumstances will require *knowledge of the truth.* Every Christian has to have a certain amount of knowledge if he/she hopes to "persevere to the end" and be saved. But now we might ask, how much knowledge is necessary? How much should the average Christian know in order to adequately fulfill his responsibilities? Here there seems to be a lot of difference of opinion among Christians! But the book of Hebrews, fortunately, spells it out for us:

> We have much to say about this, but it is hard to explain because you are slow to learn. In fact, though by this time you ought to be teachers, you need someone to teach you the elementary truths of God's word all over again. You need milk, not solid food! Anyone who lives on milk, being still an infant, is not acquainted with the teaching about righteousness. But solid food is for the mature, who

Introduction

> by constant use have trained themselves to distinguish good from evil.
>
> Therefore let us leave the elementary teachings about Christ and go on to maturity, not laying again the foundation of repentance from acts that lead to death, and of faith in God, instruction about baptisms, the laying on of hands, the resurrection of the dead, and eternal judgment. And God permitting, we will do so. (Hebrews 5:11 – 6:3)

The author is talking about **fundamentals of the faith**, the very basics of what each of us *have* to know in order to get along in God's Kingdom. We could describe it like this: we live in a new world now – God's spiritual world – that Christ brought us into at our conversion. ***These truths describe our new surroundings to us so that we know where we are, the basic rules, and the resources that are available to us.*** The Bible is literally our roadmap guiding us through this world to our destination: Heaven.

In other words, if we are ignorant about *these* things, we are like lost tourists in a strange land who don't know the language or customs. Ignorant Christians are actually wandering around lost in God's spiritual world, completely at a loss about what's going on around them. They don't know where to turn for help, and they wouldn't know what to ask for if they found someone. They don't even know much about their Lord – which is obvious when they blunder into God's presence without the necessary ceremony and blurt out whatever inappropriate thing comes to mind instead of bowing down to the Master in fear and reverence!

And notice that these things listed in Hebrews are just the fundamentals; there's more to come. The author wishes his students knew more than just the basics! For a life of service to God, in order to fully honor God in all things and bring him the glory he richly deserves, in order to build the Church into a holy

Introduction

and eternal dwelling place for the Lord, and in order to endure persecution faithfully to the end, *we have much more to learn than this simple list!* These are just the fundamentals of the faith; they're designed to give us a simplified understanding of the spiritual world that we're part of now. They are like a basic course in geography – to help us understand the lay of the land we're in – and a basic course in history – to help us understand how things got to be the way they are. Once we have mastered these basics, we need to *move on*, to *learn more*, to "go on to maturity," in order to carry out our mission on earth.

Unfortunately many Christians don't even know these basics! "In fact, though by this time you ought to be teachers, you need someone to teach you the elementary truths of God's Word all over again. You need milk, not solid food!" The author thinks it's a shame that his students know so little about the very basics of the faith. What happened? What went wrong? Did they purposely turn their backs on the teaching in the Church? Did someone fail them and not teach them these things? Whatever the reason behind their ignorance, he feels that his hands are tied: there are more important issues to deal with, issues that will involve the great work of God that we're going to be involved in, yet his readers are way behind right now. It's going to be difficult, if not impossible, to bring them up to speed and train them in what they need for coming trials.

In fact, he can see dangers here that perhaps you and I haven't been aware of. Ignorant Christians are playing dangerous games. It's quite possible to get "converted," become part of a church, enjoy the Gospel blessings, fellowship with other Christians, read the Bible, worship God and pray to him – and yet, because of ignorance of the basics of the faith, *turn one's back on Christ in the end.* Sadly, many churches have people who do this.

> It is impossible for those who have once been enlightened, who have tasted the Heavenly gift, who have shared in the Holy Spirit, who have tasted the

Introduction

> goodness of the word of God and the powers of the coming age, if they fall away, to be brought back to repentance, because to their loss they are crucifying the Son of God all over again and subjecting him to public disgrace. (Hebrews 6:4-6)

That such a thing should happen is a condemnation of our poor educational system in the Church. Christians ought to be required to learn the fundamentals of the faith as soon as they profess Christ as Savior. This would go a long way to prevent the public embarrassment that the Church often suffers when so-called Christians turn their backs on the Gospel and dishonor the "Sovereign Lord who bought them." (2 Peter 2:1)

Many more Christians in the Church suffer from ignorance in a less tragic way, though any degree of ignorance is nothing to be proud of. Without at least a basic knowledge of God and his Kingdom, the teaching that they do come under – sermons, Sunday School lessons, Bible studies, etc. – will have little or no effect on them. Truth washes over them like rain over an umbrella. In order to assimilate the lessons that church leaders give them, they have to have at least a basic understanding of the truth; but without that, what is said in Church doesn't mean much to them and they never do get the point.

> Land that drinks in the rain often falling on it and that produces a crop useful to those for whom it is farmed receives the blessing of God. But land that produces thorns and thistles is worthless and is in danger of being cursed. In the end it will be burned. (Hebrews 6:7-8)

Jesus told us that not only does he expect this from many that hear the Gospel, but he will also take measures to deny any more knowledge to those who despise the truth.

Introduction

> The knowledge of the secrets of the kingdom of Heaven has been given to you, but not to them. Whoever has will be given more, and he will have an abundance. Whoever does not have, even what he has will be taken from him. This is why I speak to them in parables: "Though seeing, they do not see; though hearing, they do not hear or understand." (Matthew 13:11-13)

Ignorance will be rewarded with God's rejection, not God's acceptance. Unfruitful professing Christians are as much a curse to the Church as briers in a flower garden.

Preserving the truth in the Church has always been a priority. Paul was constantly concerned that his spiritual charges learn the truth just as he taught it; he also expected them to pass it on unchanged, just as they received it from him.

> And the things you have heard me say in the presence of many witnesses entrust to reliable men who will also be qualified to teach others. (2 Timothy 2:2)

Christians must realize that the Lord Jesus organized the Church to preserve and pass on the truth of God. He built into its structure the necessary functions that will provide nourishment for God's children. The leaders of a church need to make sure the flow of truth inside Church functions remains free and unobstructed, so that the "pure milk of the Word" can get to all the people of God. If we don't recognize how he organized this to happen, or (what would be worse) if we work against his plan, people will shrivel up spiritually and won't be able to carry out their responsibilities under God.

> It was he who gave some to be Apostles, some to be prophets, some to be evangelists, and some to be pastors and teachers, to prepare God's people for

Introduction

> works of service, so that the body of Christ may be built up until we all reach unity in the faith and in the knowledge of the Son of God and become mature, attaining to the whole measure of the fullness of Christ. Then we will no longer be infants, tossed back and forth by the waves, and blown here and there by every wind of teaching and by the cunning and craftiness of men in their deceitful scheming. Instead, speaking the truth in love, we will in all things grow up into him who is the Head, that is, Christ. From him the whole body, joined and held together by every supporting ligament, grows and builds itself up in love, as each part does its work. (Ephesians 4:11-16)

And this fits in with one more thing that we ought to notice from the Hebrews passage: not only do we need to know these basics, *we ought to know them well enough to teach others.* The author is really pinning us to the wall about this. It's not an easy matter to teach something to someone. If you've ever tried it, you know already that you have to know it *very well* if you want your student to understand it. It's been said that a successful teacher has to know ten times more about his subject than what he intends to give his/her students; this is so that he will be able to sort through exactly what to say, and how to say it, to make it stick in the student's mind.

But not only will this deeper knowledge benefit our own understanding of the truth, we also have the responsibility to pass on the faith to the next generation. They need to know these things too. Who else will teach them except we who first learned it? If our students see that we love it enough to take it seriously and set up the church in a way that this information *will* get passed on to succeeding generations, then they will also take it seriously. Perhaps our present crisis of the younger generation turning away from the church in droves is because they can see how little importance we put on these truths ourselves. If church

Introduction

is just a matter of empty and meaningless ceremony, with little or no real knowledge behind it, that won't appeal to a generation looking for answers. *We* will be responsible for their falling away.

What we want to do in this study, therefore, is cover the fundamentals of the faith. As you go through them, notice the method:

> **First**, the material is sketchy at best. Each fundamental of the faith is a broad topic, and unless we want to write an entire book on each one, we have to keep it short. Obviously there is much that we could have looked at, but we don't have the chance to here. So it will be up to you to search the subject further in the Bible and get well-grounded in it.

> **Second**, you will find that the lessons often take the time to correct faulty thinking. It ought to be no surprise, when you think about it, that Christians who are brand new to the world of God have a lot of mistaken notions about God from their past. They have been taught for years at the feet of their former master, the great Enemy of our souls, the Father of lies (John 8:44). When they first enter the world of light, they bring with them a lot of baggage from the world's way of thinking that has to be discarded.

Finally, if some of this is new even to older Christians, that shouldn't be a surprise to you either. The modern Church hasn't been doing a very good job at training converts in the fundamentals of the faith. (One proof of this is the dismal fact that millions of new converts to the cults of our day came from mainline Christian denominations – they weren't taught the truth, so they don't know a lie when they hear one.) Usually what happens when someone is converted is that they are welcomed

Introduction

joyously to the ranks of the faithful, encouraged to worship and pray and witness, and then left to fend for themselves when it comes to Christian education or the mastery of the Bible. They struggle to understand sermons and Sunday School lessons without the benefit of an introductory Bible survey course or lessons on how to study the Bible for themselves. It should be no wonder that, even later when they've experienced a lot of Christian life, they still have holes in their Christian world view that nobody filled in for them. Hopefully we can do that here.

The Importance of Knowledge

**The heart of the discerning acquires knowledge;
the ears of the wise seek it out. (Proverbs 18:15)**

Among some people it seems to be the accepted practice to belittle or even ridicule those who value knowledge. It happens all the time in the secular world. Those who despise "knowledge" don't trust others who have an education; they argue that an education isn't necessary to get along in the world. In fact, they often accuse those who have a lot of "book learning" of not having any common sense.

But we also hear this quite frequently in the Church. Many people feel that the Bible itself warns against "accumulating knowledge," that knowledge "puffs up" and actually gets in the way of one's spiritual growth. It is far better, they say, to live the simple life and love God with all your heart. That's all that is necessary for a Christian to do.

You will often find, however, that those who think that getting knowledge can be spiritually harmful do not, themselves, have much knowledge of the Bible. Not only does this idea contradict the plain teaching of the Bible, you will probably never meet a person who had a deep knowledge of the Scriptures who regretted having that knowledge. They may regret not using it more, and they may regret not having even more knowledge, but they were never sorry about what God taught them.

The Importance of Knowledge

Some of those who teach against getting knowledge, if they were cornered, would probably admit that it isn't knowledge *itself* that is bad for us, but the way we use or don't use the knowledge we have. But, they would hasten to say, at least we ought not to be so caught up with accumulating more knowledge when we haven't yet mastered what we already know. But there are others who sincerely think that pursuing knowledge for its own sake is unbecoming to a spiritually minded Christian.

We must disagree with their argument. Not only does the Bible itself teach against this idea, it actually encourages the *accumulation* of knowledge — for many reasons. And the very thing that these people fear — the accumulation of knowledge when one hasn't yet put it all into practice — is, according to the Word of God, the mark of a *wise man*.

As is usual in such disagreements, there are at least two problems here: *first*, people have to be more careful about what the Bible actually says about something, instead of reading what they want to see into the text. *Second*, in order to magnify the problems that can be associated with knowledge, they ignore the benefits (which much outweigh the problems) and so end up with an unbalanced view of the truth. It's much safer to let the Bible speak for itself; if there are potential problems, God's Word will faithfully let us know about them without our sincere but misguided help.

Our position here is that **knowledge is fundamental to the Christian life and the Kingdom of God.** Without knowledge, there is no Christianity, no work of the Church, and certainly no glory to God in our works. Though there are problems that often arise, we have no right to despise or reject the pursuit of knowledge any more than we can the holiness of life, which is also riddled with problems. *It is our Christian duty before God to gain knowledge.*

The Importance of Knowledge

The world's knowledge

Even in the world's eyes, knowledge is critical for reaching one's goals. Education is an important building block of any society; an *educated* citizen, we are often told, is a *responsible* citizen. Businesses rely on knowledgeable employees to do their jobs well. We select leaders for our community from knowledgeable and "wise" people who have proven that they know what they are doing.

Let's look at an example. If you would walk around a construction site when people are working on a building, you would find that there are different levels of employees. There are low-level jobs for those who don't have much knowledge of construction in general; they can nail up a board somewhere or haul mortar to the bricklayers. There are more responsible jobs for those who have more knowledge. And those who understand the entire operation are overseers, the architects and senior contractors. The job level depends on one's knowledge and skills. This is true in any job or business in our society.

Why are people's jobs different according to the level of knowledge that they have? Because you can't risk ruining the job! Ignorance jeopardizes the project. If a man knows nothing more than how to haul cement, what would the building look like if he was given the responsibility of overseeing the entire project? It would be a disaster. The person who oversees the project has to be completely knowledgeable about his job: he knows how to schedule the steps of the project, and knows what the individual workmen must do, and knows the building code, and how to estimate and keep to the planned costs, and so on.

This is so obvious in the work world that almost nobody questions it. Nobody would ever put a plumber in charge of launching a rocket to the moon! Someone on a lower rung of the job ladder may be jealous of those over him who have more knowledge, and he may despise them for their knowledge, but society doesn't take him seriously. It can't afford to. Everyone has his sphere of activity for which he is skilled.

But, unfortunately, this ignorance rules too often in the Church among Christians. "Fools are put in many high positions, while the rich occupy the low ones. I have seen slaves on horseback, while princes go on foot like slaves." (Ecclesiastes 10:6-7) People who don't know what they are talking about are put in positions of leadership to make policy, while those who have a profound understanding of God's truth are despised and ignored. New-born Christians, and even immoral hypocrites, have the "right" to voice their (ignorant) opinions against the sound judgment of older and wiser believers. Why? Because knowledge is at a premium among God's people today, and popularity and reputation are the deciding factors in choosing leaders and deciding issues. This means, of course, that the work of the Church is often shoddy or even ruined compared to what it could and should be.

The Bible's testimony of knowledge

Following are most of the passages in the Old Testament and the New Testament that deal with the subject of knowledge. You should understand that these are only those passages that use the word "knowledge" — there are many more passages that use the words "knowing" and "understanding" and "wisdom."

Bezalel received knowledge to build Temple — *Exodus 31:3*
Solomon's request for knowledge honored — *2 Chron. 1:10*
the heavens declare knowledge — *Psalm 19:2*
David's request for knowledge — *Psalm 119:66*
knowledge and discretion to the young — *Proverbs 1:4*
fear of the Lord is the beginning of knowledge — *Proverbs 1:7*
fools hate knowledge — *Proverbs 1:22,29*
find the knowledge of God — *Proverbs 2:5*
God gives knowledge — *Proverbs 2:6*
knowledge is pleasant to the soul — *Proverbs 2:10*
God created world by his knowledge — *Proverbs 3:20*

The Importance of Knowledge

may your lips preserve knowledge — *Proverbs 5:2*
those with knowledge appreciate wisdom — *Proverbs 8:9*
choose knowledge rather than gold — *Proverbs 8:10*
wisdom possesses knowledge — *Proverbs 8:12*
knowledge of the Holy One is understanding — *Proverbs 9:10*
folly is without knowledge — *Proverbs 9:13*
wise men store up knowledge — *Proverbs 10:14*
through knowledge the righteous escape wicked — *Prov. 11:9*
whoever loves discipline loves knowledge — *Proverbs 12:1*
the prudent man acts out of knowledge — *Proverbs 13:16*
knowledge comes easily to the discerning — *Proverbs 14:6*
stay away from a foolish man without knowledge — *Prov. 14:7*
the prudent are crowned with knowledge — *Proverbs 14:18*
the tongue of the wise commends knowledge — *Proverbs 15:2*
the lips of the wise spread knowledge — *Proverbs 15:7*
a discerning heart seeks knowledge — *Proverbs 15:14; 18:15*
man of knowledge uses words with restraint — *Proverbs 17:27*
not good to have zeal without knowledge — *Proverbs 19:2*
rebuke discerning man, he will gain knowledge — *Prov.19:25*
don't stray from words of knowledge — *Proverbs 19:27*
lips that speak knowledge are a rare jewel — *Proverbs 20:15*
when wise man instructed, he gains knowledge — *Prov.21:11*
eyes of the Lord keep watch over knowledge — *Proverbs 22:12*
knowledge - true and reliable words — *Proverbs 22:20-21*
apply your ears to words of knowledge — *Proverbs 23:12*
rare & beautiful treasures through knowledge — *Prov. 24:4*
a man of knowledge increases strength — *Proverbs 24:5*
a man of knowledge maintains order — *Proverbs 28:2*
God gives knowledge — *Ecclesiastes 2:26*
advantage of knowledge: preserves life — *Ecclesiastes 7:12*
teacher imparted knowledge to the people — *Ecclesiastes 12:9*
the Spirit of the Lord on Christ for knowledge — *Isaiah 11:2*
the earth is full of the knowledge of the Lord — *Isaiah 11:9*
a rich store of knowledge — *Isaiah 33:6*
idol worshippers without knowledge — *Isaiah 44:19*
he will justify many by his knowledge — *Isaiah 53:11*
Israel's watchmen lack knowledge — *Isaiah 56:10*
shepherds who lead with knowledge — *Jeremiah 3:15*
senseless & without knowledge — *Jeremiah 10:14; 51:17*
God gave knowledge to Daniel & friends — *Daniel 1:17*
God gives knowledge — *Daniel 2:21*
the people destroyed from lack of knowledge — *Hosea 4:6*
Israel rejected knowledge — *Hosea 4:6*
earth is filled with knowledge of glory of Lord — *Hab. 2:14*

The Importance of Knowledge

the lips of a priest ought to preserve knowledge — *Malachi 2:7*
knowledge of Heaven given disciples — *Matt. 13:11; Luke 8:10*
John the Baptist to give knowledge of salvation — *Luke 1:77*
Pharisees took away the key to knowledge — *Luke 11:52*
Apollos' thorough knowledge of Scriptures — *Acts 18:24*
thought the knowledge of God not worthwhile — *Romans 1:28*
zeal not based on knowledge — *Romans 10:2*
the depth of the knowledge of God — *Romans 11:33*
complete in knowledge & competent to teach — *Romans 15:14*
enriched in knowledge — *1 Corinthians 1:5*
fragrance of the knowledge of Christ — *2 Corinthians 2:14*
light of the knowledge of the glory of God — *2 Corinthians 4:6*
excel in knowledge - *2 Corinthians 8:7*
demolish everything that sets itself against knowledge of God — *2 Cor.10:5*
not trained speaker, but does have knowledge — *2 Cor. 11:6*
reach unity in knowledge of Christ — *Ephesians 4:13*
love may abound in knowledge, depth of insight — *Phil. 1:9*
ask God to fill you with knowledge — *Colossians 1:9*
growing in the knowledge of God — *Colossians 1:10*
treasures of knowledge hidden in Christ — *Colossians 2:3*
the new self being renewed in knowledge — *Colossians 3:10*
wants all men to come to knowledge of truth — *1 Timothy 2:4*
may God grant repentance leading to knowledge — *2 Tim.2:25*
knowledge that leads to godliness — *Titus 1:1*
grace & peace through knowledge — *2 Peter 1:2*
everything we need through knowledge — *2 Peter 1:3*
add to your knowledge — *2 Peter 1:5*
don't be unproductive in your knowledge — *2 Peter 1:8*
grow in knowledge — *2 Peter 3:18*

As you can see, the Bible is plainly encouraging us to *get knowledge*. Each of these passages deserves a great deal of your time and study, because what they are saying about knowledge is critical for your salvation and understanding of God. Nobody can say that the Bible discourages getting knowledge. The problem is not that we have too much knowledge, but that we are *unwilling* to get knowledge — and when we are unwilling, the results are disastrous. We list all these passages here in order to convince those who despise knowledge that they do so in defiance of God's command to take it seriously.

The Importance of Knowledge

- **Getting knowledge:** The Bible teaches us that it's important to get knowledge, to store up knowledge, to seek for it with more interest than we do the riches of the world. David and Solomon both prized knowledge, and God honored their requests. The job of teachers is to impart knowledge to their students. Only fools hate knowledge and avoid the divinely-appointed methods of getting it. Israel rejected knowledge to her own hurt, and the Pharisees took away the key to knowledge from those under their spiritual care and were condemned for it.

- **Benefits of knowledge:** Knowledge leads to salvation; it gives us the information we need to know God, to know ourselves, to know the truth about our spiritual need, to know the way to Christ and how to take hold of him in faith. Knowledge also brings benefits to one's life such as prudence, discernment, new life, the treasures of Heaven, justification, grace and peace, and godliness.

- **Disasters from a lack of knowledge:** Israel turned away from the knowledge of God and suffered punishment many times, including defeat from her enemies, spiritual darkness, internal warfare, even rejection from God himself. A man without knowledge is a fool; a person who rejects knowledge is headed for trouble. Ignorant watchmen will unknowingly allow the enemy to come in and destroy the city. The Jews were destroyed because of a lack of knowledge. The Pharisees had the Jews bound up in blind legalism; they were so blind that they could not see the glory and hope in Jesus Christ

— who was their God come in the flesh. Even Peter came dangerously close to serving the purposes of the devil in his ignorance; only by the prayer of Christ was he preserved from destruction.

- **Warnings about despising knowledge:** Many people simply aren't interested in getting knowledge, but a few actually despise knowledge and do their best to prevent others from getting knowledge. The Pharisees barred the gate to knowledge; false prophets led the Israelites away from the truth; the Devil misled Eve with a lie, and so all mankind fell into sin and death. Paul condemned the legalizers who deliberately led people away from the truth of the Gospel. Israel constantly rejected the knowledge that the Prophets proclaimed to her, and so brought upon her head a severe punishment in the destruction of Jerusalem and the Exile. The Jews crucified Christ to get him out of the way, even though he brought them knowledge that would save them — and so they brought upon themselves a terrible destruction at the hands of the Romans.

Knowledge is the foundation

Jesus told us that those who worship God must worship him "in Spirit and in Truth." (John 4:24) Notice that we cannot worship him, we cannot hope to please him, we cannot serve him according to his will, if we do not have the truth. That's where knowledge comes in — knowledge is the facts we need to learn the truth about him and our service to him. Without truth we have no Christianity. And the Spirit is the only one who can reveal the truth to us in a way that we can understand it and get the spiritual point that it makes.

The Importance of Knowledge

The Kingdom of God rests on truth, so much so that the Apostle Paul says that the entire Church is "built on the foundation of the Apostles and Prophets, with Christ Jesus himself as the chief cornerstone." (Ephesians 2:20) In other words, we depend on what we have from them — their witness to the works and reality of God, which is *the Bible*. This is the truth about God and his world. This is the knowledge that we need, not what other men and religions claim is knowledge. The Bible is spiritual knowledge, revealed to our hearts by the Spirit (1 Corinthians 2:10) and is appreciated only by those who are spiritually minded.

- **The Bible is knowledge that leads to wisdom.** Knowledge is the necessary first step to wisdom. There are three different words used in the Bible to describe the process of wisdom: *first*, you must find out the facts — the data, or the truth. This is what is known as **knowledge**. It ought to be obvious that without the facts, you can't proceed to accomplish your goals. For example, if you don't get the facts about the true state of your heart, you aren't going to see that you *need* to fix your heart — you won't know *how*, nor will you know *why* you need to!

   The *second* step is **understanding**. This is being able to use the facts in some way. For example, if you know that the Spirit of God reveals the way of salvation in the Word, you will study the Word and find out what you must do to be saved. Not many people know how to use the Bible for this purpose! They can read it, but they don't know how to apply its truth to their own particular spiritual condition. But a person of understanding will know what to focus on, and how to grow in holiness by following the Spirit of God.

The *third* and final step is **wisdom**. Wisdom is knowing the <u>overall picture</u>, and how to achieve the long range goals that you have in mind. In the case of a Christian, wisdom is being fully aware of God and his glory. In order to live in his presence, you must undergo a radical transformation of character — from a sinner to a saint, from a rebel to a servant, from an orphan to the privileged position of a child of God. If we want to live in God's Kingdom, we must learn what the requirements are for living there. Wisdom knows *what* the goals are, and *how* to achieve those goals. We must eventually look like Christ:

> Do everything without complaining or arguing, so that you may become blameless and pure, children of God without fault in a crooked and depraved generation, in which you shine like stars in the universe as you hold out the word of life — in order that I may boast on the day of Christ that I did not run or labor for nothing. (Philippians 2:14-16)

We could summarize the three like this: knowledge is knowing *what* to do, understanding is knowing *how* to do it, and wisdom knows *why* and *when* it must be done.

If we could categorize people by their spiritual progress, we would have to say that only a few people know the facts, fewer still have any spiritual understanding, and it's a rare person who has true wisdom. It's just too easy to stop somewhere along the way. The proof is in the current state of affairs of Christ's Church. "For everyone looks out for his own interests, not those of Jesus Christ." (Philippians 2:21) But however we assess the situation among current Christians, it still remains that knowledge is the necessary first step in this process of becoming wise. And since so few people are concerned with studying the Bible and learning the facts, it's no wonder that so few attain wisdom in the end.

- **The Bible is designed for the head first, then the heart.** By God's creative wisdom, we first get truth into our minds — through seeing and hearing it — before it hits the heart. In other words, God speaks to us *first* through his Word, which is specially made to address our minds.

    Our minds are the front door that the Lord enters when he wants to deal with us. It receives the Bible as knowledge — as facts, propositions, truth, data, however you wish to call it. It *understands* what the Word says; the words mean something to us, thus we can act on what we understand. This is not by accident! God designed us this way; we are not creatures of instinct but of intellect. And the mind is, naturally, the first thing that must be changed if we wish to be a child of God: "Do not conform any longer to the pattern of this world, but *be transformed by the renewing of your mind.* Then you will be able to test and approve what God's will is — his good, pleasing and perfect will." (Romans 12:2)

    But our relationship with God must not stop at the mind. Like a percolator, the Word of God must continue on *through* the mind and drip into the heart where it inclines our affections and changes the inner man. We must love God, and hate sin, and love our brothers, and long for the glory of the Church, and fear the Lord. Knowledge that is stuck in the brain isn't being put to the use that the Lord meant for it. But, on the other hand, feelings that aren't based on sound knowledge can't be trusted.

- **The Bible trains us to be co-laborers with Christ.** Perhaps not many Christians realize what they have been called to do. Ours is a high calling; we are given the task of helping to build the eternal Kingdom of God. There are many aspects of this job, and they all require a great deal of knowledge and understanding if we wish to succeed. If we don't know what we are doing, however, we will either mess things up terribly or God won't allow us to help with the project. Too much is at stake for him to risk such important work to unskilled labor.

Christians are "God's fellow workers." (1 Corinthians 3:9) That's an amazing statement in light of what the job consists of and how ignorant we are by nature! We have to know what God's goals are, his building methods, the materials to be used, the timing that's involved, our exact responsibilities, and God's part of the project. We have to know when one thing is achieved and when to start the next step. We have to know what to do with people who won't cooperate and do their part. We have to know how to avoid and undo the enemy's work against us. In fact, the knowledge that we need can be overwhelming!

As we have already seen, if someone has little skill and knowledge, he will get a job that requires little from him. Responsible positions go only to those who know what is going on, who have "the mind of Christ." (1 Corinthians 2:16) Those with knowledge "will be able to test and approve what

God's will is — his good, pleasing and perfect will." (Romans 12:2)

Notice that the Lord gave greater responsibilities to those who *developed* their talents, not to those who let their talents sit unused. (Matthew 25:14-30) And you can be sure that they first *learned* how to do this; in other words, they started by gaining knowledge.

- **The Bible helps us avoid the traps of the enemy.** When you are in the middle of a battle, one good way of getting yourself captured or killed is not knowing what's going on. Ignorance is fatal in war. That's why every responsible army has a well-organized intelligence unit to keep everyone informed on the current situation.

  The devil is a liar, and the father of lies. He specializes in "counter-intelligence" — anything that contradicts the truth of the Word of God. We saw this clearly in the Garden of Eden as he led Eve into deception about God's command. Notice that it is sufficient for his purposes if we simply believe the lie; once that poison enters our minds, the rest is assured — our downfall is certain.

  Unfortunately, Peter himself, the leader of the disciples, best illustrated this danger of ignorance. When Jesus informed them of his plans to go to Jerusalem where he would be killed, Peter drew him aside in horror and counseled him to give up such a foolish idea. Jesus, however, knowing full well what his goal must be, recognized the hand of the enemy and lashed back with a sharp rebuke:

The Importance of Knowledge

> Get behind me, Satan! You are a stumbling block to me; you do not have in mind the things of God, but the things of men. (Matthew 16:23)

It's too often the case that Christians, not knowing what God is doing in their lives, actually work *against* him instead of *with* him. Unwittingly they are serving the purposes of the enemy of God. The only remedy for this ignorance is the knowledge of God and his ways and works.

The *only* way to begin fighting this deadly strategy of the enemy is to get the knowledge of God — in other words, the Word of God. The ministry of the Word among Christians is specially designed to give us what we need to protect ourselves from the enemy's lies:

> Those who oppose him [*i.e., the teacher*] he must gently instruct, in the hope that God will grant them repentance *leading them to a knowledge of the truth*, and that they will come to their senses and escape from the trap of the devil, who has taken them captive to do his will. (2 Timothy 2:25-26)

The gifts that Christ gives to his Church are exactly for this purpose:

> It was he who gave some to be Apostles, some to be prophets, some to be evangelists, and some to be pastors and teachers, to prepare God's people for works of service, so that the body of Christ may be built up until we all reach unity in the faith and *in the knowledge of the Son of God* and become

mature, attaining to the whole measure of the fullness of Christ. Then we will no longer be infants, tossed back and forth by the waves, and blown here and there by every wind of teaching and by the cunning and craftiness of men in their deceitful scheming. Instead, speaking the *truth* in love, we will in all things grow up into him who is the Head, that is, Christ. From him the whole body, joined and held together by every supporting ligament, grows and builds itself up in love, as each part does its work. (Ephesians 4:11-16)

Perhaps you aren't aware of the fact that the greatest field of prospects for the cults today are the mainstream denominations: Baptists, Methodists, Presbyterians, Episcopalians, Lutherans, etc. The problem is that the average church-goer doesn't know enough of the Bible to be able to tell where the cults are wrong. And a superficial knowledge won't help; you have to press on for the true spiritual knowledge that only the Holy Spirit can give you, if you want to be rock-solid against their attacks.

- **The Bible trains us for future trials.** Being a student of the Bible is just like being a student of a school: you must learn a lot of facts for future use. Children often complain that they will *never* use the stuff that they have to learn! So why should they have to suffer through such useless material? We adults smile, however, because we know the great demands of life and the necessity for training: we can't reach our goals without knowledge.

The Importance of Knowledge

It's no different in God's school. We have a tremendous amount of material to learn if we want to be ready for trials ahead. God has work for us to do, and we have to study for that job just as we would study for any worldly employment.

Unfortunately, when the average person graduates from childhood to adulthood, he usually puts aside his books and decides he will *never* study again! This is fatal in Christianity. We *will* have trouble in the world; we *will* be attacked by the enemy; we *will* be greatly and constantly tempted by the pleasures of life; we *will* have difficult decisions to make; we *will* be responsible for others. It isn't a possibility, but a certainty, that our lives will be filled with such things. It's the height of childish ignorance to claim that we don't have to prepare ahead of time for those days!

Think of this for a minute. In the hour of crisis, will there be time to go back and research the information that you need to meet the crisis? Isn't it instead the case that there is *no time to learn* in the middle of a crisis? When a soldier finds himself in the middle of a fierce battle, he begins to be thankful that his drill sergeant put him through those endless hours of "meaningless" drills back at boot camp! The training that he thought was for no purpose actually trained his mind and reflexes so well that the right moves come automatically. Now his life literally depends on the knowledge and skill that were drilled into him.

Keep in mind, also, that the day of death is coming for every person, even if they manage to avoid most of life's trials. On that day there will be a great need for former skills and training as we face our greatest enemy in the battle of faith. There won't be time to learn anything then.

But in today's Church, because people for the most part have become so lazy and reluctant to *study* the Word, many teaching and preaching ministries water their messages down, make the standards lower, make it more "fun," and generally reassure their people that they don't have to take the Bible so seriously. In fact, our fast-paced society demands more of students in secular areas — physics, computers, economics, etc. — than we do of students of the Word! For some reason, the Church leaders are assuring Christians that they don't have to work hard at Bible study, while the world is pressing *its* students into becoming masters of their subjects! This is not right: God's Word is the most profound book we have; it has a greater impact on our lives than any other area of study. Our job is to become masters of the Bible, not remain spiritual babies in our understanding.

It's a foolish argument to say that storing up knowledge is counter-productive to the Christian life. It isn't true that this knowledge is useless if we don't use it right away. It is *wise* to store up this knowledge for future use. "Wise men *store up* knowledge, but the mouth of a fool invites ruin." (Proverbs 10:14)

> Go to the ant, you sluggard; consider its ways and be wise! It has no commander, no overseer or ruler, yet it stores its provisions in summer and gathers its food at harvest. (Proverbs 6:6-8)

The Importance of Knowledge

Notice that it doesn't eat the food as it gathers it! It stores it away for those times that are coming when there will be great need of food, yet none will be available.

The Bible teaches us to do the same thing with the knowledge of God; in fact, children especially are encouraged to do this:

> Remember your Creator in the days of your youth, before the days of trouble come and the years approach when you will say, "I find no pleasure in them." (Ecclesiastes 12:1)

This passage is even more remarkable when we consider that it advises learning about God as a child — the age when they can least put the information to use! Obviously the point is to get the knowledge into the mind so that it will be available in the future. So, if this is true for the children, why not for the rest of us as well?

The writer of Hebrews found it frustrating to deal with ignorant students; he wanted to give them more knowledge, but they hadn't even learned the basics yet!

> We have much to say about this, but it is hard to explain because you are slow to learn. In fact, though by this time you ought to be teachers, you need someone to teach you the elementary truths of God's word all over again. You need milk, not solid food! Anyone who lives on milk, being still an infant, is not acquainted with the teaching about righteousness. But solid food is for the mature, who by constant use have trained

themselves to distinguish good from evil. (Hebrews 5:11-14)

Notice that his complaint wasn't their lack of love, or devotion, or service, but *knowledge* — that is the necessary foundation for all Christian life.

Paul reminded Timothy of the great worth of the Scriptures for the believer:

> ... and how from infancy you have *known* the holy Scriptures, which are able to make you wise for salvation through faith in Christ Jesus. All Scripture is God-breathed and is useful for teaching, rebuking, correcting and training in righteousness, so that the man of God may be thoroughly equipped for every good work. (2 Timothy 3:15-17)

No conscientious Christian who fears the Lord would purposely avoid the responsibilities that God has given them, so they *must* accept what God has provided to help them fulfill that calling — the knowledge of God in the Word.

- **The Bible is the true basis of faith.** Faith is not what most people think it is. Faith isn't believing that things will turn out like they want them to! It isn't strength of conviction, or vain hopes, or wishful thinking. Faith is based on *facts*; without the truth we could never have faith in God.

  "Now faith is being *sure* of what we hope for and *certain* of what we do not see." (Hebrews 11:1) As Paul said, we now live "by faith, not by sight." (2 Corinthians 5:7) Living by faith is *not* a life of ignorance. Our eyesight enables us to know our physical surroundings, but faith enables us to know our spiritual surroundings. It gives us facts to base our hopes upon. The truth of the matter is that we know exactly what God is, and the world he lives in and calls us to. We have that knowledge in the Bible; there are no secrets about what we can know. Faith is the ability of the soul to know the reality of those spiritual things. *Faith is living in the light of God's world.*

The Spirit is the one who reveals these things to us, and convinces us of their reality when our senses can't pick up on them. "We have not received the spirit of the world but the Spirit who is from God, that we may *understand* what God has freely given us." (1 Corinthians 2:12) Our faith is based on what we see spiritually, not physically. How does that happen? Nobody knows! Nobody can prove the reality of spiritual things, though the person who has seen them in the Spirit can no more deny their reality than he can his own existence! So you see, true faith rests solidly on facts, evidence, truths, knowledge — spiritual knowledge that only the Spirit can give us. If there is no spiritual knowledge, then there can be no true faith — and "without faith it is impossible to please God." (Hebrews 11:6) Therefore knowledge is absolutely essential to our salvation and spiritual growth.

- **The Bible helps us discern the true God from the false gods.** We cannot overemphasize the importance of knowledge when it comes to God himself. One of the greatest sins that mankind has ever committed is to make a false idol and call it God. This has been done by so many people, in so many ways, all through history that we have to believe that it's a fundamental problem in the heart of man, and therefore widespread wherever we look — including in our generation.

God is what he is. He gets glory for being the way he is. So when someone says that God isn't what he says he is, that takes away from God's glory and deeply offends him. And the lies and theories about God abound among us! Ask any three people about God, and you will certainly get four opinions about what he is really like — and probably none of them will match the Bible's description of him.

If you don't know the truth about God, it's impossible to love him, or fear him, or obey him, or worship him, or work with him, or submit to him, or relate to him in any meaningful and true way. It's as if you would marry someone that you have never seen or been close to! Who can carry on a marriage across a long distance, never knowing a single true thing about their partner? The same holds true, in a more profound sense, with our relationship with God.

We must first get the facts about God before we can hope to perform our duties toward him. The Scriptures teach us what we need to know about God: there is where we find out *why* we must fear him and love him. We read about the works he did, so that we will pray for those same things and work along with his purposes. We learn the ways to approach him and what to ask him for. All of our spiritual activities depend completely on our knowledge of God. Even our first steps of repentance and faith were based on what we first heard and learned about him.

Jesus revealed that to know God is, in itself, eternal life! "Now *this* is eternal life: that they may *know you*, the only true God, and Jesus Christ, whom you have sent." (John 17:3) So the person who despises *knowledge* will turn his back on God himself.

- **The Bible puts us under responsibility.** We've already looked at the fact that those who have little knowledge will be given small jobs; they can't be trusted with important matters, because they don't know enough to do the job well. But the person who knows a great deal about the matter is a good choice for the manager of the project.

Of course the responsibility that comes with higher positions should make one think twice! The person on the bottom of the social scale would love to have the opportunity to run things, but he doesn't know what he is talking about: he wouldn't like the headaches that come with the job. Positions of leadership and critical roles in the church's work require above-average wisdom and understanding. "Not many of you should presume to be teachers, my brothers, because you know that we who teach will be judged more strictly." (James 3:1) Too often these roles are given away in desperation to the first volunteers who want the job. It isn't long before we see the foolishness of this approach: the spiritual condition of those under their care goes from bad to worse. This is the point that Jesus was making in the parable of the drunken servant who was put in charge of things:

> Who then is the faithful and wise manager, whom the master puts in charge of his servants to give them their food allowance at the proper

time? It will be good for that servant whom the master finds doing so when he returns. I tell you the truth, he will put him in charge of all his possessions. But suppose the servant says to himself, 'My master is taking a long time in coming,' and he then begins to beat the menservants and maidservants and to eat and drink and get drunk. The master of that servant will come on a day when he does not expect him and at an hour he is not aware of. He will cut him to pieces and assign him a place with the unbelievers.

That servant who *knows* his master's will and does not get ready or does not do what his master wants will be beaten with many blows. But the one who *does not know* and does things deserving punishment will be beaten with few blows. From everyone who has been given much, much will be demanded; and from the one who has been entrusted with much, much more will be asked. (Luke 12:42-48)

Lest you get the idea that all of this is only for pastors and teachers and other leaders of the church, you should study (in addition to the parables that Jesus taught about the talents) what Paul says about gifts in the Church. Every Christian believer has gifts that he or she received from God; we are *all* obligated to work for him as servants. Just because others don't see *their* obligation, or might not agree with you about yours, doesn't excuse you from your duties in God's house. And hopefully you are convinced by now that you can't possibly carry out your spiritual responsibilities before God without a good bit of knowledge of God's Word.

The Importance of Knowledge

On Judgment Day, most people will hear that they didn't do the work that God gave them to do — they either didn't know about it, or they didn't want to do it. Of the rest, most of *them* will hear that they didn't do their job well enough. We can't presume on his good graces on that day: remember, he is a hard man, and he expects our work to be up to *his* standards. Otherwise he will burn up our "good works" as so much worthless stubble. (1 Corinthians 3:12-15)

- **The Bible is a house full of spiritual treasures.** Finally, we should address the problem of *how much* knowledge is necessary. Is it enough to know the basics of the Christian faith? Should we memorize a church catechism and then quit? Should we just memorize some well-known Biblical passages? Is what we learn in Sunday School and sermons enough to live on? And the teachers themselves — should we accept volunteers among those new to the faith, or use those who haven't grown much spiritually over the years?

  The answers to these questions should be plain. We need to know enough to do our jobs well — to please God, not ourselves or others. God called us to his work, and he is a "hard man" who expects results, efficiency, and timely fruit from our labors. In the story of the talents, the man with one talent, who did nothing to turn it to profit, said that Jesus is a hard man; amazingly, Jesus didn't deny that name! "You knew, did you, that I am a hard man?" (Luke 19:22) As Paul said, we work to please God, not man, and our work has to measure up to *his* expectations:

The Importance of Knowledge

> Am I now trying to win the approval of men, or of God? Or am I trying to please men? If I were still trying to please men, I would not be a servant of Christ. (Galatians 1:10)

This comment from Paul is instructive. In this passage, he is accusing the legalists of preaching a different Gospel than the one which Paul preached. In other words, they weren't preaching according to God's knowledge, or God's Truth. Furthermore, the Galatians, who didn't have enough knowledge to tell the difference, were believing this false gospel! Both errors give us a better idea of how much we have to know in order to avoid both.

Jesus counsels us about how much we need to learn in order to help build God's house as it should be:

> Therefore every teacher of the Law who has been instructed about the Kingdom of Heaven is like the owner of a house who brings out of his storeroom new treasures as well as old. (Matthew 13:52)

He is referring to the Law of the Old Testament — the Mosaic Law that the Israelites received. Modern Christians hardly know enough about the Gospel, let alone anything in the Old Testament! But those who have studied the Old Testament have found tremendous spiritual depth there; it is, in fact, a rock-foundation for all the New Testament history and doctrines that we are so fond of. We cannot understand the New without a sufficient understanding of the Old. Who can hope to believe in Christ without knowing about the covenant given to Abraham, and the messianic lessons in King David, and the sacrificial system of the Temple, and the warnings of the coming Kingdom of God proclaimed by the Prophets? We can't. So our job is cut out for us: we have much to learn about the God we claim to believe in, and his many works that the Bible records for our sake.

Dangers associated with knowledge

As with any precious gift of God, there are abuses that man is guilty of. Knowledge is no exception. But the abuses don't make it necessary to abolish the gift! Rather we have to isolate the abuses and find ways to eliminate *them*, and at the same time develop the gift to a purer level for God's glory.

Another thing that we must be careful to do is to define precisely what the abuses really are, instead of making up imaginary dangers and alarming people with them. It's not right to burden people's souls with rules and regulations of men, when God laid no such burden upon them. It is also wrong to teach that we are *not* responsible to God in things that he very plainly said we *are* responsible for, even under the guise of devotion to the Lord. Devotion doesn't replace duty, as Jesus taught us in his rebuke to the Pharisees. (Matthew 15:3-9)

There are well-known Scriptures that deal with the problems associated with knowledge — but we must study them carefully to determine what exactly they are warning us about.

- **"Knowledge puffs up." — 1 Corinthians 8:1** — This verse is commonly quoted by those who warn us against accumulating knowledge. Those who quote it really mean to say that knowledge doesn't do us good like love does — "Knowledge puffs up, but love builds up." Get love, they say, and you will fulfill your Christian duty; get knowledge, and you haven't done anything worth your while yet. In fact, you are probably ignoring your duty of love as you blindly accumulate knowledge!

But that blatantly ignores the context! Read further: "The man who thinks he knows something *does not yet know as he ought to know.*" (1 Corinthians 8:2) In other words, the problem is not that one *has* knowledge, the problem is not having *enough* knowledge!

Paul isn't contrasting love and knowledge. He is talking about people who know only a little and act as if they know enough; their little knowledge only gets them into trouble through pride and arrogance. The solution for ignorance is to *learn more* of what God wants us to know. This fits in with many other passages: for example, see Hebrews 5:11 — 6:2. You know that you are starting to get enough knowledge when your pride turns into humility: when you see that God is bigger and more glorious than you thought, and that you need more of his grace and mercy than you thought.

Love, on the other hand, is pure at any stage of learning, whether found in a new-born Christian or an experienced believer. It is the one grace that pleases God in any form. Whoever loves, fulfills the Law. (Romans 13:8) But no passage of Scripture teaches that love replaces knowledge; the two work hand in hand, though Christians with love may not have sufficient knowledge to work effectively in God's kingdom — a common problem in today's Church.

- **"You diligently study the Scriptures" — John 5:39** — Jesus rebuked the Jews for knowing their Bibles yet missing the point — that the Bible (which to them was the Old Testament) taught them the truth about himself.

    Again, notice that the problem was not that they had too much knowledge. The problem was that they didn't understand what they were reading. This is natural enough, when someone studies the Bible without the revealing hand of the Spirit opening their hearts to the truth that it teaches. There is a superficial level of Bible study, and a deep, spiritual level of Bible study — few achieve the second, while most are satisfied with the first.

    The answer, again, is *not* to quit studying! It's not knowledge that is the problem but a lack of spiritual understanding of that knowledge. When Paul the Pharisee became a Christian, his vast knowledge of the Scriptures suddenly filled with light from Heaven. With that knowledge and extensive training, he was able to refute the Jews and convince the Gentiles of the truth about Jesus Christ. Men of lesser knowledge and skill didn't have the advantages that Paul had.

- **"Knowledge will pass away" — 1 Corinthians 13:8** — This is another popular quote with the anti-knowledge people. But again, they aren't careful to get the context, and they are making the text say what it definitely does not say.

The Importance of Knowledge

Paul is speaking about *imperfect* knowledge again (see above under 1 Corinthians 8:1). He says first that "where there is knowledge, it will pass away," — because "For now we know *in part* ... but when perfection comes, the *imperfect* disappears." (1 Corinthians 13:9-10) What is Paul calling "imperfect?" Knowledge? Hardly! Jesus himself said that to know God is *eternal life*. (John 17:3) The "imperfection" that he speaks of here is that we *know imperfectly*. We know too little, we don't know enough to know the overall picture as God knows it. And this is precisely what he states in the next verse: "Now I know *in part*; then I shall know *fully*, even as I am fully known." (1 Corinthians 13:12)

He is, again, bringing out the unique nature of love, which is perfect at any stage of spiritual development. He isn't saying that other graces are unnecessary because of love, but that they aren't perfect — and therefore we shouldn't depend on them as if they were perfect. There is always more to learn, and what we know now is far less than what we need to know in God's opinion. Love, in contrast, does its perfect work even in such little things as a cup of cold water in time of need. An act of love is, in itself, pleasing to God. Our imperfect knowledge, however, often tests his patience with us.

As far as knowledge goes, however, our goal is still perfect knowledge, not doing away with it!

- **"God made foolish the wisdom of the world"** — **1 Corinthians 1:20** — Here we have a true assessment of the world's knowledge: it's of no spiritual use. The greatest knowledge of the wisest men can't show us the truth about God, or the work of the Spirit, or any of the issues of the Kingdom of God — for example, righteousness and salvation.

But that's an indictment against the world's knowledge, not against knowledge that comes from God. The knowledge that God gives — the Bible, in other words — leads us to life and salvation. The wise man speaks the truth about God only if he gets his information from the Word of God. As Jesus said, "Your Word is truth." (John 17:17)

- **"Nothing ... except Christ and him crucified" — 1 Corinthians 2:2** — This is also used many times in defense of the idea that we don't need a lot of knowledge to be faithful Christians. As if Paul was saying, "All I need to know is that Jesus died for me!"

    But Paul isn't saying that at all, and a little thought will make his meaning plain. When he says that "I resolved to know nothing while I was with you except Jesus Christ and him crucified," he evidently had a *great deal* in mind. Jesus Christ is the fullness of the Godhead, the great High Priest who fulfills all the Old Testament shadows and types, the sacrifice in God's Heavenly Temple (according to the strict requirements of the Law), the King of kings who follows the Messianic pattern laid down by David, the Passover Lamb, the Head of the Church, the greatest of the Prophets as predicted by Moses, the fulfillment of all the Old Testament prophecies, Yahweh come in the flesh, the Bread of Life, the great Shepherd, the Righteousness of his people, the Suffering Servant, the doom of our enemy Satan, and so on. Paul constantly refers to these and many more aspects of the huge subject of Jesus Christ, as you will clearly see as you read his letters to the churches.

He is contrasting his message of Christ against the message of the so-called wise men of his age, who spend their time on philosophical issues that don't give life to the soul or glory to God. That is, in fact, the context of this passage. One would have to close one's eyes completely to claim that Paul avoided knowledge! His knowledge of the things of God was profound and God-inspired, for the benefit of the Church, and he utilized it on every occasion.

How does one get this knowledge?

You can be sure that, for something as important as this, God put it right at our fingertips — under our noses, so to speak. He is not unfaithful, and he doesn't wish the death of any man; God "wants all men to be saved and to come to a knowledge of the truth." (1 Timothy 2:4) We will find, therefore, that the knowledge that he knows we need will be available to us. If we don't know the truth, it isn't his fault!

- ***God reveals himself.*** We cannot overestimate the importance and value of the Bible. In this book, God reveals his true nature — which is the life-giving knowledge that we so desperately need in our spiritual darkness and state of sin and death. In his light, we see things clearly: our own sin and helplessness, the dangers surrounding us in this world, the safety in Jesus Christ, the hope of Heaven, the strategy of our enemies, the constant oversight of God in our lives, and much more.

God didn't *have* to tell us any of this; he could have left us in complete ignorance and refused to show us anything. Why did he have mercy on us? We don't know! But this uncommon act of love should draw us close to him, willing to look into matters that he obviously thinks are important for us to know.

He will show us things that we *need* to know. Many philosophers and academics spend their lifetimes searching for knowledge that does them *no spiritual good*. It's not wrong to be educated, but it's a serious mistake to substitute the world's knowledge for the knowledge of God. The truth in the Bible saves us, it leads us into God's presence, it corrects the errors and lies of the world's so-called "wisdom", it leads us into life and peace and joy. Like a wise father, God gives his children what they need to grow on and makes them skillful to serve him. The only thing we need to do to get this knowledge is to take it from him, like a little child, in faith — simply believing that this is God telling us the truth, and trust in this truth alone. We must not change, add to, or take away from it —the Bible is what we need to know, exactly as it stands. If we approach his Word in this way, we are using it as he intended.

- *Ask for it.* We often miss the greatest things in life because we won't ask for them. "You do not have, because you do not ask God." (James 4:2) That just seems too simplistic. We feel that we must do it ourselves — we hate to be objects of charity. If we depend on someone else to give us what we need, that destroys our pride and self-confidence – we don't like to feel ignorant.

But in this case we can't afford to be proud. We *are* ignorant and helpless.

> You say, 'I am rich; I have acquired wealth and do not need a thing.' But you do not realize that you are wretched, pitiful, poor, blind and naked. I counsel you to buy from me gold refined in the fire, so you can become rich; and white clothes to wear, so you can cover your shameful nakedness; and salve to put on your eyes, so you can see. (Revelation 3:17-18)

The treasures of Heaven cannot be bought, or earned, with any amount of human work or earthly treasures. The only way we can have any of it is to come to God as a helpless child and ask him for it.

There are many Scriptures that encourage you to ask God for things. They focus on the fact that God is *ready* to give you what you need, he *wants* to give it to you, and he *will* give it to you when you come in humility and faith.

> If any of you lacks wisdom, he should ask God, who gives generously to all without finding fault, and it will be given to him. But when he asks, he must believe and not doubt, because he who doubts is like a wave of the sea, blown and tossed by the wind. That man should not think he will receive anything from the Lord; he is a double-

minded man, unstable in all he does. (James 1:5-10)

Ask and it will be given to you; seek and you will find; knock and the door will be opened to you. For everyone who asks receives; he who seeks finds; and to him who knocks, the door will be opened. Which of you, if his son asks for bread, will give him a stone? Or if he asks for a fish, will give him a snake? If you, then, though you are evil, know how to give good gifts to your children, how much more will your Father in Heaven give good gifts to those who ask him! (Matthew 7:7-11)

And will not God bring about justice for his chosen ones, who cry out to him day and night? Will he keep putting them off? I tell you, he will see that they get justice, and quickly. However, when the Son of Man comes, will he find faith on the earth? (Luke 18:7-8)

Since God *wants* you to have knowledge (as we have seen from his Word), rest assured that the prayer of faith for knowledge, as Solomon found, *will* be answered. What we pray about shows what we have our hearts set on; as Jesus told us, "For where your treasure is, there your heart will be also." (Matthew 6:21) He loves it when you make his priorities your priorities.

- ***Study his Word.*** Although God reveals his truth to us, and the Spirit opens our hearts and minds to receive his truth, we aren't allowed to be lazy about this matter. "The sluggard buries his hand in the dish; he is too lazy to bring it back to his mouth." (Proverbs 26:15) The rich feast that God lays out for us in his Word will do us no good at all if we don't dig in and eat.

Study is a lost art in many circles, and most people associate it with school — which they thankfully leave behind them at their graduation! What they don't realize is that their education had *two* purposes: to give them knowledge, and *to show them how to get more knowledge on their own.* Life is full of new challenges and difficult trials; if we have the ability to *keep learning*, we can achieve much more than we thought possible and get out of difficulties that will stop others.

The one textbook that you can't afford to close for good is the Bible. We've already seen how important it is for our spiritual growth and well-being. It gives us the information we need to serve God acceptably. But it isn't a dime-store novel! You can't get what you need out of it by just reading it five minutes a day. Is that the way you will learn physics or calculus? Neither will you learn anything from the Bible until you start seriously studying it.

God, in his great wisdom, put the treasures of his truth beneath the surface, so to speak. Workers have to dig deep to reach veins of gold ore, or diamonds; these things don't usually lay around on the surface for anybody to pick up. In order to keep the pagans from making a mockery of his Word, God hid the deep things of Christ in the Bible so that only by study will you begin to see the truth about him. The Lord follows his own advice: "Do not give dogs what is sacred; do not throw your pearls to pigs. If you do, they may trample them under their feet, and then turn and tear you to pieces." (Matthew 7:6) You can tell when someone is tapping into the depth of the Bible when you hear him talk about certain issues that are important to God — not to the vanity of men in their intellectual pride. Such knowledge only comes through study and the revelation of the Spirit; that's how we can know when someone is really understanding it.

It takes work to get the truth of the Bible. It's not beyond the ability of any believer, because the Spirit stands ready to give it to you when you ask in faith. But the saints of the past have found that they must pray over the Bible, meditate on it, study it thoroughly, use it and apply it, and go back to it again and again in humility, ready to learn more.

Do your best to present yourself to God as one approved, a *workman* who does not need to be ashamed and who correctly handles the word of truth. (2 Timothy 2:15)

Notice that his passage uses the word "workman" — that implies someone who labors over the Word. If you don't know how to study the Bible, there are many books, aids, and teachers who can help you learn. And will there ever be a point at which you can say, "I've learned all that there is to know!"? Certainly not: the Word of God is limitless, capable of keeping you and countless other people busy with its living truth. The more that you study it, the more that you will see is yet to be learned — that is, if the Spirit is teaching you.

The Importance of Knowledge

- ***Attend the ministry of the Word.*** We cannot avoid the fact that God has already provided a means of learning the Bible in the Church. He faithfully worked out an efficient way that we can benefit from his wisdom. The gifts of the Spirit are specially designed to give the knowledge of God to his people.

> It was he who gave some to be Apostles, some to be prophets, some to be evangelists, and some to be pastors and teachers, to prepare God's people for works of service, so that the body of Christ may be built up until we all reach unity in the faith and in the knowledge of the Son of God and become mature, attaining to the whole measure of the fullness of Christ. (Ephesians 4:11-13)

Those who teach and preach are, ideally (though not always) called and specially trained by the Spirit to give you the spiritual knowledge that you need. This is from God. It doesn't help matters when you rebel against what God is doing through them for your sake.

> Obey your leaders and submit to their authority. They keep watch over you as men who must give an account. Obey them so that their work will be a joy, not a burden, for that would be of no advantage to you. (Hebrews 13:17)

Paul was thankful for the Thessalonians because they recognized the hand of God in his ministry:

> And we also thank God continually because, when you received the Word of

> God, which you heard from us, you accepted it not as the word of men, but as it actually is, the Word of God, which is at work in you who believe. (1 Thessalonians 2:13)

Of course you have to use some discernment about this. Many "ministries" are teaching false doctrine, and they are building their own empires instead of God's Kingdom. You have no business being under such false teaching. You can tell whether God is working through a particular teacher or preacher by how closely they stick to the Bible — not in a superficial way, but in the fundamental, primary issues of the Word. But there isn't a ministry on earth that is perfect; many are faithfully teaching the Word of God in spite of some problems. Be charitable, and be sensitive to God as he teaches you through his servants.

Knowing the truth

There is a sobering reality to Christianity, whether people like it or not: God is real, and there is only *one truth* about him. Most people will be condemned on the Last Day because their "thinking became futile and their foolish hearts were darkened," and they "did not think it worthwhile to retain the knowledge of God." (Romans 1:21,28) Not everyone will be saved on that day. Most will find to their misfortune that *knowledge* was the key to salvation.

Paul very carefully describes a person who despises knowledge:

> So I tell you this, and insist on it in the Lord, that you must no longer live as the Gentiles do, in the *futility of their thinking*. They are *darkened in their understanding*

and separated from the life of God because of the *ignorance* that is in them due to the hardening of their hearts. Having lost all sensitivity, they have given themselves over to sensuality so as to indulge in every kind of impurity, with a continual lust for more. (Ephesians 4:17-19)

He knows exactly what their problem is. Their hearts are wrong because their minds are wrong, and because their minds are wrong their hearts can't be made right. Without a knowledge of the truth there is no salvation; there can only be sin and death. Ignorance naturally leads into open wickedness and rebellion against God's will.

But when a person turns to the Lord in knowledge — in other words, when he hears the truth and believes *that* — he is saved.

You, however, did not come to know Christ that way. Surely you heard of him and were *taught* in him in accordance with *the truth that is in Jesus.* You were taught, with regard to your former way of life, to put off your old self, which is being corrupted by its deceitful desires; to *be made new in the attitude of your minds*; and to put on the new self, created to be like God in true righteousness and holiness. (Ephesians 4:20-24)

This first step of salvation introduces the believer into a lifetime of learning about Christ: the Lord Jesus is a vast treasury of spiritual power and resources, and we need to know as much about him as possible so that we can be saved from our deep-seated and extensive sin. The "new attitude of our minds" is the spirit of *learning*, of *getting knowledge*. Becoming a Christian means becoming a student of God for the rest of one's life.

The Knowledge of God

Now this is eternal life: that they may know you, the only true God, and Jesus Christ, whom you have sent. (John 17:3)

The Bible is the revelation of God. It was written for that purpose alone. Here we learn about his nature, his names, his works and ways, what he loves, what he hates, how he does things. We see his glory there, and we learn to fear him there. If it weren't for the Bible, we would never know any of these important facts about God. We need a book of this size and complexity to do the subject justice.

Though many people use the Bible for many purposes, its primary purpose is to show us the truth about the true God. We can find out about other subjects from other sources, but the only reliable source of information about God is the Book that he gave us. Here is everything that we need to know about him.

Every good textbook is about a particular subject; a calculus book, for example, teaches the student calculus, not economics or art. And the Bible is a textbook too, focusing on the most difficult subject known to man – the hidden and mysterious God who has finally revealed himself in this book alone.

There are a number of reasons for needing to know about God, but the most important is this: *to know God is life.* Jesus told us this in his priestly prayer:

Now this is eternal life: that they may know *you*, the only true God, and Jesus Christ, whom you have sent. (John 17:3)

Unless we learn about God, we will die in our sins. (John 8:24) We will be helplessly lost in a deadly game between spiritual powers, in which we are only small players. But the person who gets in touch with God will "step into the light" (John 3:21) and will find all sorts of answers and resources for life's problems.

Unfortunately many people usually read the Bible for every reason but that! They look for themselves in it, they look for morality, for philosophy, for rules on running a society – everything but the knowledge of God. When they do this, they show that they don't understand its purpose. Like any good textbook, the Bible focuses on one issue – and it sticks to that issue all the way through, even though it has a lot to say about other issues. We mustn't let its great size and scope confuse us about what it's trying to do.

Man-centered religion

We were all born with a crippling spiritual problem: our attention is almost always focused on *ourselves*. We are the most important person that we know! Life is a struggle, and we feel that it's necessary to busy ourselves with fulfilling the daily needs that we have – food, clothing, shelter, education, family, jobs, etc. All these matters take up most of our waking hours, and they deal, primarily, with us and our own needs.

But we have to realize that this inward focus is because of the sin and death that our first parents plunged the human race into. Man wasn't made, originally, with himself as the center of his world. He was made in the beginning to be aware of *God* –

and to follow God's direct leading in every aspect of life. God is the Creator, the Provider, the source of all good things, the Lord who instructs us which way to go, the Comforter, the Master – he is everything that man needs. God is like the hub of a wheel, and we are the spokes that connect into him. God is the well from which we draw daily strength and wisdom. He is the light that illuminates our world so that we can see where to go and what to do. He is our constant companion. Man was made to be totally dependent on God; so much so that, if God would withdraw from man's world, man would die as a result.

> When you hide your face, they are terrified; when you take away their breath, they die and return to the dust. When you send your Spirit, they are created, and you renew the face of the earth. (Psalm 104:29-30)

As a matter of fact, that's precisely what happened at the beginning of the world! See Genesis 3 for the results of sin: separation from God, and death.

We were all born sinners, and our natural tendency is to move away from God, not toward God. That explains why we all try to get along as well as we can *without* God, though our ruined society is eloquent proof of how foolish and deadly that is. But it's particularly tragic when we try to practice our *religion* without God! For example, the purpose of the Church is to glorify God and make him known; instead, many churches say almost nothing specific about God in their ministries – sermons and lessons too often focus on man instead of God. It's so pathetic to see people focus their attention on themselves instead of carrying out their God-given mandate of glorifying God.

You can see for yourself what a lot of people are up to. There are telltale signs that reveal when they are focusing on themselves instead of God. For instance, you will often see this happening in "worship" services:

They pray *about* themselves, and *for* themselves. They ask God for a list of things that *they* want (and they already decided what they wanted, without consulting him first!). They ask for strength to go on, for faith, for holiness, for cures, for success, for blessings – things that they need, for works that they are doing themselves. It doesn't seem to occur to them to find out what God might be doing (he's building a Kingdom!), and what *he* wants of *them*!

> **For everyone looks out for his own interests, not those of Jesus Christ. (Philippians 2:21)**

They glorify themselves. There's a lot that goes on in a church that's the result of people working hard. And since they all like to get credit for what they do, they make sure that everyone knows that *they* did this thing, and how clever or intelligent or holy they were in doing it. They may make an offhand remark about how God deserves the glory, but really they're showing off *their* devotion, *their* skills, and *their* holy life when they parade their good works before men.

> **So when you give to the needy, do not announce it with trumpets, as the hypocrites do in the synagogues and on the streets, to be honored by men. (Matthew 6:2)**

Their work is easily explainable. Science in modern times has made our lives so much more comfortable and efficient. Unfortunately this mentality has also invaded the Church; zealous workers try to apply specialized methods (following a "one-two-three" kind of formula) to achieve great results – like conversions, revivals, increased church attendance, spiritual renewal, and so on. The problem with this approach to church work is that everyone is depending solely on the methods used, the zeal and strength of faith, the dedication – and they *expect* it to work out because they did the right things. In other words, follow the formula, and you're certain to get great results – God *has* to honor your efforts! About the only thing they ask of God is to "bless" their efforts! But that approach ignores the vital fact that God alone can make his church grow, and he uses methods that we will never understand. We have our part to do, to be sure, but without God's mysterious moving of the Spirit there will be no growth or success. People show whether they really believe in this by what they depend on, and whether they actually wait for God to do his part.

Unless the LORD builds the house, its builders labor in vain. Unless the LORD watches over the city, the watchmen stand guard in vain. (Psalm 127:1)

This is life without God. It's a shame that this happens even in the Church, where people ought to know better. We *have* been taught better than that: we can't save ourselves, we can't discover the truth on our own, we can't become more spiritual by working harder to please God. We can't even take care of ourselves from day to day!

The eyes of all look to you, and *you* give them their
food at the proper time. (Psalm 145:15)

The answer for all of our problems is God himself. Unless he acts, we are lost, no matter how holy or dedicated we are. Unless he reveals himself, we are blind to the truth about him, no matter how clever or intelligent we think ourselves. Unless God saves us, our sin *will* kill us, no matter how hard we try not to sin.

Change the focus

What we need is a change of focus. A religion that doesn't center on God, that doesn't reach out and touch him, that doesn't trust in and wait on him to do something real to us, is an empty and worthless religion. But when God becomes real to us, and does real things in our lives, then we can call ourselves Christians. That is, in fact, the kind of faith that the Bible teaches us. It teaches us to expect answers to our prayers – specific answers that solve specific problems that we have. God can do anything that we ask of him! And the Bible teaches us that God will deliver us from our sin, so completely that we will no longer live in it. We can expect, in other words, that our lives will change dramatically when we walk with God. Anything short of his real presence and work in our lives is a pretence and a lie; it's not Christianity.

To understand what it means to focus on God, the easiest place to start is in the church. First, browse through the hymnal and notice what most of the hymns are about. You will see that they almost always focus on God in some way. They tell of his characteristics, his works, the life of Christ, how he answers prayer, the Spirit's work in the church – a hymnal is often like a book of doctrine about God! It's strange that, while people so often spend time thinking about themselves even in church, they at least are forced to look at God when they sing hymns!

But we need to take that same spirit and spread it across the entire church service. The sermons should be about God. The Sunday School lessons should teach about God. The prayers should open up the doors of Heaven and direct our minds to God sitting there on his throne. The entire service ought to be doing the same thing that the Bible itself does – revealing the true God in such a real way that we all know we have been in his presence, that we have learned something about him, and that knowledge will change our lives accordingly. This is what Paul prayed for, and what he said will most impress others who visit us:

> And I pray that you, being rooted and established in love, may have power, together with all the saints, to grasp how wide and long and high and deep is the love of Christ, and to *know* this love that surpasses knowledge — that you may be filled to the measure of all the fullness of God. (Ephesians 3:17-19)

> And we pray this in order that you may live a life worthy of the Lord and may please him in every way: bearing fruit in every good work, *growing in the knowledge of God.* (Colossians 1:10)

> But if an unbeliever or someone who does not understand comes in while everybody is prophesying, he will be convinced by all that he is a sinner and will be judged by all, and the secrets of his heart will be laid bare. So he will fall down and worship God, exclaiming, "God is really among you!" (1 Corinthians 14:24)

The purpose of the church service is to reveal the Lord to his saints: to bring them into his presence, through the Spirit and through faith, so that they can see him, know him, fear him, trust in him, and serve him. It should be a revelation to everyone who is present.

The Scriptures teach us that this is exactly what should happen when we gather together for worship. For example, in Psalms the writers often tell us what we should focus on in public worship. Here are the subjects that the Bible says our sermons and lessons should be about:

his abundant goodness – ***Psalm 145:7***
his awesome works – *** Psalm 145:6***

The Knowledge of God

his deeds – *Psalm 73:28*
his faithfulness – *Psalm 40:10*
the glorious splendor of his kingdom – *Psalm 145:12*
the glorious splendor of his majesty – *Psalm 145:5*
his glory – *Psalm 96:3*
the glory of his kingdom – *Psalm 145:11*
the God of Jacob – *Psalm 74:9*
his great deeds – *Psalm 145:6*
his great love – *Psalm 89:1*
his holy Name – *Psalm 145:21*
his love – *Psalm 40:10*
his love that stands firm forever – *Psalm 89:2*
his marvelous deeds – *Psalm 71:17*
his might – *Psalm 71:18*
his mighty acts – *Psalm 71:16*
his Name – *Psalm 22:22*
no wickedness in him – *Psalm 92:15*
his power – *Psalm 71:18*
his praiseworthy deeds – *Psalm 78:4*
the ramparts and citadels of his city – *Psalm 48:13*
his righteous acts – *Psalm 71:24*
his righteousness – *Psalm 35:28*
the Rock – *Psalm 92:15*
his salvation – *Psalm 40:10*
his splendor – *Psalm 71:8*
he plans things for us – *Psalm 40:5*
his truth – *Psalm 40:10*
he is upright – *Psalm 92:15*
his ways – *Psalm 51:13*
what he has done – *Psalm 9:11*
what he has done for me – *Psalm 66:16*
what he did in days past – *Psalm 44:1*
his wonderful acts – *Psalm 105:2*
his wonderful deeds – *Psalm 26:7*
his wonderful works – *Psalm 145:5*
his wonders – *Psalm 9:1*
his works – *Psalm 64:9*

When the Bible says something so plainly, and so consistently, it's time to take notice. In particular, we need to examine our own forms of worship – especially prayer and praise, and teaching the Word – and see if we're doing what these passages say we ought to be doing.

The essence of our faith

Man's greatest spiritual need is to know *for certain* whether there is a God, and if so, what he is like. If you study comparative religions you will notice that deep-seated drive to know the *truth about God*. The trouble is, none of those religions agree on the subject! They all say so many different and conflicting things about God that skeptics have given up hope of ever knowing anything certain about him.

Let's think this through: if God really does exist, and man's greatest problem is knowing for certain that he does, then when one of us actually breaks through and finds God, it must please the Lord immensely. That person is one of the favored few if he can actually *see God*. And that's exactly what Hebrews tells us:

> And without faith it is impossible to please God, because anyone who comes to him *must believe that he exists* and that he *rewards* those who earnestly seek him. (Hebrews 11:6)

To the person who finds God goes the rewards. He can now know the truth about many things that used to be a mystery – for example, the nature of God, the human spiritual condition, escape from sin and death, the treasures of eternity – the mystery of the ages opens up to his mind and heart. He can see things that generations of people have never known.

> But blessed are your eyes because they see, and your ears because they hear. For I tell you the truth, many prophets and righteous men longed to see what you see but did not see it, and to hear what you hear but did not hear it. (Matthew 13:16-17)

But can we really expect that such a thing could happen? *Can* someone know God? Wouldn't it be more natural to assume that people have only imagined God, and that the thousands of religions and philosophies in the world have attempted to do the impossible? Fortunately we don't have to wonder about this: there were **eyewitnesses** who have left irrefutable testimony about God. According to them, they *have* seen God – and they told us exactly what he's like. They also told us that we, too, can see their God if we come to him in a certain way. Their testimony, of course, is written in the Bible.

Eyewitnesses have seen God do amazing things. They saw him rescue the Israelites out of Egypt and destroy Pharaoh's army. They saw him give Moses the Law at Mt. Sinai. They saw him split the earth apart and destroy the wicked. They saw him destroy Sodom and Gomorrah. They saw him lead the Israelites into the Promised Land, a land held by tenacious Canaanites that were forced to give way before a powerful God. They saw him establish David on the throne, and give Solomon uncommon wisdom. They saw him take his people into exile to Babylon. They saw him bring those people back from Exile. They saw him come as an infant, born to a virgin, and perform miracles before believers and unbelievers alike. They saw him crucified and raised from the dead. They saw him ascend to Heaven. They saw him send the Spirit and begin building the Church.

These witnesses aren't lying to us. They number in the millions; they all saw God come *in person* and do *real* things among the people. Theirs wasn't an imaginary god, like Baal or Ashtoreth were. With this God, people could get some hard-core answers about life's most serious problems. "What then shall we say that Abraham, our forefather, discovered in this matter?" (Romans 4:1)

He provides meaning. Ecclesiastes tells us that the world – and our existence in it – looks empty and without meaning on the surface.

> I, the Teacher, was king over Israel in Jerusalem. I devoted myself to study and to explore by wisdom all that is done under heaven. What a heavy burden God has laid on men! I have seen all the things that are done under the sun; all of them are meaningless, a chasing after the wind. (Ecclesiastes 1:12-14)

The Lord did this on purpose: he didn't want man to find meaning in the *world*, but in *him*. God created man with a purpose in mind; he made us to serve him. He has a kingdom to build, he has certain methods by which he wants that kingdom to be built, and he expects us to share his values, his ways and methods, so that we will work with him instead of against him. So it's no wonder that people find nothing meaningful to live for in *this* world – only as we get in touch with God, and find our place *under him*, will we discover why we're here.

He defines right and wrong. God is the standard of morality, not man. Adam and Eve made a terrible mistake when they used their own feelings and thoughts to justify eating the fruit of the Tree of the Knowledge of Good and Evil.

> When the woman saw that the fruit of the tree was good for food and pleasing to the eye, and

also desirable for gaining wisdom, she took some and ate it. (Genesis 3:6)

If everyone operates on what *they* think is right, nobody will agree and we'll have chaos on our hands – which explains the kind of society we live in nowadays. Instead, we have to look to the Creator, the Judge of the earth, to find out what's right and wrong. Since he made the world according to *his* pattern of righteousness (in other words, the Law – the description of his perfect moral character) it makes sense to find out from him what the rules of his universe are. Work with them, and your life will be a success; work against them, and not only will you not get anywhere, but you'll ruin yourself and everything around you in the process. God's moral Law makes things work together in harmony.

He sets the goal. When the Lord made the world, he had something definite in mind. He wasn't interested in simply creating things and then walking away from them! An engineer doesn't make something only to throw it away when he's done; he has something in mind for his creation – a use, a purpose.

God is the same way about his world. Whether we know it or not – and most creatures don't, though man ought to know something about what God is up to – we fit into an overall plan that's slowly but surely building up and developing into an overall picture. At the end of time, God will bring everything to a finish, and show all of us what he has been working on all this time. Only then will we understand what part we played in the design process. And we will also have to face the truth about ourselves: whether we learned what that plan was and fit into it, working along with God to achieve his goals as profitable servants, or whether we turned our backs on him and his plans to pursue our own instead. The Lord has been looking forward to Judgment Day for a long time.

What do we learn about God?

There are two ways to study the Bible: either look for what it says about God, or look for ourselves in it. Since the Bible is primarily about God, our study will be profitable only if we look for *him*. If we don't, we aren't cooperating with the Author of the book – and of course we're going to get the wrong idea about what it teaches! Perhaps this is the real reason that so many people get so many conflicting theories from the Bible: they aren't being open-minded about what it wants to show them.

So when we study the Bible and look for God in it, what do we find there? We are going to learn so much about the Lord that it will amaze us! Never will we get to the bottom of the well; there's so much to learn about the infinite God that we could spend a lifetime studying him. And it's all information that will feed us, and strengthen us, and guide us toward light and life. It's all sweet and good for the soul.

- **God's ways.** The Lord has ways of doing things, peculiar to himself. Having "ways" just means that he prefers to do things in a certain way; not any way will do.

Through the Bible we can draw close enough to God to observe his ways. We find that they aren't at all the way *we* prefer to do things!

'For my thoughts are not your thoughts,

> neither are your ways my ways,'
> declares the LORD.
> 'As the heavens are higher than the earth,
> so are my ways higher than your ways
> and my thoughts than your thoughts.'
> (Isaiah 55:8-9)

For instance, God prefers to use little things to build his Kingdom. He isn't impressed with big things like we are. We love to use millions of dollars and thousands of people to solve our problems; we think that nothing can get done unless we throw huge, expensive solutions at the problems. But God seems to delight in choosing the little things, the things that nobody notices or cares about, to solve our most serious problems. He used five small pebbles in David's sling (not Saul's armor!) to bring down Goliath. He used a common prisoner (Joseph), an alien slave, to save Egypt from a devastating famine. He used a few fish and a couple of loaves of bread to feed thousands of people. He doesn't need much of this world, because it's his miraculous power that will solve the problem anyway. When he uses little or nothing to do something astonishing, it shows him off – and gets him glory.

He has other special ways of doing things that we need to learn: he uses **time** to work out his solutions, he uses **insignificant people** to do his important work, he wins by apparently **losing**, he **builds up** instead of tears down, he works through his **Spirit**. These are critically important facts to know about God, because we need to be working with him instead of against him as we serve in his Kingdom. If we don't know the way he likes to go about things, we'll only get in his way – if not actually hurt things! The Israelites angered God because they didn't know his ways, and therefore proved useless to his plan of the conquest of Canaan.

> Today, if you hear his voice,
>   do not harden your hearts
>   as you did in the rebellion,
>   during the time of testing in the desert,
> where your fathers tested and tried me
>   and for forty years saw what I did.
> That is why I was angry with that generation,
>   and I said, 'Their hearts are always going astray,
>   and **they have not known my ways**.'
> So I declared on oath in my anger,
>   'They shall never enter my rest.'
>   (Hebrews 3:7-11)

But if we know his ways, we will prove exceptionally useful to him.

- **God's works.** Though it's obvious that God does things, often we don't think about *what* he does and *how* he does it. The record of his works span the entire Bible; we can learn a great deal about God – in addition to avoiding certain problems – by studying his works.

"Great are the works of the LORD; they are pondered by all who delight in them." (Psalm 111:2) The works of God fall into seven categories:

Creation and Providence
the making of Israel
judgment
the coming of Christ

**building up a Kingdom
the Last Day
the Word of God**

The Bible very carefully explains each of these special works of God: exactly what he did, why he did it, how he did it, and how it turned out (or will turn out!).

For example, in the *Making of Israel*, we see him making a covenant with Abraham that will be effective not only for his physical descendants, but with all of his children down through the ages, including the eternal Church that exists in our own time. He gave Israel the Law, the description of the perfect Servant of God (which not only describes our sin against God but what it will take to remove that sin.) He introduced the circumcision of the heart, symbolized among the Israelites by physical circumcision but a characteristic of all true children of God. And he made faith the key that enables anyone who will to enter into the Kingdom of God.

There are three reasons we need to not only know, but fully understand, God's works: *first*, so that we can identify his work. The problem we have in this world is that there is so much deceit going on. Everyone with a religion claims that God is blessing *them* and helping *them*, according to the rules of *their* religion! But there are lots of things going on in this world that aren't God's doing. Either man is behind it, or the world system, or our great enemy Satan. People are trying to build a perfect world, a form of righteousness, a false sense of security and peace and happiness – but it won't work. They're relying on the wrong god. Only the

God described in the Bible can make good on his promises of Heaven.

This means that we have to be able to correctly identify the works of this God; we have to be able to tell whether he's really present doing his type of work. Unless we can do this, we're going to be confused about whether he's really behind something! People will throw "every wind of teaching" (Ephesians 4:14) at us, claiming that their god is real, and try to deceive us.

But there's no reason to be deceived or confused about what is really God's work. All we have to do is study his works recorded in the Bible and learn exactly what it is that our God does. Then we take that list and compare it with what's going on in any "ministry" that claims his name – and see if they match. If not, then we don't have to take them seriously.

Second, we need to know God's works because they are food for prayer. We want what only God can do, because only God can give us what we need. Prayer homes in on God's promises, his power and wisdom, his spiritual world that overcomes our world. When we pray, we shouldn't make up things to ask for! Ask instead for what he *does*. God's treasures and works are much more powerful than anything we can imagine, and they are all carefully explained to us in the Bible. There's no point asking for things that he doesn't do!

Third, we need to know exactly what God does so that we won't try such things ourselves. God not only does what man can't do, he does what we are not supposed to even try to do. He *has* given us work to do, and he expects us to be busy about it. But he never required us, for example, to save ourselves, or change our own hearts, or defeat the enemy on our own, or make his Kingdom our way with our own efforts. Each of these important works requires *his* hand – only he has the eternal resources, and the necessary power to pull it off. If we even try, we will fail and mess things up in the process. Our job is to open ourselves up to him so that he can do his work for and through us.

- **God's glory.** God requires glory in all that he does. "Glory" is very simple: it means, who gets the credit? Who was responsible for what happened? In God's case, he is behind just about everything that happens in this world – except sin, which, unfortunately, is to our "credit."

God made the world, he provides for the daily needs of every creature in the world, he decides when and where each of us will be born and live (Acts 17:26), he raises up nations, he brings them down, he lifts up a man to honor, he dishonors others, he keeps the Church alive and strong, he regularly brings down the wicked to destruction and holds them there until Judgment (2 Peter 2:9). It's awesome to see how much God does in our world – yet he gets almost no credit for all these things. For proof, look in today's newspaper and see if it gives him the credit for *any* of this, though it's all true.

He demands glory, however; so someday he will get all this credit that we owe him. On the Last Day, he will demand an accounting from every creature in the world; that judgment will reveal the entire truth behind all that's happened in history. It will be plain on that day how much God had a hand in everything that happened. On that day, every creature will plainly see, and completely agree with the fact, that God deserves credit for all of history.

There are two reasons he demands glory: *first*, because he really is what he claims to be! He isn't being arrogant, like a proud man who actually has little to be proud about. When the Scripture says that God is Almighty, it goes on to prove that point by telling us about the miracles that he did – awesome works that beggar the human imagination. There's no question, when we study the record, that he does deserve all the credit that the Bible gives him.

Second, he wants us to hear about what he is and what he has done, so that we will *want* what we see in him and come to him for salvation. He gets glory so that *we might be saved*. When more people take advantage of what he offers us in Christ, when more people find out that he's as good as his Word, then he gets glory in the earth. A successful church will grow with more and more people who come for the life they heard about and saw in God, through us – who receive real answers to our prayers.

• **God's holiness.** God is *holy* if he's anything. That's the first thing that struck Isaiah when he saw God on his throne in Heaven:

> In the year that King Uzziah died, I saw the LORD seated on a throne, high and exalted, and the train of his robe filled the temple. Above him were seraphs, each with six wings: With two wings they covered their faces, with two they covered their feet, and

with two they were flying. And they were calling to one another:

> "Holy, holy, holy is the LORD Almighty;
> the whole earth is full of his glory."

At the sound of their voices the doorposts and thresholds shook and the temple was filled with smoke. "Woe to me!" I cried. "I am ruined! For I am a man of unclean lips, and I live among a people of unclean lips, and my eyes have seen the King, the LORD Almighty." Then one of the seraphs flew to me with a live coal in his hand, which he had taken with tongs from the altar. With it he touched my mouth and said, "See, this has touched your lips; your guilt is taken away and your sin atoned for." (Isaiah 6:1-7)

Nobody can see God and live. (Exodus 33:20) That's because he's so pure and righteous, and we are so wicked and unrighteous, that we can't coexist in the same place. The King is offended with so much of what we've done against him and his Kingdom that he *has* to straighten out the problem. He has that right – this is his world, and he has the right to decide what his house will be like. He wants his house to be as holy as he is – not a trace of sin and death, not even the elusive thoughts of sin that so often run through our minds during the day.

And since he's the Master, it's we who have to change, not him! Actually, the entire Bible can be described as God's solution of *making* us fit in with his holy nature, one way or another: the wicked will be destroyed; and the righteous will be saved, cleansed, and made holy themselves so that they can live with him.

- **God the Savior.** Hopefully when we see just how holy God is, we will be struck with the same point that Isaiah realized: how unholy we are in comparison. We can only learn the depth of our spiritual problem by learning the depth of God's holiness.

But as we grapple with the reality of our sinful nature, God won't leave us hopeless – which could easily happen when we see that there's no hope for us in our own efforts or in whatever the world offers us. God will step in with *his* solution to our problem of sin and death: the Lord Jesus Christ, the Savior who took away the sin, who renews the mind and heart and makes a "new creation" (2 Corinthians 5:17) out of a sinner. Those who see this wonderful answer and reach out to take it from the Father's merciful hand will find eternal life and light from Heaven.

Salvation is God's great business on earth. He's been busy putting the system together even from the beginning; the foundations of the Church extend back to the first books of the Bible. For those who have eyes to see, the Covenant given to Abraham was the first great building block in the salvation process. From there, the rest of the structure grew throughout the Old Testament (the Law, the making of the nation Israel, the Promised Land, King David, the Temple, the Prophets of Israel) into the finished work of Christ as he formed his Church out of the redeemed over all the earth.

There are too many Christians who glibly say, "I believe in Jesus," without giving any thought to all that went into the salvation that Jesus offers us. It's an enormous work! God used millions of people, over thousands of years, to prepare what we now have in Jesus. And we need to study that material in depth if we hope to come close to understanding the true nature of Christ and what he does for us in saving our souls for Heaven.

- **God's plans and goals.** The Bible is like the morning's schedule for the employees at work. It carefully outlines three things: where we are now, where we are headed, and how we're going to get there. With this information, we can be fully informed about what God is doing among us – and become profitable servants as we work with him. After all, God can't work with ignorant servants who don't know their master's wishes! (John 15:15)

What are God's plans? *First*, he's only using this world as a temporary measure, to work out the more serious aspects of eternity. He has little concern for what unbelievers consider crucial for life – food, clothing, shelter, pleasure. As Jesus counseled us, the Father knows that we need such things – what he wants *us* to work on are the more important matters:

> So do not worry, saying, 'What shall we eat?' or 'What shall we drink?' or 'What shall we wear?' For the pagans run after all these things, and your Heavenly Father knows that you need them. But seek first his kingdom and his righteousness, and all these things will be given to you as well. (Matthew 6:31-33)

Second, he intends to destroy this physical world at the end of time. It will have served his purposes by then, and he won't have need of it any more. (Hebrews 1:11-12) So it's no use putting our hearts on it, or spending all our energies to get more of what he intends to dispose of in the end.

Third, his great intention all along has been to solve our problem of sin and death – *his* way. He intends to destroy sin in our hearts, to free us from the great Deceiver of the world, to fill our minds and hearts with his saving Word, to put us in the company of the saints, to work out his salvation by means of the gifts of the Spirit, to put the desire for Heaven and its treasures in our hearts and take away the desire for this world's treasures – and much more. If you study *how* he plans to save us – the precise steps, the particular things he intends to do – then you won't be surprised or disappointed when he keeps hammering away at these same issues, instead of what *you* want him to do.

Fourth, he intends to wrap up everything at the end of time and judge all things. This judgment is absolutely necessary, because otherwise people will think that he hasn't had all things in control – or at least that he hasn't been fair to many of us. On that day, he intends to prove that he was always the Master, in full control of everything. Nothing happened apart from his will. Everything he did was entirely fair and just – and he'll show us why, so that we will understand and be forced to agree with his judgment. This is important to know, because it should give us confidence in how he runs his world now, and faith in him as he works things out according to *his* will – not according to *our* wishes. He knows what he's doing.

- **God's Kingdom.** If we could back up far enough to see the entire project that God is working on, we can see that he's building a Kingdom. Remember that he first made this world as his kingdom, and he gave man the responsibility to rule over it in his Name. Since that first kingdom fell, with man, into ruin and sin and death, God has been working on a second one to replace the first.

The first kingdom was based on the physical, and the frail will of man to keep it going. This second one, however, will be made of tougher materials: stones made in Heaven, not on earth; wisdom from above, not below; and made to last forever, not open to the destructive ravages of time and weather and the hand of man.

This second Kingdom is addressing some vital concerns: *first*, the heart of man. In order to have a Kingdom of peace and righteousness, the notorious criminal in God's ruined universe has to be *remade* – born of the Spirit, made holy and clean in God's sight. Then man can not only know and appreciate the holiness of God, he can love and live with the kinds of things that Heaven is made of. A willing, happy, and obedient servant doesn't happen by accident – it's the result of long years of work in the church, work done by God himself. The finished product will be a glory to God's wisdom and power, and will naturally fit in with the kind of Kingdom that God has in mind for eternity.

Second, the second Kingdom will consist of all the things that God wants for man. God wants *peace* for us – something that none of us have ever worked out on our own. God wants perfect *righteousness* for us – a claim that none of us can truly make of ourselves at this point. (Psalm 143:2) God wants us to be his *family* (Ephesians 1:5) – an astounding gift that even the angels marvel at. If we list all the things that God has planned for man in eternity, they fall into two groups: the end of all that made us miserable in this world, and the precious gift of the treasures of Heaven.

God is the source of all that we need

When we finally get a grasp of how enormous God is, we begin to realize how much we need him. This is true of anything in life. For example, children often don't like to read books because books represent school – which they hate! But as they grow up and their needs get more complex, they find that books hold the answers that they're looking for. Suddenly something that had no value becomes of great value. The same thing is true about God. Though too many people see no value in knowing God, a few have "grown up" spiritually and caught a glimpse at the unimaginable riches that are in God – and they are all free for the asking.

> Now to him who is able to do immeasurably more than all we ask or imagine, according to his power that is at work within us … (Ephesians 3:20)

> I can do everything through him who gives me strength. (Philippians 4:13)

These treasures exactly fit the needs of man. God intended that they should, since in the beginning mankind was supposed to rule over God's creation in God's Name, using God's resources to do the job according to God's specifications. Now that some people are back on track – in other words, they have been restored from the deadly effects of sin and death, and have become "co-laborers" of the new spiritual Kingdom that Christ is building – they need the treasures of Heaven even more now. What will we find in God that will help us do our jobs?

- **Resources.** "For no matter how many promises God has made, they are 'Yes' in Christ. And so through him the 'Amen' is spoken by us to the glory of God." (2 Corinthians 1:20) It's hard to believe that all the riches of Heaven are ours now, but it's true. Everything in Heaven is ours. The problem is knowing what they are, and how to get them!

Another problem that too many of us have is that we settle for a religion without answers. We pray, but we don't ask for anything specific; we too often think that if we get too specific in our prayers, God won't answer them and we'll be disappointed. So we ask for general things like "Lord, bless me!" But God's treasures are real, designed to address real problems in our lives. Get answers to your prayers, and don't be satisfied until you do. Be like Jacob who wrestled with the angel all night until God gave him what he asked for!

One way to start is to focus on the Names of the Lord. The Bible tells us many of his Names, and each one describes a particular aspect of his character or works. For example, there are (according to one count) over 125 names for Christ in the Bible – like Shepherd, Husband, King, Physician, Passover Lamb, and so on. Each of these are descriptions of what he will do for us. When we understand each of these and how perfectly he fulfills these ideas for his people, our lives have to become richer as a result.

Another resource is what Jesus referred to as the "treasures in Heaven."

> Do not store up for yourselves treasures on earth, where moth and rust destroy, and where thieves break in and steal. But store up for yourselves treasures in Heaven, where moth and rust do not destroy, and where thieves do not break in and steal. For where your treasure is, there your heart will be also. (Matthew 6:19-21)

What are those treasures? How does one store them up? What are the steps involved? What will happen if we do store them up? What will happen if we don't? If we could have some of these practical questions answered, we would be much richer as a result.

- **The Way.** "I am the Way, the Truth, and the Life. No one comes to the Father except through me." (John 14:6) One of the biggest problems in life is finding out exactly what to do with oneself. We want to be doing something, and since most people don't believe in a God, they make up a job to do – whatever pleases them, or whatever makes them feel better about themselves.

But a Christian already has the way marked out for him. *His* main purpose is to *get ready for eternity*. The Spirit's job is to lead him to Heaven; along the way, the Lord will work on his soul and mind to make him fit for when he finally arrives there. This is because God requires that all who live with him in Heaven look and act a certain way – and the pattern is Christ himself, the first Man who rose to live with the Father in Heaven. That's why the Spirit must live with us, and work on us, because such a high calling will require that we undergo many changes, and our souls must conform to the standard in Christ. At death we will finally "graduate" and "share our Master's happiness." (Matthew 25:21)

- **Instructions for the job.** "You are my friends if you do what I command." (John 15:14) As we journey through this world getting ready for the next, there are two things we must do: we must love God (which requires that we stick to the program and get ready to live with him!), and we must love our neighbor (which requires that we know God's love for him as well, and fit in with God's plans for *how* to love our neighbor and build the Kingdom of saints in the Church!).

We can't work on our salvation in our own way. Paul said to "work out your salvation with fear and trembling" (Philippians 2:12) – which means that we have to do it God's way. We mustn't do things that would anger God, or aim in directions opposite from his will, or use materials that are not of his choosing. And we can't work even in the Church in our own way; a "church" like that will be build on sand, not the solid foundation of Christ. Paul told us to build on the foundation of the "Apostles and Prophets", with Christ as the cornerstone. (Ephesians 2:20) If we follow these instructions, our work will be revealed on the last day as something worth saving; if not, God will throw it away as so much trash, because we weren't careful to do things his way. (Romans 9:22)

- **Correction and reproof.** "All Scripture is God-breathed and is useful for teaching, rebuking, correcting and training in righteousness." (2 Timothy 3:16) There are times when we have to be corrected, because we don't always do what is right. Though we all admit that we aren't perfect, it's a hard thing to admit to a particular fault.

"Wounds from a friend can be trusted, but an enemy multiplies kisses." (Proverbs 27:6) A wise person will welcome correction, because it means that someone cares enough about his soul to tell him where he's going wrong. It would be a crime to let someone go headed off into sin without telling him the consequences! The Lord is being a caring Father when he rebukes us for sin; he doesn't want his children to grow up wicked and rebellious. He wants them to be *perfect*.

If anybody knows what's wrong with us, our Creator and Redeemer does. God designed us to work a certain way, and he knows when we're spiritually broken and not working according to his original design. Christ died for our sins, and he knows what's in us that offends God and how to go about crucifying that sin.

The Bible has so much to say about our sins, and how to correct them, that many times we hate to keep reading about it – it seems too oppressive and negative. But we little realize the extent of our sin: like a cancer that spreads throughout the body, our sin, willfulness, rebellion and ignorance has affected every part of our lives. It will take an entire lifetime to work it all out. It's a mercy that the medicine for all of it is in the Word of God! How else could we be saved? We also little realize the tremendous requirements for living in Heaven – there, total and absolute perfection is the standard.

Nothing short of that can even survive in the presence of such a holy God! We have a lot to do to get ready.

- **The Big Picture.** "I make known the end from the beginning, from ancient times, what is still to come." (Isaiah 46:10) Finally, another important advantage that we get from knowing God is his viewpoint from Heaven. From there on his throne, "high above all principalities and powers," he can see the entire universe and its progress. He can see how everything fits together, and what is still needed to complete the picture.

That shouldn't be news to anybody – everyone knows that God is above all and can see everything. The amazing thing is that he invites his children – in fact, he insists on it! – to share his vantage point. In Christ we are seated at the right hand of God!

God calls his children fellow workers (1 Corinthians 3:9). We *need* to see things as he does if we are going to work on building his Kingdom. We have to see what materials to use, how to lay block upon block, when to step out of the way to let God do his part, what the goal is, when to lay this work down and start another, where the weak points are, and how to discern the destructive work of the enemy. We can see all of this from Heaven.

But how do we step up to such a height? There is where the Spirit of God comes in. He lifts us up spiritually (though a spiritual step, it's nevertheless real!) to the throne of God, where we can see God in his glory and turn around to see his Kingdom beneath his feet. With an open Bible as our guidebook, and the Spirit taking us by the hand, we enter the halls of the King to work with him on his eternal house.

How do we learn of him?

There are only three ways we can learn the truth about God, and we have got to get this right if we hope to know the truth. The reason that so many have failed to find the true God is that they didn't use the way that God gave them to know it. God has graciously given us the means of finding him; it's the height of ignorance and stupidity to turn our backs on what he himself says is the only way to find him.

First, **we will learn of God only in the Bible.** It's unfortunate that many people don't believe this. They think that they can go by their feelings, or on what their authorities or traditions tell them about God. The Bible, however, is the only reliable source of information about him.

You have to understand how the Bible does this in order to get the most good out of it. In the Old Testament we have the truth about God broken down into simple stories that deal with one or two aspects of him at a time. Through history, biography, worship ceremonies, prophecies and wisdom literature, we learn about God piece by piece. In the New Testament we have the full light of God in the Son, and the writings of the Apostles interpret who Jesus is and what he did. The more we study, the fuller the picture becomes – like putting together a picture puzzle. And you have to keep studying; you can't stop after learning only one or two things about God. The knowledge of God is like a diamond: it has many facets, which must first be turned around and looked at separately. Then back up and look at what the whole thing is.

Then you will get a balanced and useful understanding about God.

***Second*, we will learn of God only by the Spirit.** The Spirit's job is to reveal the things of God:

> The Spirit searches all things, even the deep things of God. For who among men knows the thoughts of a man except the man's spirit within him? In the same way no one knows the thoughts of God except the Spirit of God. We have not received the spirit of the world but the Spirit who is from God, that we may understand what God has freely given us. (1 Corinthians 2:10-12)

Because of the Spirit, we can actually enter into the "Holy of Holies" in God's temple in Heaven and see our Father there, with the Son at his right hand. Prayer would never work without the Spirit's help; he shows us the reality of the treasures of Heaven, and enables us to approach the Father with our requests. What was once impossible for man – to come into God's presence – is now routine for the children of God, because of the power of the Spirit. Even when we read the Bible, the Spirit must open its truth to us in a way that we are able to see God there in his glory.

***Third*, we will find God only in Jesus Christ.** Jesus came with the purpose to reveal God to us. He is eminently qualified to do this, because he himself is God's Son – one with the Father, who sends his Spirit out to us and draws us in with him and the Father. In times past, the revelation of God was done through earthly realities – the temple in

Jerusalem, the physical miracles, the Exodus from Egypt. Now, however, we have the reality in Christ that those old "shadows" were pointing at. Find Jesus, come to him, lay yourself out to him, and *you will know God* as he draws you to himself and lives in you through the Spirit.

Knowledge of God straightens things out

When the patient takes the medicine, his illness disappears. When the student studies his textbook, he passes the test. When the runner trains diligently, he wins the race. There are many examples in life that show us the importance of taking seriously the fundamentals if we hope to win the prize.

When it comes to spiritual matters, there is also a fundamental principle: ***learn about God.*** If you do this, things will go so much better for you spiritually. It may be painful – hard work is usually painful and not at all fun. It may seem pointless – training often looks pointless. It may seem like drudgery while others are having more fun doing other things. But in the end, *the knowledge of God is **life***. When hard times come that require a knowledge of God, you will be so thankful that you spent time studying about him. You will know *what* to do, and you will know *where* to go for necessary spiritual resources, when others won't have any notion of what to do or where to go for help.

> The name of the LORD is a strong tower;
> the righteous run to it and are safe. (Proverbs 18:10)

- **The knowledge of God prevents idolatry.** We mustn't think that idolatry was a problem of primitive societies only. Anybody who forms an image – whether out of stone or their imagination – of a god that is different from the God of the Bible is an idolater. The Bible describes the true God; any other god is a false god.

Since the necessary information about the true God is so plain and within reach in the Bible, there's no excuse for making up a false god. The Bible shows us his spiritual characteristics, the works he has done in the past, what he likes and what he hates, who he chooses to honor him, what he does to the righteous and the wicked. In fact, there's such a complete and wide-ranging description of God in detail there, that we can not only know a great deal about him, it will provide years of study to search out all of his ways and works. You may not know much about him at first, but the more you study about him in the Word, his picture will become clearer to you and you will be able to act on that knowledge with life-changing results. False gods can't give you any payback like this.

- **The knowledge of God produces fruit in us.** As you get to know God better, you will begin to realize what he expects of you. He's a God of holiness, a God of peace and righteousness, a God of love, a God who hates sin. It's only natural that he would want those around him to be the same way.

The angels know very well what God is like, and they dare not do anything against his will. They exist only to serve him with their whole beings – to a point of perfection. Human beings, however, since they live in a dark world with little understanding of a God they can't see, often talk themselves into turning away from God and committing sin with no remorse or stricken conscience.

But when we see this God that the Bible talks about, then (like other saints in the Bible who saw him) we know down inside what we are in comparison to him. We know that there's a lot to straighten out in our lives because he is the way he is. If we have any hope of living in his Heaven for eternity, then we understand that much work has to be done on our hearts before we'll be ready to live there – we have to be made fit for his service. As we stand now, we would never be allowed in! (Matthew 22:10-14) We have to have the robes of Christ's righteousness covering our nakedness of sin and death.

- **The knowledge of God gets him glory.** We've looked at this before, but it bears repeating. God insists on getting glory – he wants everyone to know who he is and what he can do. That's glory – giving him the credit for what he is.

When we search him out, then, and finally get to know him, we are filled with the appropriate feelings of love, fear, devotion, service, honor and praise. We can't help but relate to him in a way that honors him. Nobody can meet God and not be changed as a result!

That change in our hearts will soon become apparent not only to the Lord, but to the world around us. Others will know that we've been in the presence of God. They will see a changed life, and a new hope. They will want the same thing, and they'll ask us how and where they can find this God. You see, the process just grows and grows, as the knowledge of God spreads all around the earth. The more this happens, the more glory God gets as a result.

- **The knowledge of God shows our responsibilities.** At first just the sight and knowledge of God is overwhelming; when we actually see him, we can do nothing but stand amazed – and keep looking. Just absorbing this new revelation is a full-time work.

But it won't be long before the Lord will show us what to do with this knowledge. These are the steps: *first*, we learn about God; *then* we go out and do our work – never the other way around. When we learn who the Lord is and what *his* works are, that reveals what *our* place is in his plan – and we do have a place. We must never do his work; due to our ignorance it's too easy to think that we can and must act first and save ourselves. But while we wait on him to do his part, and trust that he will keep his promises and do what we can't do for ourselves, we also must take his command seriously to go out and do those things that he has given us to do. Of course, if we know him and his works well, we will know exactly what it is that we must do – we won't be confused, or in the dark, about his will for our lives.

- **The knowledge of God guides prayer.** Little do most people understand this powerful concept! Prayer needs something to grind on, like a meat grinder working on meat. We must put the ways and works of God into our prayers if we hope to say anything intelligent to the Almighty during prayer time.

When you read in the Bible about what God did in the past for his people, that's what you need to pray for in your time. (Habakkuk 3:2) When you read about God's utter holiness, you obviously need to look at your own heart and pray that he would make you fit to live with him in eternity. The point is that you must focus on what *he* considers important; and the Bible shows us very clearly what's important to God. If we pray while giving no thought at all to God's nature, his works and promises to us, or his overall plan for the Church, then how can we expect him to take our prayer seriously if we don't take him seriously? How can he let us help him work on his Kingdom if we don't know what's going on?

The Point

We've spent a lot of time here looking at how much the Bible shows us about God. The reason for that is because people are so prone to look for everything except God when they study the Bible. That has to change: our only hope is **God**, and the Bible mercifully shows us our hope in clear pictures, in a way that we can see him and put our trust in him.

Therefore, when you **read the Bible**, *look for God there*. He's on every page. The purpose of the Bible is to show us God, in many ways. Don't miss the point and use the Bible for everything but that!

When you **worship**, focus your thoughts on God and get him clearly in view. He's what you really need. "Who have I in Heaven but you? And earth has nothing I desire besides you." (Psalm 73:25) He deserves all glory, and he always listens to those who get him clearly in view and honor him for what he is.

The Knowledge of God

When you **pray**, find out first what *he* wants to do, and what he has available there in Heaven, and then ask for *that*. Don't make up your own list of things to ask for! He knows, as the Creator, what you need and what you must do. Your job is to report in to the Master and give him the credit for knowing what he's doing. Turn your prayer over to him, and let him do the talking for a change while you listen.

The Fear of the Lord

**Let all the earth fear the LORD;
let all the people of the world revere him. (Psalm 33:8)**

I once had a discussion with someone about the fear of the Lord. He insisted that New Testament Christians don't need to fear God anymore. "Perfect love casts out fear," he quoted to me. So I went home and did a search on my computerized Bible for all the references on fearing God – about a hundred verses all told – and took the printout to him the next day. After looking over what the Bible actually says about it, there wasn't much he could say except it was clear that he was wrong!

We're going to look at many of those references here, and I believe that you too will see how important and proper it is for a Christian to fear God. He *commanded* us to fear him, we must *understand* what this fear is, we must *serve* him in fear, we must be *zealous* to fear him – even *Jesus Christ* himself feared the Father!

What is the fear of the Lord?

When you fear God, it means simply this:

You are careful to do everything that God commands, because you know that if you don't there will be dire consequences.

We fear God in the same way that we fear other things, like losing our jobs, or war, or disease, or great social upheavals. Fear means that we know we could get hurt if we aren't careful; so, knowing that, we *are* careful and live so that we won't get hurt. Fear is, in fact, a built-in characteristic in almost all living creatures: it's a failsafe measure that we fall back on to avoid pain, injury and death. It's being alert about our surroundings and finding the safest way through the dangers. If it weren't for fear we would walk calmly into destruction without any hesitation.

There are certain unique reasons for fearing God, however:

- **God is the Creator:** God made us, which means he can unmake us any time he wants to. He knows how we're made, he knows us inside and out, and therefore he knows what he can expect out of us. If we don't operate as he designed us, he will be extremely displeased with us. This is what made the Apostle Paul write the following difficult passage:

> Therefore God has mercy on whom he wants to have mercy, and he hardens whom he wants to harden. One of you will say to me: "Then why does God still blame us? For who resists his will?" But who are you, O man, to talk back to God? "Shall what is formed say to him who formed it, 'Why did you make me like this?'" Does not the potter have the right to make out of the same lump of clay some pottery for noble purposes and some for common use? What if God, choosing to show his wrath and make his power known, bore with great patience the objects of his wrath — prepared for destruction? (Romans 9:18-22)

God forms us according to his will, not ours. He decides when and where all of us will live. (Acts 17:26) God decides what the circumstances of our lives will be. He literally formed us in the womb, according to his will. (Psalm 139:13-16) He knows the day of our death, and how we will die to glorify him. (John 21:19) If God has such complete control over us as our Creator, who wouldn't fear him? What has he planned for us? What has he already decided that we should live through? Will we have suffering or blessing, joy or sorrow, life or death? Will we even have a chance to hear the Gospel and be saved, or will we never hear it? All these events and times are in his hands; we are helpless before him.

- **God is the King:** The universe is God's Kingdom, and he alone sits on the throne. Scientists think that the universe runs according to built-in laws and principles of physical existence. In reality, God rules over all.

> He is before all things, and in him all things hold together. (Colossians 1:17)

> I have installed my King
> on Zion, my holy hill.
> I will proclaim the decree of the LORD:
> He said to me, "You are my Son;
> today I have become your Father.
> Ask of me,
> and I will make the nations your inheritance,
> the ends of the earth your possession.
> You will rule them with an iron scepter;
> you will dash them to pieces like pottery."

> Therefore, you kings, be wise;

> be warned, you rulers of the earth.
> Serve the LORD with fear
> and rejoice with trembling. (Psalm 2:6-11)

The King is guiding the universe according to the blueprint that he drew up in the beginning. He provides for his creatures (Psalm 145:15-16). He publishes his Law – both physical and spiritual – and demands obedience from all creatures. He protects his subjects. He expects righteousness and justice – morality and ethics are built into the fabric of our world, and none of us can deny that. And the universe is slowly but surely headed for Judgment Day when the King will wrap it all up as a finished product, a Kingdom in which he alone rules and gets all glory. (1 Corinthians 15:24-25) If God is this much in control of the world, who would not fear the King?

- **God is the Judge:** A judge plays a vital role in a courtroom. Since almost nobody tells the truth about themselves, especially when punishment is at stake, the judge is appointed to hear the testimony from both sides of the argument and review the evidence. Then he issues his *judgment* – his official opinion of **what really happened**. Then the law proceeds on *his* opinion, not on anybody else's.

Since we are all sinners, none of us can be trusted to tell the whole truth about ourselves before a holy God. Not only do we fear the consequences of what might happen to us if found guilty by God, none of us realize the full extent of our moral crimes. God alone knows what we've done and the damage we've caused. He alone knows what it would take to satisfy the Law's demands. He alone knows what we need to be fixed. Therefore, God is the only

Judge that we have. Paul taught us never to judge ourselves:

> I care very little if I am judged by you or by any human court; indeed, I do not even judge myself. My conscience is clear, but that does not make me innocent. It is the Lord who judges me. Therefore judge nothing before the appointed time; wait till the Lord comes. He will bring to light what is hidden in darkness and will expose the motives of men's hearts. At that time each will receive his praise from God. (1 Corinthians 4:3-5)

- **God uses terrifying standards:** For all the above reasons, a reasonable man could easily see that it's wise to fear God. We can go wrong in so many ways before such a God that it would be a good idea to live his way instead of our way.

But we little realize how serious the problem really is. God uses terrifying standards to judge us by. His Law is like a measuring stick that he puts alongside our lives. When he does that, we fall so far short of the standards that it's a miracle that he doesn't throw us out as so much worthless junk and start over again! Anybody who thinks that they are something ought to look carefully into the Law; it's a frighteningly deep well of righteousness and justice that we have little concept of.

Jesus, for example, showed us the unreachable standards of the Law in his Sermon on the Mount:

> You have heard that it was said to the people long ago, 'Do not murder, and anyone who murders will be subject to judgment.'

> But I tell you that anyone who is angry with his brother will be subject to judgment. Again, anyone who says to his brother, 'Raca,' is answerable to the Sanhedrin. But anyone who says, 'You fool!' will be in danger of the fire of hell.(Matthew 5:21-22)

Who hasn't felt the temptation to harbor ill feelings against another human being, for whatever reasons? And whatever your reasons, what if God felt that it was unjust for you to have those feelings? If he did, he judged you guilty of murder and hell is your punishment! What kind of standards of perfection does this God expect of us?

It's this surprising severity in the Law, this perfection that we can't possibly reach, that most bothers people about God when they read about him in the Bible. And the Bible also shows God's full intent to thoroughly punish the wicked (remember, the "wicked" are those whom God calls wicked, not what we call ourselves) in violent and sudden punishments.

In other words, God is not playing games with us. He means exactly what he says. If we fulfill the Law then he will reward us; if we break his Law, he reacts in wrath and promises to destroy us. This is the God of the Bible, and this is the God that many people have been avoiding. This is the primary reason that people make up false gods – they want someone who isn't so harsh with impossible standards.

Does the Bible teach the fear of God?

Contrary to popular opinion, the Bible not only teaches us the duty of fearing God, it does so from beginning to end – both in the Old and New Testaments.

Here are some of the passages of the Bible that teach us to fear God. This isn't by any means the entire list that I showed my friend; there are many more that use the word "fear" as well as many passages that use the words "feared" and "fears." But you will get the point from this shortened list all the same.

> **Do not take advantage of each other, but fear your God. I am the LORD your God. (Lev. 25:17)**
>
> **The LORD commanded us to obey all these decrees and to fear the LORD our God, so that we might always prosper and be kept alive, as is the case today. (Deut. 6:24)**
>
> **And now, O Israel, what does the LORD your God ask of you but to fear the LORD your God, to walk in all his ways, to love him, to serve the LORD your God with all your heart and with all your soul. (Deut. 10:12)**
>
> **Their children, who do not know this Law, must hear it and learn to fear the LORD your God as long as you live in the land you are crossing the Jordan to possess. (Deut. 31:13)**
>
> **He did this so that all the peoples of the earth might know that the hand of the LORD is powerful and so that you might always fear the LORD your God. (Joshua 4:24)**
>
> **Now fear the LORD and serve him with all faithfulness. Throw away the gods your forefathers worshiped beyond the River and in Egypt, and serve the LORD. (Joshua 24:14)**
>
> **But be sure to fear the LORD and serve him faithfully with all your heart; consider what great things he has done for you. (1 Samuel 12:24)**

The Fear of the Lord

He gave them these orders: "You must serve faithfully and wholeheartedly in the fear of the LORD." (2 Chron. 19:9)

He sought God during the days of Zechariah, who instructed him in the fear of God. As long as he sought the LORD, God gave him success. (2 Chron. 26:5)

And he said to man, 'The fear of the Lord—that is wisdom, and to shun evil is understanding.' (Job 28:28)

Serve the LORD with fear and rejoice with trembling. (Ps 2:11)

... Who despises a vile man but honors those who fear the LORD, who keeps his oath even when it hurts. (Ps 15:4)

The fear of the LORD is pure, enduring forever. The ordinances of the LORD are sure and altogether righteous. (Ps 19:9)

You who fear the LORD, praise him! All you descendants of Jacob, honor him! Revere him, all you descendants of Israel! (Ps 22:23)

The LORD confides in those who fear him; he makes his covenant known to them. (Ps 25:14)

Let all the earth fear the LORD; let all the people of the world revere him. (Ps 33:8)

But the eyes of the LORD are on those who fear him, on those whose hope is in his unfailing love. (Ps 33:18)

Fear the LORD, you his saints, for those who fear him lack nothing. (Ps 34:9)

Teach me your way, O LORD, and I will walk in your truth; give me an undivided heart, that I may fear your name. (Ps 86:11)

As a father has compassion on his children, so the LORD has compassion on those who fear him. (Ps 103:13)

Let those who fear the LORD say: "His love endures forever." (Ps 118:4)

The Fear of the Lord

The LORD delights in those who fear him, who put their hope in his unfailing love. (Ps 147:11)

The fear of the LORD is the beginning of knowledge, but fools despise wisdom and discipline. (Prov. 1:7)

Do not be wise in your own eyes; fear the LORD and shun evil. (Prov. 3:7)

The fear of the LORD is a fountain of life, turning a man from the snares of death. (Prov. 14:27)

Through love and faithfulness sin is atoned for; through the fear of the LORD a man avoids evil. (Prov. 16:6)

Do not let your heart envy sinners, but always be zealous for the fear of the LORD. (Prov. 23:17)

The LORD Almighty is the one you are to regard as holy, he is the one you are to fear, he is the one you are to dread. (Isaiah 8:13)

He will be the sure foundation for your times, a rich store of salvation and wisdom and knowledge; the fear of the LORD is the key to this treasure. (Isaiah 33:6)

Listen! The LORD is calling to the city — and to fear your name is wisdom — "Heed the rod and the One who appointed it." (Micah 6:9)

Then the church throughout Judea, Galilee and Samaria enjoyed a time of peace. It was strengthened; and encouraged by the Holy Spirit, it grew in numbers, living in the fear of the Lord. (Acts 9:31)

When this became known to the Jews and Greeks living in Ephesus, they were all seized with fear, and the name of the Lord Jesus was held in high honor. (Acts 19:17)

Since, then, we know what it is to fear the Lord, we try to persuade men. What we are is plain to God, and I hope it is also plain to your conscience. (2 Corinth. 5:11)

The Fear of the Lord

> Who will not fear you, O Lord, and bring glory to your name? For you alone are holy. All nations will come and worship before you, for your righteous acts have been revealed. (Rev. 15:4)

Notice several things about these passages. ***First***, there's no question that it's our duty to fear God. Only a fool would ignore all these commands, promises and threats. ***Second***, some of these passages actually promise rich blessings to those who fear God. Fearing him isn't what many think it is – as if it's a matter of terror and hiding from him. As we shall see, godly fear is the first step to a healthy relationship with God! ***Third***, look at the last four passages in the list – they are from the *New* Testament, not the Old. The book that teaches us about Christ and the New Covenant, the one that many suppose is encouraging us to give up our fear of God, is actually doing the opposite. It *supports* the Old Testament theme of fearing God; it even teaches us to fear the Lord Jesus!

Why do many people not fear God?

"The fool says in his heart, 'there is no God.'" (Psalm 53:1) It's surprising how little fear there is among people, when you consider the reasons that we ought to fear God. It's plain in Scripture that he is so awesome, so demanding, and so ruthless against the wicked that only a fool would ignore such warnings. But even in light of the threats and commands and promises about the fear of God, many people have no fear of God. Why is that so?

First, they can't see God. God is Spirit, and that presents our physical senses with a problem that we can't solve. If we can't see God, how do we know for sure that he exists? If all we have are the words of men – honest men, to be sure, but still only human beings – how do we know for sure that this God spoke through them? Unless we see for ourselves the miracles that he did, we refuse to believe. Why believe in someone who doesn't seem to want to present himself for our inspection? Why worship a God that we can never see?

So, people don't believe in him. They believe in and fear money for the power it has over their lives, they believe in and fear great armies, they believe in and fear governments that hold absolute power over them – but they won't believe in a God who seems to be someone's imagination from thousands of years ago. Expecting them to believe in the God of the Bible is asking too much of the modern man, who has been trained to trust only his senses and scientific instruments and principles.

Second, they make up a false god that they're not afraid of. False gods abound; they've been around since the beginning of time, when man first turned his heart toward the forces of nature and worshiped them. A false god is 100% the product of man's imagination; nobody can prove they exist. There is no God but Israel's God.

False gods are handy things to have around, though. They provide a person with just enough religion to ease the conscience. We can give our false god certain qualities to make him god-like, but not too much so as to interfere with our lives. False gods make no demands on the soul, just on the outward life where it's easy for us to do something to make it happy – like with prayers and ceremonies and pilgrimages and church buildings. False gods allow us to change the rules – to call good evil and evil good. So as long as we've convinced ourselves that our "god" isn't what the Bible says he is, we don't have to pay any attention to the Bible's God.

But unfortunately false gods can't save us either. While we're busy worshiping our false gods, they don't answer us – they can't, since they're not real. They certainly can't help us with our problems; we will have our problems answered by "luck" or Mother Nature just as quickly as a false god could do it. But since false gods don't make extreme demands on our souls, we cling to them in spite of their silence, in spite of the plain teaching in the Bible of who the real God is.

Third, many people in the Church have been led astray by false teachings about Jesus Christ. They've been taught that God is love now, in the New Testament age, and Jesus came to bring that love of God to us. There's no more reason to fear him, only love him. Fear, they say, was appropriate only for the Jews in the Old Testament who were under the Law. Now that we aren't under the Law, fear is out of place. What is there to fear?

But this completely ignores huge realities in the New Testament. For one thing, it has been noted that Jesus taught more about Hell and eternal punishment than any other single subject. He evidently wanted to get our attention! God is not playing games, and he is just as ready to condemn the wicked now as he ever was in Old Testament times. Let the wise heed the warning. Second, the New Testament Church rests just as much on the Law of God as the Old Testament saints relied on God's love. Both subjects are taught in both books; Jesus didn't come to destroy the Law but to fulfill it. It isn't our obligation to the Law that has changed, but *how* it will be fulfilled. But more on that later. The point now is that God demands that we fear him for the same reasons that he demanded it from the Israelites: he still has expectations of us, and we had better be busy fulfilling our duty to him – or else! This is what Jesus taught – see John 8:24 for an example.

Our fundamental problem

We all know that people all around the world have problems in life, but it's rare to meet someone who understands what humanity's biggest problem really is. We are told constantly that if we just had better education, more democratic governments, more business opportunities, or a fairer distribution of wealth, then most or all of our problems would be solved. But the Bible disagrees with all of these viewpoints. The problem behind all of our other problems is **sin**.

Sin is simple to understand and impossible to escape. But we have to see this problem clearly if we hope to solve it. One of our major failings is this stubborn refusal to think about sin the way God sees it – and that's why sin still rules us. We have to name the demon before we can be rid of it. We can't go into the subject of sin at length here, but we can at least give an idea of the nature and scope of our sin.

The Bible defines sin for us in clear terms:

Everyone who sins breaks the Law; in fact, sin is lawlessness. (1 John 3:4)

As we have already seen, this world is a Kingdom with God as the supreme King over all. And he naturally will govern his Kingdom according to Law – the laws of Creation, the laws of Providence, and the laws of ethics and morality. All of these laws are necessary for a well-balanced, happy, productive Kingdom. For example, the Creator made mankind upright (Ecclesiastes 7:29) – righteous and sensitive to what is right and wrong. He made man to be a reflection of himself, able to rule over God's world in God's Name. (Genesis 1:26) He made families (Psalm

68:6) for many reasons: an extension of God's authority, for populating the earth, to bring more "rulers" into the realm with special skills to participate in the work, and so on. He gave each creature certain characteristics that make it fit perfectly into the entire creation: it lives and moves according to its original design.

But if someone violates one or more of these laws, he's jeopardizing the well-being of everyone around him – as well as rebelling against the King who made the laws. This is sin: when man decides to ignore the laws of God, at whatever level, and set up his own laws instead. Creatures operate under instinct and can't rebel against God's instructions for them; but man *can* rebel, because he operates with his mind and will. What makes this rebellion worse in God's eyes is that man was supposed to be the ruler of Creation, not the destroyer! When the ruler himself rebels, what will be the results in the rest of Creation?

Following is a description of sin and the sinner – which describes all of us when we are not in Christ and his salvation:

- **The nature of sin** – Sin is outright treachery against God, treason against God's righteous Kingdom. The reason that God made mankind was to take care of the world according to God's Law. We were given the minds and will to accomplish this. Now, however, we have rebelled against our King and refused to do his will. We have set up our own kingdom, with laws that we like better, and we're ignoring God's Law. This is pure and simple treason. In any righteous government on earth, treason and treachery against the state is punishable by death – there can be no mercy for someone who wishes the destruction of the state and purposely works against it.

    This rebellion against God (which we've inherited from Adam and Eve, the first to rebel against him) has twisted our natures to the point that now we wouldn't think of making up with God on his terms. We hate the world of God, we hate his Law, we run and hide from him when he demands an accounting of what we've done. (Genesis 3:8) Because of our pride we don't want to even admit that we're living in sin: everyone thinks well of themselves in some way, and we certainly don't believe that we're as bad as the Bible makes us out to be. And speaking of the Bible, we all have some reservation about some or all of it: most of us would be willing to admit that the Bible may be true in some places, but none of us wholeheartedly accept the entire thing, as it stands, as the Word of God. In our rebellion we've turned away from the only place where we will hear the voice of God; but without faith (and that comes through the Word) it's impossible to please God. (Hebrews 11:6)

We all sin in many ways, and we all know that we "fall short of the glory of God." (Romans 3:23) Here are some examples of common sins:

We ignore the Bible – which is the Word of God (John 17:17), or reject its teaching in some way. The Bible is our communication with our Master with full instructions about carrying out our responsibilities under him. None of us fully carry out those instructions – which means that we are, simply put, rebels.

We give God almost no glory, especially in those areas where he most deserves it. Instead we glorify ourselves. Check the newspapers to see if they gave God the credit for feeding everyone, raising up rulers and tearing them down, bringing new souls into the world and taking out others. They won't, even though he was behind all these events and much more.

We make up our own rules for living instead of living by those rules that the Lord gave us. That is, we make up our own system of morality without first bothering to see if it's taught in the Bible.

We give no thought to our calling in life, the work that our Master has given us to do – as if we are here only to enjoy ourselves!

Even if we repent for some sin, we usually end up right back in it. "A sow that is washed goes back to her wallowing in the mud." (2 Peter 2:22)

Whatever crime we might read of in the newspapers has probably gone through our own hearts and minds at some point in our lives. Others may be doing it, but we all have felt or thought it ourselves – which demonstrates that all sin comes from the heart. (Matthew 15:18-20)

The angels know God very well, because they stand before him continuously and worship him. They can see how holy he is, that he is the Master with all authority, that he must be obeyed at all costs. They have no opinions of their own on anything because they stand on God's Word. They wouldn't dare to do anything on their own! So they live only to serve him, exactly in the way that he demands that they serve him. We humans know nothing of this fear, this awe of his Majesty, this 100% devotion to the work and glory of God. Our sin has buried us in self-centeredness so that we don't even know God, let alone have any feelings of worship toward him. And while the angels know exactly what God thinks about us, and they even know what God has in store for his enemies (angels are often sent out as the messengers of God's wrath), we are completely in the dark about our dangerous standing in God's universe. Like fools with our heads in the sand, we can't see the storm clouds gathering over us. Doom is approaching and we still play our games of immorality, rebellion and destruction.

- **The results of sin** – Sin leads to death in God's Kingdom. You have to understand the nature of the crime to appreciate God's solution. If this is treachery, then the culprit must be found and put to death before he does any more damage. Remember that God cut off Adam and Eve from the Tree of Life – "He must not be allowed to reach out his hand and take also from the Tree of Life and eat, and live forever." (Genesis 3:22) A criminal on the run is a danger to society and must be caught, tried and punished. Justice is of supreme importance in God's Kingdom.

God acted swiftly when Adam rebelled. The man's soul died immediately, as well as the souls of all his offspring. "When you eat of it you will surely die." (Genesis 2:17) This means that now none of us are able to sense God's presence; we don't have any way of communicating with him with any certainty. Just as a dead man can't know his surroundings, none of Adam's children can know anything of God or his spiritual world. We are dead to God – "without hope and without God in the world." (Ephesians 2:12)

Sin brought physical death for man as well. God never intended for man to die; it was an extraordinary punishment against the "head of state" that God had set up over the world. Scientists and sociologists tell us that death is a normal part of life, that we have to approach it with dignity as the last phase of our lives. In reality, however, it's a punishment for what we've done against God – there's nothing normal about it. It's a precaution that God took to make sure we wouldn't live forever in sin. And we all know, in our hearts, how destructive death is: we fear it as the "king of terrors" and do everything we can to avoid it.

God became our enemy the day that man rebelled. He immediately declared war against the rebel:

> Cursed is the ground because of you;
>   through painful toil you will eat of it
>   all the days of your life.
> It will produce thorns and thistles for you,
>   and you will eat the plants of the field.
> By the sweat of your brow
>   you will eat your food
> until you return to the ground,
>   since from it you were taken;
> for dust you are
>   and to dust you will return.
>   (Genesis 3:17-19)

What he did was the same as the kings did in the old days: they would have posters made and nailed up around the kingdom, declaring someone an outlaw and putting a price on his head. Now, in the courts of Heaven, man is a criminal and to be treated as such. The angels were often sent out in pursuit of the enemy: for example, two angels were sent out to destroy Sodom and Gomorrah. (Genesis 19) And whenever God came near someone, or called someone into his presence, he always treated them as they were: sinners, rebels, outlaws. If he intended to do good to them, he first had to change their hearts to cleanse them, to put spiritual life in them, to kill the rebellion in their hearts. (Isaiah 6:5-7) He never brings us into his presence without either changing us or condemning us.

Another result of our sin is the way we have remade the original world that God first created. Not content to accept God's works as they are, we have been busy "redesigning" creation to suit our own needs. This is what the Bible refers to as "the world" – that creation of ours that we love so much, that "reality" that God never meant for us in the beginning.

> For everything in the world — the cravings of sinful man, the lust of his eyes and the boasting of what he has and does — comes not from the Father but from the world. The world and its desires pass away, but the man who does the will of God lives forever. (1 John 2:16-17)

The "world" is a place where *we* are king, where we fill our lives with pleasures, where we can hate our neighbors, where everything is twisted around to suit ourselves, where the old rules are broken and new rules made to allow our heart's desire. Our "creation" is filled with misery and death, disease and suffering, crime and punishment, hatred and jealousy, murder and thievery, war and famine, sexual perversity and adultery, failure and frustration – not at all a pretty place. And all of this simply because we didn't want to live by God's Law! Our "new world" bears no resemblance to the world that God first intended for man. We've ruined what he gave us, and rebelled against our responsibility to work for his goals – we have our own agenda now.

- **The scope of sin** – Looking at what sin is and what it does to us is only the first step toward understanding it. The next step is to see how far the problem has spread. This is what really makes us wonder if there could ever be a solution for it.

Sin is in every human being. We were born with the inclination to sin. None of us want anything to do with the God of the Bible. This may sound harsh, especially when talking about "innocent" children, but growing up reveals the true nature of a child's heart – sin was there all along waiting for the opportunity to bloom in later years.

Sin is in the entire human race. Everywhere you go in the world there are rules for ethics and morality. The reason we need laws is because, without them, wretched people are going to destroy themselves and others – civilization is impossible without law and order in light of sin.

Sin is in every action of life. We can't do the simplest thing without being guilty of something.

God's Law is so complex, it covers such a wide area of human activity, that all we have to do is *not* do the Law in some point and we have broken it again. Who in the entire world isn't guilty of breaking the Law – in light of the fact that they don't even know what the Law is? Sin is not only **commission** (actually doing something forbid-den) but **omission** (not doing something that God commanded). And if God insists on the strict observance of the Law, every one of us will be guilty of something in it.

> There is no one righteous, not even one;
>   there is no one who understands,
>   no one who seeks God.
> All have turned away,
>   they have together become worthless;
> there is no one who does good,
>   not even one.
> Their throats are open graves;
>   their tongues practice deceit.
> The poison of vipers is on their lips.
>   Their mouths are full of cursing and bitterness.
>   Their feet are swift to shed blood;
>   ruin and misery mark their ways,
>   and the way of peace they do not know.
> There is no fear of God before their eyes.
>   (Romans 3:10-18)

Our guilt is not only on the outside with our actions, it lives in our hearts with our thoughts and feelings. You have no doubt had thoughts and feelings of immorality, hatred, spiritual laziness, self-glory – even if, on the outside, you have the most outstanding moral character. Have these things gone through your mind at some point in your life?

> ... sexual immorality, impurity and debauchery; idolatry and witchcraft; hatred, discord, jealousy, fits of rage, selfish ambition, dissensions, factions and envy; drunkenness, orgies, and the like. (Galatians 5:19)

Or how about these?

> They have become filled with every kind of wickedness, evil, greed and depravity. They are full of envy, murder, strife, deceit and malice. They are gossips, slanderers, God-haters, insolent, arrogant and boastful; they invent ways of doing evil; they disobey their parents; they are senseless, faithless, heartless, ruthless. Although they know God's righteous decree that those who do such things deserve death, they not only continue to do these very things but also approve of those who practice them. (Romans 1:28-32)

James says that we are *lawbreakers* even if we've broken only *one single law*. (James 2:11) Like a criminal caught in the act, his former life of good works won't help him when brought to account for the crime he committed. He must pay.

- **Punishment for sin** – This is God's answer to sin: the criminal must be punished. He can't do any less and be a just God! I've often heard people complain that God isn't just, when they look at the misery and suffering in the world. But then they don't want to hear about God's justice when the discussion comes around to their sin! They want God to forget justice and let them off the hook.

God has to punish sinners. For one thing, to let rebels back out into society again would be asking for more trouble. Our own society recognizes the need for prisons, to keep dangerous criminals off the streets and the citizenry safe. God must do the same.

His punishment will be according to their crime. They didn't want God? Then he'll completely withdraw himself from them! Then they will realize that all good things in life came from God, when they have to do without all of them. They were at war with God? Then God will destroy them as a commander does his enemies. They didn't want the blessings of Heaven? Then they will have the curses of Hell. They didn't want to live with God? Then he will throw them out of his presence. (Matthew 8:12)

God's punishment, Jesus told us, will be unimaginable misery – since sinners don't want God's mercy and grace. They will experience the fire of his wrath – they will be, as Paul describes so graphically, "without hope and without God." (Ephesians 2:12) They asked for this.

Talking about sin is never easy, because it strikes at the heart of what we are. We are corrupted with sin, yet none of us want to admit it. Like dead corpses, we are incapable of knowing our true state; we're only lying around helpless until someone buries us. In fact, this is the hardest part of evangelization. Unless the Spirit of God opens a person's eyes to the true state of his heart, we will never convince him of the fact that he is wicked and offensive to God. We all have too high an estimation of our character to listen to that.

> An oracle is within my heart
> > concerning the sinfulness of the wicked:
> There is no fear of God before his eyes.
> For in his own eyes he flatters himself
> > too much to detect or hate his sin. (Psalm 36:1-2)

But we *must* listen. God is disgusted with our spiritual state. He holds us all responsible for what we've done to his world and against his honor. And we must understand the danger of our position: God is under no obligation to forgive us. He would be entirely just to get rid of us all, as he did in Noah's day with the Great Flood. He *is* obligated, however, by his own Law to punish us severely and without mercy – we deserve nothing good from him.

He has no use for any of us in our current state; depending on us to do his work in the Church would be like leaning on a rotten stick. He can't trust us with anything in his Kingdom with the kind of performance we've shown so far.

So, we have come to the point of the problem, the crisis, the "zero hour" when something has to be done. You show that you understand the terrible situation that we're in when you realize that **the next move is God's**. There are no appeals, no diplomacy, no excuses possible. There is nothing you can do yourself to fix things. Either he destroys you, or he decides to do something entirely different with you. Either way you are in his hands.

The terrible solution

Sin is such a disastrous turn of events in a world designed for perfection that God has to take drastic measures to root it out. A cancer kills, and the doctor can't afford to take any half measures against it if he wants the patient to survive. In the same way, sin destroys the world as well as mankind, and God will not hesitate to use whatever measures are at his disposal to get rid of it.

The Law tells us what must be done: whoever rebels against his parents must be *put to death*; whoever kills someone intentionally must be *put to death*; whoever works on the Sabbath must be *put to death*; whoever makes sacrifices to false gods must be *put to death*; whoever commits adultery must be *put to death*; whoever blasphemes the name of the LORD must be *put to death*; whoever approaches the sanctuary uninvited must be *put to death*. There are many more crimes that require death besides this short list. God is serious, in other words, about us obeying his Law.

Whoever breaks the Law must be punished. Almost always that meant the lawbreaker must be put to death. Death was a severe penalty, to be sure, but it showed two things:

> **First**, the sin, in God's eyes, is nothing less than treason and dangerous to the well-being of the community. We may consider it "sowing one's wild oats" or "having a little fun," but God doesn't see it that way. Sin destroys what God created. Its destructive power may not be immediately obvious, but over time we will always see its results twisting good into evil and bringing misery and frustration. There are no such things as "little" sins to God – that's like talking of "a little poison" in one's drink! Just a little germ will eventually kill someone.

> **Second**, that God isn't playing games with us. He meant what he said when he commanded us to obey him. When someone receives the death penalty, it makes everyone else wake up to the seriousness of the crime. They might not have thought it a terrible sin, but evidently God does! The King strengthens his authority over the

Kingdom when he backs up his threats with sudden and powerful action; everyone is put on notice that they had better obey the King or else.

The Old Testament describes two solutions that God has for dealing with sin: **first**, he kills the sinners outright. The first massive judgment against mankind was the Flood in Noah's day. We are told that –

> The LORD saw how great man's wickedness on the earth had become, and that every inclination of the thoughts of his heart was only evil all the time. The LORD was grieved that he had made man on the earth, and his heart was filled with pain. So the LORD said, "I will wipe mankind, whom I have created, from the face of the earth — men and animals, and creatures that move along the ground, and birds of the air — for I am grieved that I have made them." (Genesis 6:5-7)

This was the first of many demonstrations of God's wrath against sinners all through the Bible. In fact, the "final solution" in the book of Revelation will be even more catastrophic than this one in Genesis was! It's unfortunate that many people have to be so stubborn in their sin; God won't hesitate to send terrible punishment on sinners when he deems it necessary. Does the "Judge of all the earth," who always does what is right, have the right to do this to people? Yes – since he's the Creator and they're ruining his Creation, since he's the King and they're rebelling against his authority, he has every right to solve the problem in the way he sees fit. He wants a *perfect* Kingdom, not an imperfect one.

The **second** method he uses is just as destructive and startling to us, but the outcome is amazing and life-giving. He instituted a system of sacrifice to take away our sin. The sinner would bring his sacrifice – usually an animal of some sort – to the

Temple, and there the priest would slit its throat and offer the blood and flesh as a *substitution* for the sinner. In other words, according to the Law the sinner should die – but God in his mercy will accept the death of the animal in his place. We call this the **atonement** – the substitution of the death of an animal for a man's or woman's death.

Israel's sacrifices weren't like the sacrifices of pagan nations. People offered sacrifices to false gods in order to please them, as if the gods thought the animal flesh tasty – or the willingness to give up good meat for religious purposes a noble gesture. But the true God requires sacrifice because *someone must die for sin.* This sacrifice was a punishment, not a noble gesture. If the Israelites didn't offer these sacrifices for their sin, then God would demand *their* deaths! The Law demands death for sin, and the sacrificial system was a merciful way out of death for the Israelites.

In the book of Hebrews we read that God accepted those animal sacrifices for the time being, even though everyone knew (at least those who had the "eyes to see!") that the blood of animals can't really take sin or guilt out of the heart:

> It is impossible for the blood of bulls and goats to take away sins. (Hebrews 10:4)

What they symbolized, for the time being, was the staggering sacrifice that God had in mind even before he set up the Temple in Israel – the sacrifice of his only Son, Jesus Christ. In Christ we have *a man* dying for the sins of man – the only just way of taking care of the problem of sin. And we have *the Son of God* dying for the sins of man, which means that he will be able to finally clean the hearts of his people and change them from sinners to saints. But more on the sacrifice of Christ later.

The point here is that God always deals with sin in the same way – *someone must die.* Either the sinner himself must die, or a substitution for the sinner. In any case the Law wouldn't be fulfilled, and justice wouldn't be done, if there wasn't a punishment.

A life of repentance

The first step in salvation is to see our wretched state of danger before God. When a criminal realizes that his name is on every wanted poster, that every citizen is on the lookout for him, that the king seeks him out to destroy him, then life turns into a cycle of hiding, fear, lies and deceit, more crime, loneliness and wandering. We are all in this state of danger, whether we know it or not. The mercy is that God allows some of us to see this.

It's a mercy because God has a plan to save us from our sin and not destroy us. We will look at the process of salvation later, but here we must see the heart of God as he calls wretched, hardened rebels to his throne. Jesus showed us the Father's heart in the story of the prodigal son – he welcomed the rebel with open arms. (Luke 15:12-24) It's almost too much to believe, in light of what we are and the state of things in God's world. But that's exactly what we *have* to believe to take the first step back to restoration.

God has a plan to save us. And he calls us to give up, now, and come to his throne in **repentance** if we want to be saved. Repentance is doing an about-face and coming to God – the very one we've been offending all of our lives. James tells us what we should do:

> Come near to God and he will come near to you. Wash your hands, you sinners, and purify your hearts, you double-minded. Grieve, mourn and wail. Change your laughter to mourning and your joy to gloom. Humble yourselves before the Lord, and he will lift you up. (James 4:8-10)

Only a shaken, awe-struck sinner will come to God like this, but there are a few. Too many people are like the Pharisees who didn't think they had anything to repent of! But those like the fearful tax collector, who knew very well he was an offence to God, will find forgiveness from the King:

> Two men went up to the temple to pray, one a Pharisee and the other a tax collector. The Pharisee stood up and prayed about himself: 'God, I thank you that I am not like other men — robbers, evildoers, adulterers — or even like this tax collector. I fast twice a week and give a tenth of all I get.'
>
> But the tax collector stood at a distance. He would not even look up to Heaven, but beat his breast and said, 'God, have mercy on me, a sinner.'
>
> I tell you that this man, rather than the other, went home justified before God. For everyone who exalts himself will be humbled, and he who humbles himself will be exalted. (Luke 18:10-14)

The act of humiliating yourself before God is pleasing to the King. It shows him that you know how holy he is and can see his glory, that you know your crimes against him, that you know your helplessness to change, and that you know that he is your only hope. He responds positively to those who fear him and throw themselves on his mercy; it's those people he can help and use to build his Kingdom. But those who are too proud to bend their knee and ask for forgiveness will get none.

Many Christians are under the mistaken notion that once they've repented of their sins, there's no more need of it. They just continue in merry enjoyment of life assuming that all is well now. They're dead wrong: that first act of repentance was to *open the door* to God's healing hand. There is still much sin, rebellion, ignorance, pride, jealousy, envy, adultery, hatred and scores of other sins in our hearts – *even after conversion*. The job is only started at that first meeting with the King. From now on, our lives will consist of rooting out those persistent sins and putting them to death. Paul counseled the Colossians about this matter:

> *Put to death*, therefore, whatever belongs to your earthly nature: sexual immorality, impurity, lust, evil desires and greed, which is idolatry. Because of these, the wrath of God is coming. You used to walk in these ways, in the life you once lived. But now *you must rid yourselves* of all such things as these: anger, rage, malice, slander, and filthy language from your lips. Do not lie to each other, since *you have taken off your old self* with its practices and have put on the new self, which is *being renewed* in knowledge in the image of its Creator. (Colossians 3:5-10)

Sanctification – the life-long pursuit of changing your nature to resemble the perfection of Christ – is a daily business. That means that we have to daily repent; we must live the *life of repentance* if we hope to overcome our sin. There is much to crucify in our hearts. The wise Christian will realize, when he comes to God daily in prayer, that "taking care of sin" is *always* the first item on God's agenda. He is determined to save us from our sins.

It may help, in order to see the tremendous importance of living in repentance, to see what God is doing in this process. Since he's so holy that he can't allow the least sin into his presence, since he's so holy that he can't tolerate a single sinner into the border of his land of perfection – and since he is determined to bring *us* there – he has to get us ready first. Life here in this world isn't for the purpose of enjoying the pleasures of this world, or doing whatever pleases us. *We are preparing for our life in Heaven*. And there is a tremendous amount of work to be done before we're ready. We have to quit all of our sin, even the hidden sin of our hearts; we have to learn about and store up treasures in Heaven; we have to see and help build up the Kingdom of God, especially God's children – our brothers and sisters. We have to get skilled at working with spiritual materials, doing God's work in his way, glorifying him in all that we do. Only when he decides that we are ready to live with him will he take us – and not a moment before.

Which brings up another point. Our lives there in Heaven with him will consist of unending service. We will exist only to *serve him*. This isn't what we're used to! We have been trained all of our lives to serve ourselves, not God. (Philippians 2:21) But there with him we will be as the angels are, and as Revelation shows us about the elders around the Throne:

> Whenever the living creatures give glory, honor and thanks to him who sits on the throne and who lives for ever and ever, the twenty-four elders fall down before him who sits on the throne, and worship him who lives for ever and ever. They lay their crowns before the throne and say:
>
> "You are worthy, our Lord and God,
>   to receive glory and honor and power,
> for you created all things,
>   and by your will they were created
>   and have their being."
>   (Revelation 4:9-11)

If you don't get the point about why they're doing this to God, then you have a lot of training to go through – because this is what he wants *you* to do when you arrive there! Serving God is the whole reason we were made in the first place. What we have to learn here, before we are called to it in Heaven, is to submit to God and serve him *in all things*.

The benefits of fearing God

We haven't the space here to explore this subject much, but you can study the passages dealing with the fear of God and what benefits it will bring you. This may surprise many people – that fearing God is profitable business! God blesses and rewards those who fear him, because they show some wisdom in their dealings with him.

For example, one of the most precious promises dealing with the fear of God is in Isaiah:

> He will be the sure foundation for your times,
>   a rich store of salvation and wisdom and knowledge;
>   *the fear of the LORD is the key to this treasure.*
>   (Isaiah 33:6)

This is plainly saying that anybody who wants salvation, wisdom and knowledge from God must first learn to fear him. In other words, fear of God is the necessary first step to salvation. How can this be? Because a sinner realizes that he has no hope except to plead for mercy from the very God he offended. He knows that God receives a *repentant* sinner, that he has a plan to save him from his ingrown sin. A sinner knows where to go for help, and humbles himself to get that help. Fear doesn't mean running away from God, but running toward God and giving up before it's too late.

Another passage shows the delight that God has toward those who come to him in fear:

> The LORD confides in those who fear him; he
> makes his covenant known to them. (Psalm 25:14)

If you know anything about the Covenant, you will know that it's an agreement that God made with Abraham and all his children. It included all the rich treasures of salvation in Christ. God has spent the last 4000 years fulfilling that Covenant for his people! If it's that important to him, with whom will he share it? With whom will he open his heart of love and compassion and richly bless with the fullness of Heaven's treasures? *Only with those who fear him.* Only to those who know they have to do something about their sin, about this broken relationship with the Master, and come to him in fear and humility and put themselves in his hands to do with as he wills. These will find the Covenant blessings.

In 2 Chronicles 26:5 we find that as long as Uzziah feared the Lord, God gave him success in everything he did. In Psalm 34:9 we are told that those who fear God will lack nothing that they need. Psalm 103:13 tells us that God shows compassion on those who fear him. And in case you thought that fear is just an Old Testament concept, we read in Acts 9:31 that the Church lived in the fear of the Lord (and this is Jesus!) and as a result enjoyed peace, strength, encouragement, and growth in numbers.

Finally, you will notice when you look over the Scriptures dealing with the fear of God that the words "love" and "joy" and "peace" keep appearing. These aren't exactly what we would have expected alongside fear! But again we have to see what fearing God really means.

> Serve the LORD with fear and rejoice with trembling.
> (Psalm 2:11)

For example, in this verse we see two ideas joined with fear: to serve the Lord, and to rejoice in him. The serving part we've already looked at, and we know why we must serve this King. But to rejoice in him requires more insight. The beginning of Psalm 2 describes what the rulers of the earth think of the King of kings – they despise him, they want to throw off his rule over them and rule themselves. God won't allow it! He therefore gives authority and power to his Son that extends over the entire earth. It's the kind of power that will enable him to break all resistance to his rule. What kind of government will he set up in place of man's rebellion? Isaiah tells us:

> For to us a child is born,
>   to us a son is given,
>   and the government will be on his shoulders.
> And he will be called
>   Wonderful Counselor, Mighty God,
>   Everlasting Father, Prince of Peace.
> Of the increase of his government and peace
>   there will be no end.
> He will reign on David's throne
>   and over his kingdom,
> establishing and upholding it
>   with justice and righteousness
>   from that time on and forever.
> The zeal of the LORD Almighty
>   will accomplish this. (Isaiah 9:6-7)

A kingdom of justice, righteousness and peace is a welcome change from the misery and death of man's kingdoms! We will finally have a ruler who will do good for his people. It will be a time when all tears will be wiped away, people will rejoice in God, and all problems will be solved. But this won't happen without war: the Lord must first destroy the enemies of God to make room for the new Kingdom. This is the fear part: to those who submit now, he will show himself merciful and even "abounding in love and faithfulness." (Exodus 6:6) But those who rebel will find that "his wrath can flare up in a moment." (Psalm 2:12) He intends to set up his righteous Kingdom no matter what it takes; he will not play games with us.

Jesus himself feared the Father

To show how essential the fear of God is in God's Kingdom, the Spirit of God revealed an amazing truth in a prophecy of the coming Messiah. This is what it says of him:

> A shoot will come up from the stump of Jesse;
> from his roots a Branch will bear fruit.
> The Spirit of the LORD will rest on him —
> the Spirit of wisdom and of understanding,
> the Spirit of counsel and of power,
> the Spirit of knowledge and of the fear of the LORD —
> *and he will delight in the fear of the LORD.*
> (Isaiah 11:1-3)

Now this passage is a prophecy of Christ. He's the "stump of Jesse," the predicted "Branch" that would bear fruit in the Church. And according to this passage, he *delighted* in the fear of the Lord.

What could this mean? Jesus was the perfect man, the Son of God, supposedly the only man in history who had no reason to fear God! But if we read the account of his life carefully, we will see that he was careful to do things exactly as his Father told him. In fact, he seemed to have (to us!) an obsession to do nothing at all apart from the Father's specific instructions – as if he kept checking in and making sure he had this thing right in every detail.

Only a man who fears God will be so careful to follow God's Word to the letter. Fear, again, doesn't mean running from God but taking extreme care to do things God's way – keeping in mind that God is the Creator, the King, the Judge. He alone rules, he alone has all authority. We exist only to serve him. If we do anything at all to take away from this glory of his – like live according to our own opinions or rules – disaster will be the result and God will be justifiably angry with us, and obligated by Law to punish us.

For example, even though Jesus had no need of repentance and cleansing from sin, he insisted that John the Baptist baptize him: "Let it be so now; it is proper for us to do this to fulfill all righteousness." (Matthew 3:15) Again, when the disciples came back from looking for food and wondered what Jesus meant when he said he had eaten, he answered them with this: "my food is to do the will of him who sent me and to finish his work." (John 4:34) In the Gospel of John he repeatedly claimed that he didn't come to do his own will, but his Father's will. (John 8:28-29)

When Jesus went to Gethsemane to pray, he struggled with his Father about the upcoming crucifixion. Everything in his body screamed against the thought of such a death – especially since it would be so unnatural for the Son of God to be punished for crimes he didn't commit! But he willingly submitted in fear (remember, he *delighted* in this fear!) to God the Father: "Yet not as I will, but as *you* will." (Matthew 26:39) As Hebrews describes it –

> During the days of Jesus' life on earth, he offered up prayers and petitions with loud cries and tears to the one who could save him from death, and he was heard because of his *reverent submission*. Although he was a son, he *learned obedience* from what he suffered and, once made perfect, he became the source of eternal salvation for all who obey him and was designated by God to be high priest in the order of Melchizedek. (Hebrews 5:7-10)

Jesus knew that, though he himself was the fullness of the Godhead, he must at all costs submit to and obey the Father – the One who is in authority. That's the fear of the Lord, and our Master teaches it to us.

The Fear of the Lord

Is it proper for Christians to fear God?

Does the Bible teach Christians to fear God? Absolutely! We can take one of the New Testament letters as an example. Peter counsels us *five times*, in plain language, to fear God. Here are the references:

- Since you call on a Father who judges each man's work impartially, live your lives as strangers here in ***reverent fear***. (1 Peter 1:17)

- Show proper respect to everyone: Love the brotherhood of believers, ***fear God***, honor the king. (1 Peter 2:17)

- But even if you should suffer for what is right, you are blessed. "Do not fear what they fear; do not be frightened." But in your hearts set apart Christ ***as Lord***.(1 Peter 3:14-15) [*If you look up this Old Testament reference that Peter quotes – Isaiah 8:12-13 – you'll see there that "setting apart Christ as Lord" means "**he** is the one you are to fear."*]

- For it is time for ***judgment*** to begin with the family of God; and if it begins with us, what will the outcome be for those who do not obey the gospel of God? And, "If it is hard for the righteous to be saved, what will become of the ungodly and the sinner?" So then, those who suffer according to God's will should commit themselves to their faithful Creator and ***continue to do good***. (1 Peter 4:17-19) [*Although the word "fear" isn't used in this passage, being careful to do the right things because of Judgment Day is the definition of the fear of God.*]

- "God opposes the proud but gives grace to the humble." ***Humble yourselves***, therefore, under God's mighty hand, that he may lift you up in due time. (1 Peter 5:5-6) [*Again, though the word "fear" isn't used here, only one who fears God will humble himself before God – just because of his "mighty hand."*]

Now let's address this problem of "perfect love casts out fear." First let's quote the entire passage:

> God is love. Whoever lives in love lives in God, and God in him. In this way, love is made complete among us so that we will have confidence on the day of judgment, because in this world we are like him. There is no fear in love. But perfect love drives out fear, because fear has to do with punishment. The one who fears is not made perfect in love. (1 John 4:16-18)

First, it's obvious that those who don't "live in God" still have plenty of reason to fear God! They can't assume that just because others have discovered the depth of God's love that this means that all mankind need not fear God anymore. This is the same thing as saying that all prisoners should feel relieved when one prisoner gets a pardon from the governor! No, the rest of them are still in jail and likely to remain there without a change of heart of their own.

Second, this passage doesn't say that fear of God is bad or unscriptural. It says that God's love will eventually drive that fear of punishment away. We still have to come to God, in the first place, with fear. Modern ministries have so perverted the gospel message that they've virtually eliminated any need for sinners to fear God. "God loves you," they proclaim, with no Scriptural authority to claim that. What sinners have to hear first is that God is *angry* with them – that they're in dreadful danger and they have to come to the King in *fear and trembling* and plead for his mercy. *Then*, because the King is merciful, they will find the love of God. And when he shows his love by forgiving them, and restoring them, and making them into new creatures, they will lose their fear of him and live in his love. The love of God means nothing to a sinner until he sees how startlingly unexpected it is in light of God's holiness and his own wicked state.

Third, I would like to challenge any Christian to claim that he lives totally in God's love with no fear of having offended God in anything that he does or thinks. This passage describes the *ideal* state with God – a spiritual state that (hopefully) all Christians will experience at some point in their lives; but that state doesn't last very long, unfortunately, for most of us. As John himself told us at the beginning of this same letter:

> This is the message we have heard from him and declare to you: God is light; in him there is no darkness at all. If we claim to have fellowship with him yet walk in the darkness, we lie and do not live by the truth. But if we walk in the light, as he is in the light, we have fellowship with one another, and the blood of Jesus, his Son, purifies us from all sin. If we claim to be without sin, we deceive ourselves and the truth is not in us. If we confess our sins, he is faithful and just and will forgive us our sins and purify us from all unrighteousness. If we claim we have not sinned, we make him out to be a liar and his word has no place in our lives. (1 John 1:5-10)

All of us "fall short of the glory of God." It is always fear that brings us back to an offended God, even after years of walking in the Spirit. Fear not of rejection, but of his authority and throne, and having grieved him with our disobedience. And once again, when we tremble at the thought of what we've done to the one who loved us on the cross, we find that he loves us still and calms our hearts.

There's a perfect example in the Bible for the correct procedure to approach God. The Apostle John was the Lord Jesus' favorite while on earth; he was called the "beloved disciple" of Jesus. You would think that after several years of a close and loving relationship, John would be at least on speaking terms with Jesus whenever he might meet him. Not so! In Revelation we are told that John saw Jesus again, this time in a vision, and this was his reaction:

> I turned around to see the voice that was speaking to me. And when I turned I saw seven golden lampstands, and among the lampstands was someone "like a son of man," dressed in a robe reaching down to his feet and with a golden sash around his chest. His head and hair were white like wool, as white as snow, and his eyes were like blazing fire. His feet were like bronze glowing in a furnace, and his voice was like the sound of rushing waters. In his right hand he held seven stars, and out of his mouth came a sharp double-edged sword. His face was like the sun shining in all its brilliance. When I saw him, I fell at his feet as though dead. (Revelation 1:12-17)

His reaction, his position before the Lord, his speechlessness and fear, was all entirely proper and expected – when he saw the true nature of his God. Only after he fell down before the Lord in complete humility and fear did the Lord take the next step:

> Then he placed his right hand on me and said: "Do not be afraid." (Revelation 1:17)

The Fear of the Lord

John had no right to presume on Christ's goodwill in light of the fact that Christ is King and deserves all homage and worship. Only when Christ responds with the mercy of a King, the boon and blessing of a King, the authority of a King to make his subject rise and be honored, do we experience the "perfect love that drives out fear." Come on your knees in fear; he will raise you up with love.

Faith in Christ

I have been crucified with Christ and I no longer live, but Christ lives in me. The life I live in the body, I live by faith in the Son of God, who loved me and gave himself for me. (Galatians 2:20)

Jesus Christ is the object of a Christian's faith; we believe that we need nothing else but Jesus to be saved. As Paul put it, "For I resolved to know nothing while I was with you except Jesus Christ and him crucified." (1 Corinthians 2:2) A person's faith doesn't have to be complex, or bound up in bewildering doctrine, or take years to figure out. If we have Jesus, we have everything we need.

On the other hand, Jesus is a profound reality; saying "all we need is Jesus" is like saying "all we need is the universe!" Too many people think that it's enough to say "I believe in Jesus" and that will save them. *What is it* about him that they believe? Why do they think that Jesus is all that they need? Have they looked "beneath the cover" yet and seen "how wide and long and high and deep is the love of Christ, and to know this love that surpasses knowledge?" (Ephesians 3:18-19) Do they realize that Jesus is as mysterious and as complex as the God of the Bible — that he is "the radiance of God's glory and the exact representation of his being?" (Hebrews 1:3) Do they know *how much* God has put in Christ for us? "For no matter how many promises God has made, they are 'Yes' in Christ." (1 Corinthians 1:20) They say that we must have a simple faith in Jesus, but can they say (as Paul did), "I *know* whom I have believed, and am convinced that he is able to guard what I have entrusted to him for that day?" (2 Timothy 1:12) Did they know that Jesus is the righteousness of God, the work of God, the ways of God, the names of God, the Prophet, Priest and King, and many more offices and functions?

Our "faith" needs to be more than just saying, "I believe in Jesus." We need to know who he is, and what he does. We need to know why believing in Jesus is the key to our faith. In fact, the more we know about him the more we will believe in him — faith and knowledge *must* go together when it comes to believing in Jesus. Paul said that our goal is that "we all reach unity in the faith *and* in the knowledge of the Son of God and become mature, attaining to the *whole measure* of the fullness of Christ." (Ephesians 4:13) What we need is a well-rounded, filled-out picture of who Jesus is — then our faith will be based on what we *know* about him. Then we will trust him for things that are true about him, not for things that we have made up.

Knowing Jesus — whether you mean knowing him personally or knowing facts about him — will save you and spiritually enrich you, if you use that knowledge in the way that God intended. The Gospels primarily, and of course the rest of the Bible as well, show us what is in Jesus that we can lay claim to and use. It's like buying a tool at the hardware store: it usually comes with instructions on how to use it, so that you don't have to figure it out yourself. The Scriptures teach us what is in Jesus that we can use to grow spiritually and grow closer to God. This isn't just a frill, something that we could use *if* we want to; it's the whole point of the revelation of Christ in the Word. Unless we learn the whole truth about him, and how to have faith in him, we will never get any benefit from knowing him.

That knowledge comes, of course, from studying God's Word — the Bible. In fact, this is the only purpose of the Bible — to teach us about Jesus. The whole book is about him, from first to last. This may surprise you; it certainly surprised the Jews when Jesus told them! "You diligently study the Scriptures because you think that by them you possess eternal life. These are the Scriptures that testify *about me*, yet you refuse to come to me to have life." (John 5:39-40) The covenant with Abraham is sealed in Christ's work, the Law talks about Christ as King and his government, the Prophets announced the coming of Christ's kingdom, Joseph and David were types and examples of Christ — everything in the Old Testament teaches us something we need to know about Jesus. And of course the New Testament continues the story and teaches us much more about him that we need to know, so that our faith will be based on knowledge and not just guesses and feelings. The little pieces in the Old Testament that the saints of those days learned were actually previews or snapshots of the whole truth that is in Jesus; in the New Testament we see the entire picture brought together.

What is Faith?

But before we can hope to understand who Jesus is, we first have to understand what faith is. Faith is the tool that God has given us to probe the depth of the mysteries of Heaven. It's a skill from Heaven; without it we will never see who Jesus really is.

Christians are people of faith. Our religion requires that we "live by faith" (Romans 1:17) — and the reason for that is the nature of our God and the works that he does. Other religions have visible gods, idols of stone and wood and the imaginations of man, and it doesn't take faith to believe in what you can see and touch and think up on your own. But we Christians believe in what we *don't* see: "blessed are those who have not seen and yet have believed." (John 20:29)

Faith is a profound and mysterious experience. Not everyone who claims to have faith really has faith! The Bible clearly defines what true faith is; there is no mystery in that. The problem is that someone just can't step into faith whenever they like. It's a spiritual experience, it touches the world of God, it deals with things that you can't see with your physical eyes. It's the one sign that proves that you are in touch with God. It is, perhaps, the most important characteristic of a Christian because it makes a new creature out of him, and separates him from all other people who don't have faith.

As far as God is concerned, there isn't another thing that we could do that would please him as much as simple faith. He loves to see faith in us, and he will give us whatever we ask for if we just ask him in faith. (John 16:23) Faith has the power to move mountains — it moves God to do miracles for us. This simple yet powerful characteristic of a Christian is the key that unlocks the treasuries of Heaven. But it isn't something that just anybody can do! True faith is a rare jewel, even in today's Church, and you won't see it as often as you might expect. Jesus was surprised to see it in a Roman centurion. The Jews, he said, who ought to have had it, showed no signs of faith. (Matthew 8:10)

Faith is so characteristic of God's people that, once we understand what it is, we are going to see it all through the Bible. The Bible is the book of faith telling about the people of faith. It describes a new spiritual world where faith is the only way of communicating with God. At the very beginning of the works of God, as he first started building a spiritual kingdom for his people (in the Old Testament, where most Christians wouldn't have thought that faith would be so important!), the Lord set it down as a principle that his people would *live by faith*. Only the saints who did live by faith inherited the promises — both in the Old Testament and the New Testament.

You could say that faith is the currency of the Kingdom of God. With it, you can get whatever you want from him; without it, you are spiritually poor and can't expect to get anywhere with God. But also like money, there is a counterfeit variety of faith that our enemy has produced in the hearts of many people; and at first glance it can fool us into thinking that it's genuine.

The "faith" that most people have is this: they just believe in something very strongly — it doesn't matter what. The common expression is that "it doesn't matter *what* you believe, just that you *do* believe." That's wrong on at least two counts, however: ***first***, it's obvious that you can't believe in lies! If you are content with just believing the things you want to believe in, you are an easy target for whoever wants to spread his propaganda around — like the devil. There really is such a thing as the truth, and if you don't believe in that then your faith isn't worth anything. In God's universe there is one truth: what *he* says is true. If you don't believe that, then you believe in lies. Ignorance is *not* bliss; it is the first step toward death. This is *God's* world, and there is only *one* truth; whoever believes in lies are the children of the father of lies (John 8:44) and will someday share in his destruction. (Revelation 20:15)

Second, even if you believe the Bible (which, by the way, is the *only* truth — "Your Word is truth" — John 17:17) that doesn't mean that you are automatically a Christian. For example, some believe that there is a God, and they feel that they are doing God a favor in that. "You believe that there is one God. Good! Even the demons believe that — and shudder." (James 2:19) You see, you are in bad company if all you believe are a few facts about God! You believe that Jesus was a real man, who lived among men and preached the truth about God. Good! You believe the history books then; but that doesn't make you a Christian. Whenever you hear a sermon about a particular passage or read a book that discusses some part of the Bible, it seems reasonable to you and you accept it as true. Good! But the Bible has sounded very reasonable to people of many religions and nationalities; most of them, however, were never Christians and never even claimed to be.

So faith isn't just a matter of believing what the Bible says; it's true that you must believe what it says to have true faith, but you must also do *more* than that. This is why so many people are deceived into thinking that they are believers when really they don't have any faith at all.

The writer of Hebrews tells us what true faith is:

Now faith is being sure of what we hope for and certain of what we do not see. This is what the ancients were commended for. (Hebrews 11:1)

We could put it like this:

Faith is living in the light of God's world.

Faith is the special ability to see things as God sees them (with spiritual eyes — our physical eyes can't see them, as Hebrews 11:1 says). From his throne in Heaven, he can see this world in its entire scope, through the mists that normally cloud our eyes from seeing things clearly. God's world is all light, and whoever has that light can see all things as they really are. Faith is walking in the searchlight of Heaven that casts no shadows, that clearly lights the way in front of you.

When you have true faith, you see things that others can't see. For instance, you can see the realities of Heaven itself — God is there, in all his glory, surrounded by angels and other creatures that continually praise him. He sits on his throne, in the Temple, and the sacrifice for sins that Jesus made is forever on the altar there. There are the treasures that God has for his people, waiting for them. With faith these things are visible spiritually, they are real — they aren't just a story or even a wishful hope. That's why the writer of Hebrews paints such a vivid picture of what it's like in Heaven right now — because it's something that both he and we can see through faith:

Faith in Christ

> But you have come to Mount Zion, to the Heavenly Jerusalem, the city of the living God. You have come to thousands upon thousands of angels in joyful assembly, to the church of the firstborn, whose names are written in Heaven. You have come to God, the judge of all men, to the spirits of righteous men made perfect, to Jesus the mediator of a new covenant, and to the sprinkled blood that speaks a better word than the blood of Abel. (Hebrews 12:22-24)

This passage is all the more significant because it's in the book of faith, right after the famous chapter of faith (Hebrews 11). In that chapter we have the testimony of many saints who saw the promises of God. In other words, faith *sees* God's real world.

Faith is designed to address a specific problem that all people suffer from. From the day we were born, we were blind to, ignorant of, and totally unaware of the spiritual world of God. We can know our world only on the physical level, with our senses; but we have never been able to discern the spiritual level of existence. That's why unbelievers still think that there is no God — they can't see him. They think that this world is running on its own, as if it were a clock that somehow got wound up and will run for a long time until it decides to unwind. They see no more purpose to life than to eat, drink and be merry — for nothing means anything anyway.

The downside of this theory is that they don't have anybody but themselves to look to when trouble comes. If there is no God, then how will we solve our problems? Only by our own strength and cleverness — until that runs out, and then we just fail and die. There's no hope in this "belief" of how the world works; it's with profound truth that Paul says these people are "without hope and without God in the world." (Ephesians 2:12)

What they lack is spiritual insight — the ability to see the "other dimension" to the world. That's faith: seeing that there is more to this world than just physical things. Faith sees that God created this world, and therefore it has meaning and purpose. Faith sees what kind of God he is and why we need to live in such a way as to please him. Faith sees that this world is destined for destruction and therefore we need to put our hope on an inheritance that will never fade — a Heavenly treasure.

Someone isn't going to get this spiritual insight simply by wishing it. We are blind and ignorant of the truth because we are *dead spiritually* — that's the tragic truth of all humanity. We don't have time to get into a full discussion here of our natural spiritual state. But we are *all*, since we are descendants of Adam and Eve (who first spiritually died when they ate of the fruit of the Tree of the Knowledge of Good and Evil), dead to God and all spiritual things. We are alive for a while to the physical side of the world, but we are completely dead to the reality of God and our souls. If we get faith it's because God reaches down and touches our dead souls and makes us alive to him:

> But because of his great love for us, God, who is rich in mercy, made us alive with Christ even when we were dead in transgressions — it is by grace you have been saved. (Ephesians 2:4-5)

Just as a baby that takes its first breath in the world and opens its eyes to the light of day, a newborn Christian opens his eyes of faith and sees things that he didn't see before. He sees his Father (and the rest of the family of God!), he sees food, he sees his soul, he sees many more things that don't make sense to him right away. As he grows and develops he learns more about how this spiritual world works and how he can best get around in it. The analogy is exactly the same between physical and spiritual birth, and would make a fruitful study in the Scriptures for you sometime (start with John 3!). This is the life of faith.

When a person lives in faith, it's as if a strong searchlight shone down from Heaven and lit his surroundings so that he can see. He is aware that God is there above him, guiding him with light and life. He sees that the issues of life are spiritual. He sees what sin is, and why it's such a curse on man. He sees the emptiness of this world and the glory of the next. That sight of spiritual realities is what makes him live as he does. In fact, it's frustrating when one talks to an unbeliever who doesn't see these things. It's not just an argument or an idea, as it is to them — it's real, and we know it. We can't be talked out of it any more than of our own existence! But the unbeliever doesn't see any of it.

Faith knows that God exists and that all the spiritual truths that the Bible talks about are real. And you can also see why someone who doesn't have faith will never please God: "And without faith it is impossible to please God, because anyone who comes to him must believe that he exists and that he rewards those who earnestly seek him." (Hebrews 11:6) Without faith we will never know him, we will never hear or obey him, we will never go to him with the right requests — none of our "religion" will work without true faith. But with faith, everything becomes plain and we can go about our spiritual duties with complete confidence.

The difficulty in knowing Christ

Jesus is the most misunderstood person of all history. From his birth, through his strange ministry, to the shameful death he suffered on the cross, his entire life was filled with perplexing circumstances that confused not only the people of his day, but all the world since then. And the root of the problem is that he refused to display his glory to us while he was here.

Jesus is the Son of God, the Creator, the Heir of the Father's glory, in whom "all the fullness of the Deity lives in bodily form." (Colossians 2:9) He existed with the Father from before eternity; the Father, Son, and Holy Spirit make up the eternal, One God. Naturally he would appear just as glorious as the Father, just as terrifying as the Judge of all the earth, to anybody who could have seen him there in Heaven.

But when he came to earth, he purposely put aside that glory:

> ... Christ Jesus ... who, being in very nature God, did not consider equality with God something to be grasped, but made himself nothing, taking the very nature of a servant, being made in human likeness. And being found in appearance as a man, he humbled himself and became obedient to death — even death on a cross! (Philippians 2:5-8)

He was determined to put aside his glory, and he did a remarkable job of it. The Pharisees were dumbfounded about him: he did miracles, and argued them into theological corners, yet he was so humble and unpretentious in his work. He was an ordinary man, the carpenter's son – where did he get his education? He had no place to lay his head, yet he claimed to be God's Son. He said he could call down legions of angels to protect him, yet he let himself be led away to the terror of crucifixion.

People spoke all kinds of evil things about him; he even predicted that they would. (Matthew 12:32) When he died, the Romans and Jews both thought they were finally rid of him – all the while remembering that he *claimed* that his death wouldn't be enough to hold him down.

Now Jesus is in Heaven – or so the disciples claim. People read the story about Jesus, find inspiration in it, and then live as if he was just a storybook figure in an old history. There are still innumerable theories about who he really was: it's a never-ending controversy about who Jesus is, how much he affects our own world, and what his role will be till the end of time.

When he first came to Israel, they should have known who he was, because he was their God come in the flesh! They should have recognized him, bowed down to him in fear, and worshiped him. Instead, he got no welcome at all – he had to convince his few followers to believe his words.

> He was in the world, and though the world was made through him, the world did not recognize him. He came to that which was his own, but his own did not receive him. (John 1:10-11)

He gets almost no glory at all for who he is and what he does in this world. Glory, remember, means who gets the credit. Though Jesus created the world, he gets no credit for that. Though Jesus is the Head of the Church, most Christians don't even consult him on church matters. Though Jesus sends his Spirit to sustain his people with the treasures of Heaven, most of them don't even know what the treasures of Heaven are, let alone take seriously his command to store them up. For too many people, Jesus was the gate who let them into the Kingdom of God – but now they've left him behind and are spending their time and energies pursuing more interesting or important matters in Christianity. Over and over again, Jesus is being forgotten, left out, left behind, ignored, rebelled against, and shut out of his own Church.

The whole problem is that he insists on wearing this cloak of humility when dealing with us. We're confused by his gentleness, his willingness to wait on us, his being a man like us – and we don't or can't see the magnificence, the power, the terror, the unlimited wisdom behind the man. Always he insists that we deal with him in *faith*, not by sight. (2 Corinthians 5:7) He has his reasons for doing that; but it completely throws so many people when they hear about his greatness but they can't see it. Even though the Scriptures say that he's the Son of God, the King of kings, the righteous God who saves his people from their sins, none of that seems to happen – the world goes on as always, with people doing exactly what they want in this supposed Kingdom of his, and it seems as though he does nothing at all.

In order to see the truth about Jesus, we have to look at him *in faith*. We need the Bible to tell us the truth about him; we need to pray "in the Spirit" in order to find him. If we can't see that Jesus is everything to us – the fullness of God, the treasures of Heaven, our only hope and salvation for whoever will come to him – that means that we're not looking at him in faith, and of course then we'll never see the point about him. Unfortunately this happens in churches a great deal. Since it takes faith to lay hold of Christ so that he becomes the center of one's life, and faith isn't something that comes easily to people (especially when they aren't really interested in growing spiritually), people *say* that they love and honor Christ but really they know little or nothing about him. And when they know hardly anything about him, let alone depend on him in real ways to do real things in their lives, naturally they're going to turn their attention to other matters. Church is often where we hear about politics, social events, economics and business, education, family matters – and almost nothing about Jesus himself.

Even the leaders of the church ignore him to a large extent. I once read the book of Ephesians and marked all the places where Paul mentions Christ in some way. I was getting the feeling that modern preachers don't understand Jesus as much as they think they do, because they never seem to talk about Christ; it's always about duties of Christians, or our sins, or social issues. Sometimes they drop his Name around in their sermons but without any purpose – only to sanctify, it would seem, the other subjects that they would rather talk about. One could easily take Christ's Name out of their sermon and it would still make sense! I wanted to see if that held true of Paul's letter as well.

I found 100 places where Paul refers to Christ in some way. Examining each one I found that, far from simply using his Name to make the letter more "Christian," Paul was appealing to something in Christ to make his point. The letter would be nothing, in other words, if you took out the references to Christ. He *is* the argument of the letter.

This is all the more significant when one realizes that the letter to the Ephesians is the equivalent of a 20-minute sermon! For Paul to have used so many things about the Lord that many times in such a short span shows an amazing depth of knowledge of Jesus Christ. We simply are unequal to Paul's insight of the Lord; we are doing well when we form an entire sermon around one or two verses from his letter!

Here are the 100 occurrences of the references to Christ. I present them to show you that Jesus was constantly the theme for the Apostles when they wrote the books of the New Testament. Only if you get well grounded in the Gospels will you begin to appreciate how the Apostles founded their Church letters on the doctrine of Christ.

Eph. 1:1	Paul was an Apostle of *Christ Jesus*
Eph. 1:1	the letter was written to those who were faithful in *Christ Jesus*
Eph. 1:2	Paul blesses them with grace and peace from the *Lord Jesus Christ*
Eph. 1:3	Paul praises the Father of the *Lord Jesus Christ* ...
Eph. 1:3	... for the spiritual blessings he gave us in *Christ*
Eph. 1:4	the Father chose us in *him* before the world
Eph. 1:5	he predestined us to be adopted as his sons in *Christ Jesus*
Eph. 1:6	he has freely given us grace in the *One* he loves
Eph. 1:7	in *him* we have redemption through his blood
Eph. 1:9	the mystery of his will, purposed in *Christ*
Eph. 1:10	he will bring all things under one head, even *Christ*
Eph. 1:11	in *him* we were also chosen
Eph. 1:12	the Apostles were the first to hope in *Christ*
Eph. 1:13	and we also were included in *Christ* when we heard the gospel
Eph. 1:13	we were marked in *him* with a seal, the promised Holy Spirit
Eph. 1:15	Paul heard about their faith in the *Lord Jesus*

Faith in Christ

Eph. 1:17	Paul prayed that the God of our *Lord Jesus Christ* might give the Spirit
Eph. 1:20	the mighty power which God exerted in *Christ*
Eph. 1:20	he raised *him* from the dead ...
Eph. 1:20	... and seated *him* at his right hand
Eph. 1:22	God placed all things under *his* feet ...
Eph. 1:22	... and appointed *him* to be head over everything for the church
Eph. 1:23	the church is *his* body ...
Eph. 1:23	... the fullness of *him* who fills everything in every way
Eph. 2:5	God made us alive with *Christ*
Eph. 2:6	God raised us up with *Christ* ...
Eph. 2:6	in the Heavenly realms in *Christ Jesus*
Eph. 2:7	his grace expressed in his kindness to us in *Christ Jesus*
Eph. 2:10	we were created in *Christ Jesus* to do good works
Eph. 2:12	once we were separate from *Christ*
Eph. 2:13	now in *Christ Jesus* we have been brought near ...
Eph. 2:13	... through the blood of *Christ*
Eph. 2:14	for *he himself* is our peace
Eph. 2:15	abolished the Law in *his* flesh
Eph. 2:15	*his* purpose was ...
Eph. 2:15	... to create in *himself* one new man out of the two
Eph. 2:16	*he* put to death their hostility
Eph. 2:17	*he* came and preached peace
Eph. 2:18	through *him* we both have access to the Father
Eph. 2:20	*Christ Jesus himself* is the chief cornerstone
Eph. 2:21	in *him* the whole building is joined together
Eph. 2:22	in *him* we too are being built together to become a dwelling
Eph. 3:1	Paul is a prisoner of *Christ Jesus* for the sake of the Gentiles
Eph. 3:4	Paul's insight into the mystery of *Christ*
Eph. 3:6	the Gentiles and Israel share in the promise in *Christ Jesus*
Eph. 3:8	Paul preaches to the Gentiles the unsearchable riches of *Christ*
Eph. 3:11	God accomplished his eternal purpose in *Christ Jesus our Lord*
Eph. 3:12	in *him* and ...
Eph. 3:12	... through faith in *him* we may approach God
Eph. 3:17	that *Christ* may dwell in our hearts through faith
Eph. 3:18	how wide and long and high and deep is the love of *Christ*
Eph. 3:21	to him be glory in the Church and in *Christ Jesus*
Eph. 4:1	Paul is a prisoner for the *Lord*
Eph. 4:5	there is one *Lord*
Eph. 4:7	each one of us has grace as *Christ* apportioned it
Eph. 4:8	when *he* ascended on high ...
Eph. 4:8	... *he* led captives in *his* train and gave gifts to men
Eph. 4:9	*he* also descended to the lower earthly regions
Eph. 4:10	*he* who descended is the very one who ascended higher than Heavens

Faith in Christ

Eph. 4:11	it was *he* who gave some to be Apostles, etc.
Eph. 4:12	so that the body of *Christ* may be built up
Eph. 4:13	so that we reach unity in the knowledge of the *Son of God*
Eph. 4:13	attaining to the whole measure of the fullness of *Christ*
Eph. 4:15	we will grow up into the Head, that is, *Christ*
Eph. 4:16	from *him* the whole body grows and builds itself up
Eph. 4:17	Paul insists in the *Lord*
Eph. 4:20	we did not come to know *Christ* that way
Eph. 4:21	surely you heard of *him* and were taught in *him* ...
Eph. 4:21	... in accordance with the truth that is in *Jesus*
Eph. 4:32	just as in *Christ* God forgave you
Eph. 5:2	just as *Christ* loved us and gave *himself* up for us
Eph. 5:5	no idolaters have any inheritance in the kingdom of Christ and of God
Eph. 5:8	now we are light in the *Lord*
Eph. 5:10	find out what pleases the *Lord*
Eph. 5:14	wake up, O sleeper, and rise from the dead - *Christ* will shine on you
Eph. 5:17	understand what the *Lord's* will is
Eph. 5:19	sing and make music in your heart to the *Lord*
Eph. 5:20	giving thanks for everything in the Name of our *Lord Jesus Christ*
Eph. 5:22	wives, submit to your husbands as to the *Lord*
Eph. 5:23	the husband is the head of the wife as *Christ* is the head of the Church
Eph. 5:24	the Church submits to *Christ*
Eph. 5:25	*Christ* loved the Church and ...
Eph. 5:25	... gave *himself* up for her
Eph. 5:27	*he* presented her to *himself* as a radiant Church
Eph. 5:29	*Christ* feeds and cares for the Church
Eph. 5:30	we are members of *his* body
Eph. 5:32	the union of *Christ* and the Church is a profound mystery
Eph. 6:1	children, obey your parents in the *Lord*
Eph. 6:4	bring your children up in the training and instruction of the *Lord*
Eph. 6:5	slaves, obey your masters just as you would obey *Christ*
Eph. 6:6	like slaves of *Christ*, doing the will of God from the heart
Eph. 6:7	serve wholeheartedly, as if you were serving the *Lord*
Eph. 6:8	the *Lord* will reward everyone for whatever good he does
Eph. 6:9	*he* who is both their Master and yours is in Heaven ...
Eph. 6:9	and there is no favoritism with *him*
Eph. 6:10	be strong in the *Lord* ...
Eph. 6:10	... and in *his* mighty power
Eph. 6:21	Tychicus, the faithful servant in the *Lord*
Eph. 6:23	Paul blesses with love and faith from Father & *Lord Jesus Christ*
Eph. 6:24	grace to all who love our *Lord Jesus Christ* with an undying love

The Creator and King

Every kingdom has a king, and you can usually tell what the king is like by looking at how his kingdom runs – he spreads his influence all through the kingdom. If things are running smoothly and everyone is happy, then obviously the king knows what he's doing and he's a good king. But if things are in a bad state, and there's a lot of discontent among the subjects, then the king isn't doing his job. The king is in the position to affect the well-being of all his subjects; from his throne he can touch the lives of everyone in the realm. He has powers that no one else has; he has responsibilities and position that nobody else can claim.

The universe was made, the Scriptures tell us, by God's command, for God's purposes, and it's headed for Judgment Day where it will be examined closely to see if it conforms to God's eternal will. All we lack to finish this picture is the King himself, the One who sits on the throne over the world and directs its affairs. The Bible very clearly shows us Christ in this position; he is called "the ruler of God's creation." (Revelation 3:14)

In our day it's hard to picture what a kingdom must be like, because we are used to equality and public rule. We usually have a negative picture of a kingdom: we imagine a self-indulgent tyrant who has no concern for his subjects, who only lives to tax his people into poverty for the sake of his own comforts and enjoyments. But there have been good kings in history.

The ideal king was David who ruled over God's people. David was even called "a man after God's own heart." So, what would life be like in the ideal kingdom?

First, the king would naturally have the well-being of his subjects on his heart. **Second**, the king would make sure that everyone can make a living, and that their business efforts would be profitable. **Third**, the king would make sure that everyone has the basics of life: food, clothing, shelter. **Fourth**, the king would set up a system of law and order, giving out justice to the wicked and the righteous alike. **Fifth**, the king would do whatever necessary to protect his people from their enemies. **Sixth**, the king would lead his people to God in true worship.

David was the pattern for Christ, the model king through whom we learn what kind of King rules over God's people through all the world and throughout time. On the surface, we may not pick up on the fact that Jesus was a king like David just from reading the Gospels. But Christ not only *is* the King of the universe, he acts like it, according to this list of duties of a good king. Let's apply this standard of a good king back to the Gospel descriptions of Jesus' ministry.

- As he lived and worked among men on earth, he demonstrated kingly qualities that are easy to see. For example, he cared about his people constantly – providing for them, praying for them, teaching them, protecting them – his love for his people was the thing that motivated all his efforts on their behalf. It was for them that he came to earth. His highest sacrifice on the cross was only for them!

- We can also pick out examples of the King taking care of his own. He fed them when they had nothing to eat; he protected them from the "wolves in sheep's clothing" – the Pharisees; he paid their taxes for them; he helped them find catches of fish; he taught them the truth about God and poured out the Spirit on them so they could see God; he laid the law down – *his* Law – and demanded that his subjects obey him. If we have our eyes open, we can easily see that his entire ministry was actually the King working on behalf of his subjects.

- He still takes care of his people. He continues to send the Spirit to them so that they can know God, so that they can come before God in Heaven and present their requests in person. He sends them food and other necessities of life. He protects them now from greater spiritual dangers. He teaches them through his Word, by means of the Spirit. He rules by means of his spiritual government, complete with laws and administrators under him who care for us in his Name. Since he is still King over the world, he hasn't grown lax in his duties or cold in his care for us. He is constantly overseeing his vast kingdom and making sure things run smoothly according to his will.

But Christ's connection with the universe is even more important than his political role as King. The world was actually made *through* him; it exists day by day because of his direct, constant action upon it. In other words, he himself made the world in the beginning; it's his special creation, the work of his hands. And he made it in such a way that it depends completely on his daily care for it. Without his constant attention to its structure and affairs, the world would cease to exist. (Colossians 1:16-17)

From the very beginning, Christ has maintained a rigid hold on the universe that it can't escape. In fact, that explains why the universe is still running exactly according to God's original plans. Christ rules over the universe with intimate knowledge of every detail, with full responsibility for its progress, with full power to direct everything according to his will. Earthly kings can't possibly attend to every detail of their kingdom, nor can they directly affect every circumstance in the life of each subject in the kingdom. Christ, however, can and does work at that level throughout his kingdom. He determines when and where people will live (Acts 17:26), he gives them the food they eat every day, he leads them daily through circumstances of his own choosing. Through his wisdom and power he maintains complete control over Creation.

Hebrews tells us the unique relationship that Christ has with the Father:

> In the past God spoke to our forefathers through the Prophets at many times and in various ways, but in these last days he has spoken to us by his Son, whom he appointed heir of all things, and through whom he made the universe. The Son is the radiance of God's glory and the exact representation of his being, sustaining all things by his powerful Word. (Hebrews 1:1-3)

- **First**, the way that God makes himself known to his creatures is by means of Christ. Since none of us can see God directly, we instead look at Christ to learn about God. He is the manifestation of God, the fullness of God in the flesh, the way we learn about God. In him we learn the character of God. By his actions we understand the works of God. He's an accommodation to our limitations, so to speak, since unless God revealed himself in this way to us we would never know God.

> ... God, the blessed and only Ruler, the King of kings and Lord of lords, who alone

is immortal and who lives in unapproachable light, whom no one has seen or can see. (1 Timothy 6:15-16)

So, since God himself is unapproachable, Christ is the special way that God has provided for us to know him: we *can* approach Jesus, hear him speak, touch him, and know through him that God exists:

> That which was from the beginning, which we have heard, which we have seen with our eyes, which we have looked at and our hands have touched — this we proclaim concerning the Word of life. The life appeared; we have seen it and testify to it, and we proclaim to you the eternal life, which was with the Father and has appeared to us. We proclaim to you what we have seen and heard, so that you also may have fellowship with us. (1 John 1:1-3)

- **Second**, God made the universe *through Christ*. This was to be Christ's Kingdom, and *he* will be its absolute ruler. We can better understand this if we think about a new market that a business wants to get into. The board of the company will assign a certain department head to lead the new project: it will be up to him to hire new employees, buy the supplies needed, set up the production line, set the schedule, take care of the finances, and make regular progress reports back to the board. In short, he's responsible to make a profit – using the resources of the company, with the board's blessing, acting in the name and authority of the board but doing the work himself.

In Psalm 2 we read about this same kind of business transaction when God turned over this new Kingdom of Creation to the Son, for him to manage and build up:

> "I have installed my King
> on Zion, my holy hill."
> I will proclaim the decree of the Lord:
> He said to me, "You are my Son;
> today I have become your Father.
> Ask of me, and I will make the nations
>   your inheritance,
> the ends of the earth your possession.
> You will rule them with an iron scepter;
> you will dash them to pieces like pottery."
> (Psalm 2:6-9)

Notice the degree of control that the Son has over his Kingdom: even rebellion by earth's rulers is useless, because he intends to rule all with an iron scepter. This is *his* world now.

- **Third**, God made Christ the heir of all things. It all belongs to him to do with as he pleases. He especially proves his ownership in what he is *able* to do with it. Ownership isn't just a matter of possession for him, as it is for us; all the world lays bare under his hand, under his scrutiny, and he uses it to serve his purposes. He speaks and it obeys, instantly, and does whatever he demands of it. For instance, a dog will obey its master but it will ignore a stranger. In the same way, the universe responds immediately to Christ's word of power. He wields *miraculous* power over his kingdom. Since no part of the universe can resist his commands, it's clear who is the Master and who is the subject; he proves his authority by his power.

- **Fourth**, Christ sustains the universe through his Word. The same Word that created the universe supports it and keeps it going day by day. The power of that Word is illustrated in the fact that, unknown to them, and in spite of their disobedient hearts, people and nations nevertheless end up doing exactly what he wants from them all through history. "For he must reign until he has put all his enemies under his feet." (1 Corinthians 15:25) His Word is that of a King; he commands, and his subjects *must* obey. But what he's making out of all this is a well-balanced kingdom: in the end, when it's all over, he will be pleased with the results and he will then turn it all over to the Father.

The point in Hebrews 1:1-3 is that, from the very beginning, Christ has been the head of the universe; God relates to his Creation at all times and in every way through the powerful and effective administration of Christ.

Other Scriptural testimony teaches the same truth.

> In the beginning was the Word, and the Word was with God, and the Word was God. He was with God in the beginning. *Through him* all things were made; without him nothing was made that has been made ... He was in the world, and though the world was made *through him*, the world did not recognize him. (John 1:1-3, 10)

> ... yet for us there is but one God, the Father, from whom all things came and for whom we live; and there is but one Lord, Jesus Christ, *through whom all things came* and *through whom we live*. (1 Corinthians 8:6)

> For *by him* all things were created: things in Heaven and on earth, visible and invisible, whether thrones or powers or rulers or authorities; all things were created *by him* and *for him*. He is before all things, and *in him* all things hold together. (Colossians 1:16-17)

But even the Old Testament only gave hints about this King, so that when Paul writes about him he calls Jesus the "mystery of God." It wasn't made plain that Jesus himself was the Master until he came in the flesh "to his own" – when he came into his Kingdom in the same outward form as his subjects.

> He was in the world, and though the world was made through him, the world did not recognize him. He came to that which was his own, but his own did not receive him. (John 1:10-11)

Over time, especially after the resurrection when they finally understood the true nature of Christ, the Apostles saw *the Creator* in Jesus. They wrote their Gospels reminiscing about the *kind* of work that Christ did among them – a work that no one except the King could do.

- Only the **Creator** of the world could do miracles. The kinds of things that Jesus did reflected not only the same kind of work that happened at Creation, but in the same *way* that it was done. For example, he created enough bread and fish to feed thousands of people immediately – out of *nothing*. The original loaves and fishes that he had were only a pitifully meager starting point that represents how useless the world's contribution is to God's purposes; there just wasn't a natural explanation for how he did such a thing. And he brought the dead back to life with a *command* – remember the original Commands of Creation in which something that couldn't obey God found power in his Word to obey his wish? He *cursed* the fig tree, and *blessed* the food he used to feed the crowds, both acts in which his Word had power in itself to either kill or proliferate – again, the same kind of work that God did in the beginning. See Genesis 1-3 for the description of God working through blessing, command, curse, and miracle.

- Only the **King**, through whom the world was made, could speak with such authority and wisdom. The people were astonished at his teaching, because he spoke with an authority that ordinary teachers didn't have:

    When Jesus had finished saying these things, the crowds were amazed at his teaching, because he taught as one who had authority, and not as their teachers of the Law. (Matthew 7:28-29)

    That authority had power and conviction to it; his words stab the conscience, so that we know we are in the presence of the One to whom we must give account of ourselves. We belong to him; that's why he has the right to speak to us as he does, and why we know that we must do as *he* says, no matter what others may tell us.

- Only the **Lawgiver** could rightfully expect such complete obedience from men. Our obedience isn't allowed to be superficial because Christ's realm, and the depth to which he reaches in our hearts, isn't superficial. An ordinary ruler can only hope to make our outward actions conform to his laws; but Christ, who rules all of Creation with infinite precision, requires obedience *from the heart*. His Sermon on the Mount is an excellent analysis of how far-reaching his realm is over men. "Surely you desire truth in the inner parts; you teach me wisdom in the inmost place." (Psalm 51:6)

There are two areas where it's necessary that Christ be the Creator. **First**, he has to have such power and authority over the first Creation that he can destroy sin and its effects. "The reason the Son of God appeared was to destroy the devil's work." (1 John 3:8) And that's exactly what we see in his ministry, as he tackled sin and its destruction head on. He has the authority to name sin and rebuke it; he undoes the effects of sin – misery, destruction and death; and he lays the ax at the root of sin so that it can't continue to destroy his people. For such work he needs absolute power and authority, as he claimed several times:

> All authority in Heaven and on earth has been given to me. (Matthew 28:18)

> But take heart! I have overcome the world. (John 16:33)

Second, and this is the amazing part, *he himself* will lead the first Creation through death and resurrection into the second Creation. The first Creation is doomed to destruction, because of the sin and death that entered the world at the beginning. We need a new model, a new world, and a new nature because the old nature is no good anymore. That model is Christ: we know what we *will* be by looking at what he is *now* after his resurrection.

The world itself, as well as the sons of God, wait for the day when the old Creation will be shaken out (Hebrews 12:26-27) and we will be made new – in the image of the Son of God who rose from the dead as a spiritual man:

> The creation waits in eager expectation for the sons of God to be revealed. For the creation was subjected to frustration, not by its own choice, but by the will of the one who subjected it, in hope that the creation itself will be liberated from its bondage to decay and brought into the glorious freedom of the children of God. We know that the whole creation has been groaning as in the pains of childbirth right up to the present time. Not only so, but we ourselves, who have the firstfruits of the Spirit, groan inwardly as we wait eagerly for our adoption as sons, the redemption of our bodies. For in this hope we were saved. (Romans 8:19-24)

> For since death came through a man, the resurrection of the dead comes also through a man. For as in Adam all die, so in Christ all will be made alive. But each in his own turn: Christ, the firstfruits; then, when he comes, those who belong to him. (1 Corinthians 15:21-23)

And in what Paul calls a mystery, Christ represents in his own body the passage of the first Creation to the second Creation. The first physical kingdom will change into a new spiritual kingdom; the King himself puts his physical body to death (the first Creation must be put aside) and then leads his subjects into a new life. That new life is what we will be like, if God joins us to him. So, he became one with us physically so that we could become one with him spiritually.

> Since the children have flesh and blood, he too shared in their humanity so that by his death he might destroy him who holds the power of death — that is, the

devil — and free those who all their lives were held in slavery by their fear of death. (Hebrews 2:14-15)

So will it be with the resurrection of the dead. The body that is sown is perishable, it is raised imperishable; it is sown in dishonor, it is raised in glory; it is sown in weakness, it is raised in power; it is sown a natural body, it is raised a spiritual body. If there is a natural body, there is also a spiritual body. So it is written: "The first man Adam became a living being"; the last Adam, a life-giving spirit. The spiritual did not come first, but the natural, and after that the spiritual. The first man was of the dust of the earth, the second man from Heaven. As was the earthly man, so are those who are of the earth; and as is the man from Heaven, so also are those who are of Heaven. And just as we have borne the likeness of the earthly man, so shall we bear the likeness of the man from Heaven. (1 Corinthians 15:42-49)

Finally, we know that his resurrection into a new Creation was planned *before* the first physical Creation. Obviously God had all this planned out from the very beginning. Therefore Creation was the first step to an overall plan which included Christ's physical life, death, resurrection, and our union with him to form a Second Creation.

> He was chosen before the creation of the world, but was revealed in these last times for your sake. (1 Peter 1:20)

> … the Lamb that was slain from the creation of the world. (Revelation 13:8)

To summarize, the world was made *through Christ* because, **first**, it must be totally under his control. **Second**, he intends to destroy it completely, because as it stands – under the effects of sin and death – it can't continue into eternity in God's plans, nor can it contribute anything of value to a new, eternal, spiritual kingdom. **Third**, when the time is ripe (and in himself he already took the first step) he will do away with the physical creation that we are familiar with and replace it with a perfect spiritual Kingdom, resurrected from the dead. The universe then is a kingdom in which Christ is working out his own agenda, from beginning to end.

Other roles of Christ

The fact that Jesus is the Creator and the King doesn't by any means exhaust the depth of his abilities, authority and power. There are so many things to take care of in God's Kingdom, things that only God himself can do, that Jesus has to assume many roles on our behalf. The entire foundation of God's church consists of the works of Christ from first to last; without him we would have nothing to depend on.

- *Fullness of the Godhead* – In the divine economy, Jesus is the Son of God – one of three persons. But when he came to us, the Father put all the person and authority and power of God into Christ, so that we could truly say *Immanuel* – our God *is* with us.

    > For in Christ all the fullness of the Deity lives in bodily form, and you have been given fullness in Christ, who is the head over every power and authority. (Colossians 2:9-10)

    > The Son is the radiance of God's glory and the exact representation of his being, sustaining all things by his powerful Word. (Hebrews 1:3)

The reason is that we need God himself, not just a representative. We need to deal directly with God, for several reasons: *first*, it's God that we offended with our sin, so we need to get this straightened out with him. When Christ forgives our sin, we can be assured that he has God's authority to relieve us of our guilt. Only the offended party can forgive us our sins. *Second*, the needs in our lives require the power of Heaven. We need God's hand, the miracles of the Creator, to help us with our problems. We haven't been able to find solutions to our problems in this world; Christ however brings the power and treasures of Heaven to bear on our problems. The treasures all belong to him anyway, and he has the right to give them away to us.

It's important, however, that God comes *all the way* to us – we need him to be so close that we can touch him, see him, and hear him. We need him to be like us, a man that we can see and deal with. This is what John is so amazed at and grateful about:

> That which was from the beginning, which we have heard, which we have seen with our eyes, which we have looked at and our hands have touched—this we proclaim concerning the Word of life. The life appeared; we have seen it and testify to it, and we proclaim to you the eternal life, which was with the Father and has appeared to us. (1 John 1:1-2)

- ***Lamb*** – The Old Testament sacrificial system was a complex affair, as you well know if you've tried to make sense of the first few books of the Bible. But it all boils down to this: someone, or something, must die for sin. There's just no way around the Law's demand for shedding blood to atone for guilt.

   Ordinarily the sinner himself must die for his sin; that's only just and right. But God in his mercy gave the Israelites a way out – otherwise they would all have to die, since they were all sinners. The way out was that they could bring certain kinds of animals to the Temple and put *them* to death. It wasn't exactly the same as the sinner having to die for his own sin, but at least it was a death, the shedding of blood for a crime committed.

   The reason God accepted this sacrifice was that he was laying the foundation for an eternal principle for all of God's people: Jesus is our sacrifice, our alternate who stands in our place in the execution dock. He takes our guilt upon himself and dies, so that we don't have to. The sacrifices of the Old Testament symbolized this eternal sacrifice.

   The most powerful example of a sacrificial victim offered for sinners is the Passover Lamb, first instituted when Israel was getting ready to leave Egypt. The Israelites were to kill a lamb without blemish, one per family, and sprinkle its blood around the doors of their houses:

> The blood will be a sign for you on the houses where you are; and when I see the blood, I will pass over you. No destructive plague will touch you when I strike Egypt. (Exodus 12:13)

When the destroying angel saw the blood, it "passed over" that house; if it didn't see blood, it killed the firstborn son of the household. On that night Israel saw a graphic example of the power of the lamb's blood to save them from disaster.

Jesus is that Passover Lamb for us:

For Christ, our Passover lamb, has been sacrificed. (1 Corinthians 5:7)

Of course he's the other sacrifices of the Temple too. The animals offered there were only symbols of what God had in mind for his people:

> But those sacrifices are an annual reminder of sins, because it is impossible for the blood of bulls and goats to take away sins. (Hebrews 10:3-4)

> How much more, then, will the blood of Christ, who through the eternal Spirit offered himself unblemished to God, cleanse our consciences from acts that lead to death, so that we may serve the living God! (Hebrews 9:14)

What we have to do now is use that sacrifice when we approach God. There is no forgiveness for sin without blood; in fact, we aren't even allowed into God's presence without a sacrifice making us clean and acceptable to God. Laying claim to Jesus is the only way we will get close to our God. (Hebrews 10:19)

- **_High Priest_** – Another aspect of the Old Testament sacrificial system is the priest of the Temple. In fact, nobody was allowed into the Temple except for the priest. He was, literally, the people's lifeline to God. He was a special representative of both sides: he represented man in presenting the sacrifices to God and asking for blessings; he also represented God when he took that forgiveness and the blessings back to the people.

  The priesthood of Israel descended from Levi, one of the 12 sons of Jacob. The Law stipulated that only Levites could minister in the Temple as priests. But Jesus wasn't a descendent of Levi – his ancestor was Judah. How could he be a priest, then, and satisfy the Law's demands? The answer is in what happened *before* the Law was given:

  > And what we have said is even more clear if another priest like Melchizedek appears, one who has become a priest not on the basis of a regulation as to his ancestry but on the basis of the power of an indestructible life. For it is declared: "You are a priest forever, in

the order of Melchizedek." (Hebrews 7:15-17)

> Now there have been many of those priests [*that is, Levites*], since death prevented them from continuing in office; but because Jesus lives forever, he has a permanent priesthood. Therefore he is able to save completely those who come to God through him, because he always lives to intercede for them. (Hebrews 7:23-25)

In other words, the Father made Jesus our high priest because, *first*, he lives forever to intercede for us; *second*, he himself isn't a sinner, as the Levites were.

Now Jesus is at the throne of Grace pleading for our lives, asking for God's mercy and grace on us. He's getting answers, too – the Son of God always gets answers to his prayers! And as the faithful priest, he comes away from the throne with his hands filled with the things he asked for; he then distributes these blessings, these answers to his prayers, among his people.

The Bible describes Christ

Faith opens the window into Heaven; it lets us see things in God's spiritual world that we can't ordinarily see with our physical senses. But that open window itself is the Bible. God graciously gave us his Word so that we have truth to look at. There's no such thing as faith without the Bible, and it takes faith to understand the Bible. The two work hand in hand to reveal the truth about Christ to us.

How, then, can they call on the one they have not believed in? And how can they believe in the one of whom they have not heard? And how can they hear without someone preaching to them? ... Consequently, faith comes from hearing the message, and the message is heard through the word of Christ. (Romans 10:14,17)

What do we discover about Christ when we study the Bible? That he is like a diamond: he has many sides, many facets, to his character and work. In order to fully understand and appreciate who he is, we have to turn the diamond around and examine each facet. He plays many roles in the Kingdom of God. For example, he is not only the gentle Shepherd but also the Judge of all the earth. We can't just focus on one aspect of Jesus and expect to understand him! All the parts fit together into one beautiful whole. After we've explored the many truths about Christ, we can begin to appreciate just how much we all depend on him – and we'll start giving him the credit he deserves.

Names

The names of Christ can be found both in the Old Testament and the New Testament. They of course describe who he is and what he does just as God's names do. These are just a few of the scores of names that we learn from the Scriptures.

Messiah — This special Hebrew word means "the anointed one." It refers to the way a king was called and prepared for office: someone would pour oil over his head (we don't understand this custom in our day, but it meant a lot to them!) as a ceremony of taking office. David was anointed into office as Israel's king. But even the Jews realized that someone would come to sit on David's throne again who was anointed from on high — anointed with the Spirit of God — who would be king over Israel and defeat their enemies. Jesus did that very thing: his anointing took place at the beginning of his ministry (Matthew 3:16) and he sat down on the throne of God to rule over the earth, especially his people. (Hebrews 1:3)

Son of God — This name irritated the Jews, because they knew exactly what it meant. God is one God, and we aren't polytheists (believers in many gods). "Hear, O Israel: The LORD our God, the LORD is one." (Deuteronomy 6:4) But God himself reveals in the New Testament that believing in God the Father, God the Son, and God the Spirit isn't believing in three Gods. How that is true, nobody knows but him; but we must believe it if he says so. "This is my Son, whom I love. Listen to him!" (Mark 9:7) This means that whatever Jesus says is the very Word of God, and whatever he does is the work of God; he, therefore, really is the Savior of men.

Wonderful Counselor — We get this name from Isaiah's prophecy that was given long before Jesus came: "And he will be called Wonderful Counselor." (Isaiah 9:6) Jesus had the words of life. Whoever would listen to him would find life and peace and joy, but whoever ignored his words of counsel would only find death and failure. A counselor knows what he's talking about and he's in the business of helping others solve their problems with his knowledge. Christ is the ultimate counselor: "The words I have spoken to you are spirit and they are life." (John 6:63) There are other passages that teach the importance of Christ's counsel to men: John 6:68; John 12:47-48; John 14:24; John 15:7.

Shepherd — Everyone knows this name of Christ, if for no other reason than we have seen the picture of the gentle Shepherd on the walls of our churches. It teaches us how helpless God's people are to take care of themselves, and how carefully and completely Jesus provides for all their needs.

The Gate — This name also irritates many people, because it means that there is only *one way* into Heaven — through the gate that God provided. "I am the gate; whoever enters through me will be saved." (John 10:7) "Salvation is found in no one else, for there is no other name under Heaven given to men by which we must be saved." (Acts 4:12)

Cornerstone — Every building needs a point of reference: a fixed spot from which the builders can determine where the rest of the stones will extend. Jesus is the point of reference in the Church, which is the building that God is making for his home. Christians rely on Christ for truth, for direction, for purpose, and for strength. (Ephesians 2:19-21)

Types

The purpose of types in the Old Testament is to teach us spiritual truths in pictures – using the things of this world to illustrate the things of God's world. I hope you realize that the realities of Heaven are not made up of what makes up our world! That would be a cheap victory, to get to Heaven only to discover that we have fought and hoped for the riches of this world warmed over. Christ died for something more permanent and valuable than what God has always intended to destroy at the end of time!

Nevertheless, the Lord uses impermanent things to illustrate truths about the permanent. Not only are types useful, they may be absolutely necessary to learn – the New Testament writers may feel that the type did the job so well that they simply won't go over the same ground twice. In order to learn this particular aspect of Christ or God's kingdom you *must* study the type; it won't be discussed again in the New Testament!

Following are some of the types of the Old Testament and how they illustrate God's spiritual world.

The Tree of Life To eat of this tree meant to live forever. In Revelation 2:7 and 22:14 we read that all who enter into God's eternal city will eat of the Tree of Life. Christ himself points out that he is the vine that gives life and we are the branches. (John 15)

The marriage relationship Paul teaches that the union between man and woman is a lesson on the union between Christ and his Church. (Ephesians 5:22-33)

The cherubim & flaming sword Man was denied access to the Tree of Life. (Genesis 3:24) People throughout history have looked for eternal life and not found it; only when God was pleased to open the way to life in Christ did we have another chance at it. Even now, only those who approach Christ with faith will find him (John 6:40); only those whom the Father draws will come to life in Christ. (John 6:44)

The blood of Abel Innocent blood shed on the ground (like Christ's during his crucifixion) still speaks its powerful

Faith in Christ

message to a God who hears and will act on it. (Hebrews 12:24)

The Seed of Promise The seed promised to Abraham was actually Christ. (Galatians 3:16)

Melchizedek He was a priest without birth or death, to whom Abraham gave tithes and honor. (Hebrews 7)

Joseph There were prophecies of his exaltation, but he had to go through humiliation first. (Philippians 2:1-11)

Deliverance from Egypt The troubles that the Israelites went through, who they suffered under, and who led them out and by what means – all this is a picture of our deliverance in Christ. (Ephesians 2:1-10)

Manna The bread from Heaven tells us something of how Christ is food for his people. (John 6)

Water from the Rock The rock in the desert that refreshes the Lord's people. (1 Corinthians 10:4)

The Tabernacle The Tabernacle was built after the Heavenly pattern and resembles the salvation we have in Jesus' work. (Hebrews 8:1 - 9:5)

The system of sacrificial worship The sacrifices, the way they were done, and the forgiveness they got – all these revealed the power in Jesus' sacrifice. (Hebrews 9:6 - 10:39)

The Sabbath The Lord required his people to rest on the Sabbath, as a picture of the rest of faith in Christ that he also requires. (Hebrews 3:7 - 4:11)

Faith in Christ

Joshua the conqueror Joshua led the people of God into the Promised Land, clearing out the inhabitants and dividing up the land for the tribes. Jesus leads his people too into the Kingdom of God through warfare. (1 Corinthians 15:12-34)

King David In his duties, his character, and his experiences, David was a picture of the perfect King to come. (Luke 1:32-33)

Joshua the High Priest A priest of Israel is also the king. (Zechariah 3; Hebrews 8:1; Revelation 17:14)

Prophecies

The Prophets of the Old Testament gave a clear but piecemeal picture of what Jesus would be like. The Spirit revealed all sorts of things to them about the Christ; an astute Jew would actually have known a great deal about the Messiah if he had bothered to study the prophecies. In fact, the Jews did know many of the details, but they seem to have completely missed the picture – the details, on the surface, painted some pictures that seemed contradictory, as if they were talking about more than one person.

Here are several Old Testament prophecies about Christ and the New Testament passage that proclaims its fulfillment in him:

Prophecy	Fulfillment	Prophecy	Fulfillment
Genesis 3:15	Galatians 4:4	Psalm 16:10	Luke 24:6
Genesis 22:18	Ephesians 2:13	Psalm 22:6-8	Matthew 27:43
Genesis 49:10	Luke 3:33	Psalm 22:16	John 19:18
Numbers 24:17	Luke 3:34	Psalm 22:18	Mark 15:24
Deut. 18:15	John 6:14	Psalm 27:12	Matthew 26:60-61
Psalm 2:6-9	Ephesians 1:20-22	Psalm 34:20	John 19:33
Psalm 2:12	Philippians 2:10	Psalm 41:9	Mark 14:10

Faith in Christ

Psalm 68:18	Luke 24:50-51	Isaiah 53:9	Matthew 27:57-60
Psalm 69:4	John 15:23-25	Isaiah 53:12	Matthew 27:38
Psalm 69:21	John 19:29	Isaiah 61:1	Matthew 11:4
Psalm 109:4	Luke 23:34	Jeremiah 23:5	Revelation 11:15
Psalm 109:7-8	Acts 1:21	Jeremiah 31:15	Matthew 2:16
Psalm 110:4	Hebrews 6:20	Hosea 11:1	Matthew 2:14
Psalm 132:11	Ephesians 1:20	Micah 5:2	Matthew 2:1
Isaiah 7:14	Matthew 1:18	Haggai 2:7	Matthew 12:6
Isaiah 9:1-2	Matthew 4:12	Zechariah 9:9	John 12:13-14
Isaiah 9:6-7	John 18:37	Zech. 11:12-13	Matthew 26:15;
Isaiah 11:1-2	John 1:32		Matthew 27:6-7
Isaiah 42:1	Matthew 3:16	Zech. 12:10	John 19:18
Isaiah 50:6	Mark 14:65	Zechariah 13:7	Mark 14:50
Isaiah 53:3-5	Matthew 8:16-17	Malachi 3:1	John 1:29
Isaiah 53:7	Matthew 26:62-63		

Though the facts about Christ are pretty clear to see when *we* read the Old Testament prophecies, they weren't always so obvious to the Israelites who first heard them! In fact, even the disciples didn't understand their meaning until the Lord explained it to them:

> They still did not understand from Scripture that Jesus had to rise from the dead. (John 20:9)

> "How foolish you are, and how slow of heart to believe all that the Prophets have spoken! Did not the Christ have to suffer these things and then enter his glory?" And beginning with Moses and all the Prophets, he explained to them what was said in all the Scriptures concerning himself. (Luke 24:25-27)

Though it's good to know these prophecies, there's a reason that they are so important to the story of Christ. *They prove that we have here the Christ that God had been promising all along.* They serve to identify him; nobody else can claim to have fulfilled all these prophecies, so nobody else can claim the title of the Messiah that the Prophets predicted. They were saying, in effect, "here is how you will know him when he comes — he will do this, and look like this, and say this, and so on."

Faith in Christ

The Jews made a terrible mistake when they overlooked all the prophecies coming true before their eyes in the person and work of Christ. They *were* careful to identify the true Messiah in one detail — remember that the Pharisees knew the Messianic prophecies too: "Look into it, and you will find that a prophet does not come out of Galilee." (John 7:52) If they cared to explore the matter further, however (which they didn't), they would have found out the truth of Jesus' birth and seen that it *was* a fulfillment of prophecy.

What most people often don't realize, however, is what the Prophets were *really* saying about Christ. They weren't just predicting that he would come; if that were all that they were doing, they could have predicted the coming of Caesar and created as much excitement. Jesus is the King of kings, however — they prophesied the coming of the King from Heaven who would lay waste the kingdoms of this world and set up his own in their place.

> For to us a child is born, to us a son is given, and the government will be on his shoulders. And he will be called Wonderful Counselor, Mighty God, Everlasting Father, Prince of Peace. Of the increase of his government and peace there will be no end. He will reign on David's throne and over his kingdom, establishing and upholding it with justice and righteousness from that time on and forever. The zeal of the Lord Almighty will accomplish this. (Isaiah 9:6-7)

The Lord is salvation

Of all the names that Christ was given, the name "Jesus" is his most important name. It's based on the Old Testament Hebrew name Yahweh (יהוה) that the Lord revealed to Moses in Exodus 34.

Faith in Christ

The LORD, the LORD, the compassionate and gracious God, slow to anger, abounding in love and faithfulness, maintaining love to thousands, and forgiving wickedness, rebellion and sin. Yet he does not leave the guilty unpunished; he punishes the children and their children for the sin of the fathers to the third and fourth generation. (Exodus 34:6-7)

Jesus is the Greek way of saying the Hebrew name **Joshua** (you pronounce it as "Yehoshua"), which in Hebrew means "the LORD is salvation." Now we have the connection between *Jesus* of the New Testament and the *LORD* of the Old Testament: that same name – Yahweh – reveals the *same God* at work. It's no wonder then that Jesus was such a perfect example of the God who is "compassionate and gracious, slow to anger, abounding in love and faithfulness!"

Remember what Peter said about the name of Christ? "Salvation is found in no one else, for there is no other name under Heaven given to men by which we must be saved." (Acts 4:12) When he said that to Jews, they should have flinched — they knew the utter holiness of the Name, and they were jealous for its glory. Here was Peter claiming the same glory for Jesus' name! He was calling up visions of the God of the Old Testament, the one to whom the Israelites called for help in their time of need. He was claiming that Jesus would save us just as the Lord did in the Old Testament, because we are dealing with the same God. The only difference now is that we can see our God, and touch him, and hear him clearly as he speaks to us. His power and ability to save his people remain the same, however.

Speaking of calling on the name of God, remember the verse that told the Israelites to do that? "And everyone who calls on the name of the Lord will be saved." (Joel 2:32) Some of the Israelites understood this and they called on him when they needed help. Most, however, turned to other gods and refused to call on him. "No one calls on your name or strives to lay hold of you." (Isaiah 64:7) Well, both of these truths are also in the New Testament church. In order to find salvation from our sins, we have to call on the name of Jesus Christ. Only he can save us; only he can rescue us from sin and death. There is nobody else who can do that for us. But we *have* to call on him or he won't do it!

He told us many times the importance of coming to him:

> Come to me, all you who are weary and burdened, and I will give you rest. (Matthew 11:28)

> All that the Father gives me will come to me, and whoever comes to me I will never drive away. (John 6:37)

> If anyone is thirsty, let him come to me and drink. (John 7:37)

If we will just come to him and call him by name, he will respond immediately. The stories in the Gospels about the many people who came to him with their diseases are designed to show us this about him — his willingness to answer when people come to him.

But most *won't* come to him. After three years of ministry, he looked over Jerusalem and the hard-hearted Jews who refused to listen to his message of mercy:

> As he approached Jerusalem and saw the city, he wept over it and said, "If you, even you, had only known on this day what would bring you peace — but now it is hidden from your eyes. The days will come upon you when your enemies will build an embankment against you and encircle you and hem you in on every side. They will dash you to the ground, you and the children within your walls. They will not leave one stone on another, because you did

not recognize the time of God's coming to you." (John 19:41-42)

The Lord had come to them, and they still refused to call on him for help. So now they were going to experience some other realities of the names of God — the God of Justice, the Lord of Hosts, the jealous God.

Jesus' names are so important to understand and start using that he once pointed out that the disciples weren't taking advantage of them.

> Until now you have not asked for anything in my name. Ask and you will receive, and your joy will be complete. (John 16:24)

Most twentieth century Christians think that this means attaching the phrase "In Jesus' name, Amen" at the end of their prayers. Although I wouldn't want to upset anybody's faith in the Lord who answers prayer, I might point out that none of the disciples used that phrase at the end of their prayers — not even *after* he encouraged them to use his name! You won't find that phrase anywhere in the New Testament. What you will find, however, are examples of the disciples using Jesus' name *throughout* the prayer, starting at the beginning. We see an excellent example of how to do this in Acts 4. To them, his name wasn't a ceremonial afterthought to close things up nicely. *His name revealed something that they wanted.* They called on the Light, the Shepherd, the Lord of lords, the Resurrection, because they needed these things that were in his name. I like to think that this is what Jesus meant when he told them to use his name in prayer: pray for *what is in* his name. Then you won't be using his name to no purpose (which is forbidden in the Third Commandment), but instead for the purpose that he intended when he revealed it to us.

There is one more thing about Jesus' name that we should look at. His names reveal the truth about him — we've seen this already. That truth, however, will often surprise us; it doesn't always match our preconceived notions of who he is. When God announced the birth of Christ through the angels, he told Mary and Joseph what to name the child:

> She will give birth to a son, and you are to give him the name **Jesus**, because he will save his people from their sins. (Matthew 1:21)

That name reveals why he came — to save us from our sins. Not from our bills, or our neighbors, or our lack of free time, or whatever else may be bothering us. God looks at us and sees our sin like a glaring light in his eyes; he can't think of anything else. *We* can, though — we would rather think of anything else but our sins; but to him it's the first order of business. He has to do something about our sin before he can do anything else for us. So when you call on the name of *Jesus*, remember what he is waiting for you to ask him for.

Christ who lives in me

Jesus Christ is such a mysterious person that it's no wonder that so many people miss the significance of his life and work. In fact they do it all the time: very few people understand why he came to the earth, which is proved by the fact that they take almost no advantage of this amazing gift that God gave the world. It's like a treasure that remains underground, even though we all know where it is.

But the mystery behind Christ goes even deeper. For example, Paul was an expert in the truth about Christ. He received deeper knowledge about Jesus that he shared with the rest of the Church:

> Now I rejoice in what was suffered for you, and I fill up in my flesh what is still lacking in regard to Christ's afflictions, for the sake of his body, which is the church. I have become its servant by the commission God gave me to present to you the word of God in its fullness — the **mystery** that has been kept hidden for ages and generations, but is now disclosed to the saints. To them God has chosen to make known among the Gentiles the glorious riches of this mystery, which is *Christ in you, the hope of glory*. (Colossians 1:24-27)

If Christ was all the things that we've studied so far but no more, he would certainly deserve all glory. But God's mercy goes even further – to a point that no human being could ever have imagined. The mystery that drove Paul to spread the Gospel to the nations was that *God will live his life in us*. Jesus literally puts his life, with all his richness and power, inside our hearts.

What we will find, then, is a strange power and understanding in us that we're not used to feeling. The Spirit of Christ lives inside us, guiding us along the paths of life and giving us new strength to do what we couldn't do before. It's as if two lives are inside us:

> I have been crucified with Christ and I no longer live, but Christ lives in me. The life I live in the body, I live by faith in the Son of God, who loved me and gave himself for me. (Galatians 2:20)

It's the perfect answer to the problem that people have always had. We live in God's Kingdom, but God expects perfection, he commands us to love him with our whole being, he has spiritual work for us to do. All these things are good and proper, *but we can't do them*. Man has never been able to please God with his actions. Now, however, by putting the Spirit of Christ in us, we have that ability and understanding to live a life holy and pleasing to God. Christ already walked that road; now he holds us by the hand and directs us in the same way. Paul, again, shows us the principle of this mystery:

> For it is God who works in you to will and to act according to his good purpose. (Philippians 2:13)

> May the God of peace, who through the blood of the eternal covenant brought back from the dead our Lord Jesus, that great Shepherd of the sheep, equip you with everything good for doing his will, and may he work in us what is pleasing to him, through Jesus Christ, to whom be glory for ever and ever. (Hebrews 13:20-21)

When Paul was distressed about the Galatians, he was worried that the mystery of the Gospel was lost on them. They were trying to please God by their own acts – by following the commandments of the Law in their own strength. No Christian is called upon to please God by their own works! Christ lives the works of righteousness in us, so that all we have to do is show God what Jesus is doing in us. Paul pleaded with the Galatians, "for whom I am again in the pains of childbirth until *Christ is formed in you.*" (Galatians 4:19) This isn't our imagination; we literally need the Spirit of Christ living in us doing what we can't do on our own.

What happens when Christ lives in us? We can do the impossible: we live a life of righteousness, holiness to God, purity, the fruit of the Spirit, everything that makes us like a sweet-smelling garden to the Lord. Paul describes the process: Christ's Spirit now lives in us,

> ... in order that *the righteous requirements of the Law might be fully met in us*, who do not live according to the sinful nature but according to the Spirit. (Romans 8:4)

If you think about this a minute, you will begin to see the powerful possibilities that we have due to this mystery. Whatever Jesus did, we can do; whatever Jesus was, we can be; wherever Jesus goes, we can go. As Paul describes it, "I can do everything through him who gives me strength." (Philippians 4:13)

Conclusion

This was a lot of material, but I hope you realize that we could have gone on without stopping. Christ is such a huge subject that there's no end to the treasures in him! Our aim here was to open this up for view, like spreading a feast before us; we wanted to see the richness in him that's ours for the asking.

The other thing that we were after was to understand the way we will see this richness in Christ: only by *faith*. Faith is the ability to see past this world's cloudy darkness into God's world of light. And because Christ insisted on coming in humility, setting aside his glory, the *only* way we will ever know who he really is and what he can do is by faith.

Finally, we wanted to make the point plain that the only way we can know the real truth about Christ is in the Bible. The Word of God opens the door to our faith so that we can see the facts. The Bible is the revelation – the only revelation – of the true nature of God. And when we use the Bible to look at Jesus – both Old and New Testaments – we learn that everything we need is in him. When we are led to trust in him for *all things*, that's a sign that we really are walking in faith in the Son of God.

The Christian and the Law

So the Law was put in charge to lead us to Christ that we might be justified by faith. Now that faith has come, we are no longer under the supervision of the Law.
(Galatians 3:24)

Christians have always had trouble deciding what to do with the Law. The Law is in our Bible, but we don't know whether we have to obey it or ignore it. Even if we are supposed to take it seriously, *how much* of it do we have to do? To make matters worse, each denomination has a different interpretation on the subject, and respectable Bible teachers will disagree on the Law even if they agree on other basics of the faith.

I believe that there are at least three reasons that the Law causes so many problems for Christians:

- ***The Law is in our Bibles.*** It's hard to argue against something when it's in the Bible. We have been taught to take all the Scriptures seriously; we know that we ignore God's Word at our peril. And the Law isn't just a problem verse or two but an entire section of the Old Testament. Not only that, the rest of the Bible takes the Law very seriously — Jesus as well as the Apostles deal with the Law in some form or another. The Law, whether we like it or not, is a foundation in God's Kingdom and we simply can't ignore it unless we have a really good reason — preferably only if God himself tells us to!

- *The Old Testament and the New Testament overlap.* During the ministry of Christ and the Apostles, the Old Testament system was still in full force. Jesus as well as the disciples went to worship at the Temple; the beginning of the Church included Jews as well as Gentiles. It was a time when the Old Testament realities were still in place, and at the same time the New Testament realities were beginning to take shape. There are some confusing statements about the Law in the Gospels — and it's because of this overlap period. We Gentiles look at this period and wonder if anything changed when the last of the Apostles died — or whether nothing changed, and the Old Testament system is still in force for us today in the same way it was for Christ and his followers. Or did the ways of the Old Testament officially end with the coming of the new?

- *The Law appeals to human nature.* This might sound strange, since the Law condemns sinners. But the root idea of the Law is for *us* to *do* something: do *this*, it tells us, and you will be pleasing and acceptable to God. And we *love* to do things; we are natural-born workers, and idleness doesn't suit us well. The Law very clearly outlines things we can do, and we eagerly set about working on those things. So when the New Testament tells us to quit working and *rest*, that doesn't appeal to us nearly as much as the Law's demands. We feel much better about things when we're in control.

Because of these facts, it's going to be difficult to understand the true relationship between the Christian and the Law. The Law has always been a major part of the works of the Lord, and since we're sensitive about pleasing the Lord in all that we do, it's not going to be easy to find out our responsibilities when it appears that the foundations in the Bible are shifting. But we have to dig into the Bible and understand this subject. In spite of the surface arguments in favor of taking the Law at face value, there are many Scriptures that teach a new approach to the Law — the approach that every Christian must take in order to please God.

It's a mistake to roll over and let the legalists tell us what to believe about the Law. If it's wrong to obey the Law in the same way that the Old Testament saints did, then we must find out what is the right way. And if it's wrong to ignore the Law, then we must find out how to deal with it. We have to avoid both extremes and discover the truth about this.

It's also a mistake to argue over particular details in the Law and overlook the broader principles. The Law is God's work, and it reflects his limitless wisdom; and I doubt that anybody will understand it so well that he will know how every law relates to a Christian. Our duty is to obey what is plainly taught about it, not fight over obscure details. Paul warns us about fighting about the Law: "Some have wandered away from these [*that is, the more important things of our faith*] and turned to meaningless talk. They want to be teachers of the Law, but they do not know what they are talking about or what they so confidently affirm." (1 Timothy 1:6-7)

Our approach here will be this: we want to back up, like the Apostle Paul did in Galatians and other passages, and see the forest for the trees. We want to learn the basics of the subject first, before tackling particular issues. Get the principles down, and we will be able to deal with the less important issues correctly. As I said, Paul took the same approach: though he did some things in regard to the Law that positively baffles modern Christians, he laid down the fundamentals of our relationship with the Law in Galatians that we should study first before we try to untangle some of the stickier issues.

Definitions

Let's define some terms first. By the ***Law*** we mean this: the commands that God gave Israel through Moses. Moses was the one who brought the Law from God and gave it to the Israelites. "For the Law was given through Moses." (John 1:17) "Has not Moses given you the Law?" (John 7:19) And the Law isn't just the Ten Commandments, but the entire four books that record the commands of God: Exodus, Leviticus, Numbers, and Deuteronomy. For proof of this, see the passages in the Gospels that refer to the Law that Moses gave — they quote verses found all through these four books.

Teachers of the Bible have found it convenient to split the Law into three types: moral, ceremonial, and civil. The problem with this is that the Bible itself makes no such division of the Law. One *might* argue that the Temple laws focused on ceremony, and the relationships that a man had with his neighbor dealt with civil matters; but the fact is that *all* of it was called the Law of Moses. For example, a *ceremony* was called the Law of Moses (Luke 2:22), a *prophecy* of Christ was called the Law of Moses (Luke 24:44), and a *civil and moral* issue comes from the Law that Moses gave (John 8:5). Furthermore, almost all the laws had multiple levels: one law would have both moral and civil aspects to it. The Jews have always understood this. For example, in the introduction to a modern translation of the Talmud, the Jewish author explains:

> The Torah *[that is, the Law]* makes no essential distinction between "matters between a man and his Creator," and those "between man and his fellowman," because the structure of relationships between human beings is intimately connected to the relationship between man and his Creator ... the various laws are interrelated and intermingled. Ritual matters are connected with civil disputes; moral instruction is

interwoven with laws of ritual purity and impurity, etc.[1]

The main reason that the Bible doesn't make a hard distinction between the three types is because it's *all* the Law of God; the Jews were responsible to keep them all – none of the laws were less important than the others. It's not fair to separate the laws into more and less important parts; when someone does that, they are just conveniently explaining away large parts of the Law that they *don't* want to be responsible for. For example, many people agree that we should keep the Ten Commandments, some people think that we need to follow the dietary laws and civil laws, and almost nobody thinks that the sacrificial laws apply to us today.

A **Christian** is someone who trusts in Christ alone for his or her salvation. Christ is, for them, their "all in all" — meaning that in him they have everything they need spiritually. They are forgiven and delivered from their sins in him, they are delivered from death and Hell in him, they are adopted as sons of God in him, they are made holy and righteous and justified in God's sight in him, they have a future hope of glory in him, and they have his Spirit. What more could they want? If they did not have Christ, they would not have anything.

You see, of course, what we are getting at here. If Christ is everything that a believer needs, this casts a doubt over whether a Christian needs anything more from the Law. If he can please God and gain a hope of Heaven by having Christ alone, what need is there of dealing with the Law about anything? The Law has nothing more to say to someone like this – and certainly nothing to offer him!

---

[1] *Adin Steinsaltz, The Talmud: The Steinsaltz Edition*; Vol. 1: Tractate Bava Metzia, 1989; Part 1; pp.1-2.

The purpose of the Law

One great purpose of the Law is this: to condemn mankind. Paul tells us in Romans what the Law does to us:

> Indeed I would not have known what sin was except through the Law. For I would not have known what coveting really was if the Law had not said, "Do not covet." (Romans 7:7)

The Law tells us exactly what sin is. We need that, because until the Law came, people didn't exactly know what offended God about human behavior. They made up their own definitions of what is right and wrong, and as a result there were as many systems of morality and ethics as there were men and nations! What was "right" in one culture, was "wrong" in another. People were confused about the true nature of sin.

So, God gave the Law in order to clear up the confusion. "Here is what sin is," he told us. And with that definition of sin, he condemned every human being who has ever lived, because nobody has ever kept *this* Law perfectly. We are all guilty of breaking God's Law in some way, during some time in our lives. Even such a simple version of the Law as the Ten Commandments is enough to prove every one of us a sinner. The Law isn't trying to make us friends with God; it is proving, without a shadow of a doubt, that we are already his enemies.

Keep in mind that the Law has a double edge. Not only does it define what sin is, it also demands a penalty for anybody who commits sin: punishment. The Law is no friend! If we fulfill the Law in every way, it will leave us alone. But if we offend God in even one matter, it rises up in wrath and condemns us.

So then, the Law is holy, and the commandment is holy, righteous and good. Did that which is good, then, become death to me? By no means! But in order that sin might be recognized as sin, it produced death in me through what was good, so that through the commandment sin might become utterly sinful. (Romans 7:12-13)

Why some people feel so comfortable living in the shadow of the Law, I will never understand. They don't know that they live under the shadow of *death*. The Law means trouble for sinners; going to the Law for help or comfort is like reaching out to pet a guard dog that is trained to kill strangers.

The Law hurts. The only way that it wouldn't hurt anybody is if that person kept the whole Law, perfectly, all his life. With such a person the Law has no argument or problem. But if it finds the least blemish in him, the smallest offense, then the Law becomes a fierce enemy. That sin has challenged the glory of God, and the Law will not rest until there is blood shed. "In fact, the Law requires that nearly everything be cleansed with blood, and without the shedding of blood there is no forgiveness." (Hebrews 9:22)

Picking and Choosing

A *legalist* is someone who finds it necessary to obey the letter of the Law. This means that they read the Law in the Old Testament and feel that they must obey exactly what it says. They also try to make others feel that same obligation.

Legalists tell us that all of us must obey the Law in some way; we may not have to obey *all* of the Law, they tell us, but at least the more important parts of it. They teach that the Ten Commandments are essential for every Christian. Some of the more extreme legalists even pick out other parts of the Law and try to obligate Christians to live by those too — for example, the Sabbath laws, and the laws concerning food, and the "clean and unclean" laws. Some legalists pick out the "ceremonial" laws that they feel we should use in church, and the "civil" laws that modern societies should use.

The biggest problem about legalists is this: they pick and choose the laws that they say we must obey. The reason that they are so choosy (which they usually won't be honest enough to tell you!) is that, when you read the Law of Moses, it becomes obvious to you that *nobody* can keep all those laws. Even if we wanted to, it would be impossible in our modern society to obey everything that the Old Testament Law demands. Even the legalists will admit this!

For example, in Exodus 20:2-17 the Lord gave the Ten Commandments to the Israelites. Then in verse 23 he repeats Commandments one and two; so far the legalists are staying right with the text. Then in verse 24 he commands them to make an altar and sacrifice animals to him; the altar must be formed without tools, and it must not have steps. Now the legalists are in trouble! What are they going to tell us about *this* command? If they say that Christ has offered all the necessary sacrifices for us and now we don't have to obey this additional command of sacrifice, then how is that different than the first part of the Law given here in the same text? If they say that we must keep this sacrifice *spiritually* and the other commands *literally*, they must show why they think one is literal and the other spiritual — they must give the principle that guides them into interpreting the text this way so that we can use that principle later on with other commands. Any way they go, they are in trouble.

Another example: one law that the legalists are fond of enforcing is the command about tithing. There are several passages that make tithing a necessary obligation on the Israelites; they didn't have any choice about the matter. The Law is never a matter of choice: it's a binding obligation which the legalist *must* do or else he is in instant trouble as a law breaker. The tithing laws, since they are also part of the Mosaic Law, were binding on the Israelites; they had to do it or be guilty of breaking the Law.

But there were other laws in the Old Testament that were just as binding; why aren't the legalists pressing us about those as well? For example, all the males twenty years old and older were obligated to pay the half-shekel tax to support the tent of meeting. (Exodus 30:11-16) They weren't to pay any more than this, nor any less than this. Also, each family was supposed to pay, under penalty of the Law, a five-shekel tax for each firstborn son in Israel. (Numbers 18:15-16) Now these laws were just as binding as the tithe law; why then aren't the legalists demanding those taxes from us as well? There is nothing in the Scripture that says the tithe law is still binding and these are not. If they answer that those had to do with specific "ceremonies" that we don't have to worry about now, then how is that different from the tithing law which also paid for those *same kinds* of ceremonies in the Temple?

If you look carefully into the tithing law, you will notice what the tithe was supposed to consist of: not money, but *food*. The tithe was used for a specific purpose. When all Israel collected in Jerusalem three times a year for the yearly feasts, they had a logistics problem on their hands. There was no way that the merchants of Jerusalem could support millions of pilgrims! The tithe was designed to address that problem. The priests were to collect the tithe from everyone in Israel *as food*, not money (it makes a special point about that — Deuteronomy 14:24-26 — people can't eat money!), and store the food in Jerusalem. Then when the people showed up for the yearly feasts, they would have enough to eat during their stay there. (Deuteronomy 12:17-19; Deuteronomy 14:22-29) Now if we are obligated to keep this law, why is it that we aren't doing exactly what the law says to do? Why are we twisting it into exactly what the law says *not* to do, and ignoring its most important elements? Are we free to twist God's law around to suit our own tastes like this?

The best-known passage about the law of tithing is Malachi 3:8-10. It is a powerful incentive to take tithing seriously, and many a preacher has used it against his congregation to get them to start giving more to the church. But the problem is that this isn't the *only* sin that Malachi accuses the Israelites of breaking! Again, legalists pick and choose what they want out of the text and conveniently ignore other things that are there. Malachi accuses 1) the Israelites of bringing crippled animals to the sacrifice (Malachi 1:8); 2) the priests of violating the covenant with Levi (Malachi 2:8); and 3) Judah of desecrating the sanctuary in the Temple. (Malachi 2:11) Why is only one of the scathing denunciations of Malachi picked out and the rest of them ignored? If someone answers that these other issues are spiritual for us Christians, then why isn't the tithing law spiritual for us too? What goes for one must apply to them all!

You can't pick and choose the laws that you want to obey. They are all one body of Law; it was God's Word given through Moses, all of it, and as the Scripture says, "Whoever keeps the whole Law and yet stumbles at just one point is guilty of breaking all of it." (James 2:10) When once you have set your hand to keeping the Law, you are obligated to keep *all* of it. "Cursed is everyone who does not continue to do *everything* written in the Book of the Law." (Galatians 3:10) The Lord will not be impressed with your arguments that you thought you only had to keep part of it; that's not what *he* said to do with it!

There are important reasons why you can't pick and choose the laws that you want to obey and ignore the rest. ***First***, there is the fact that these laws are all part of the great body of Law that the Lord gave the Israelites through Moses. It was all given to Israel, as the rules of the Kingdom of God, and none of them were given to other nations. It was the way the nation was to operate, the government over God's people. The Israelites were bound to keep the *whole* Law, not just the parts that they liked best. Now if any of those laws are still binding today, then they all are, since it's all the Law of God. There is nothing in Scripture which says that parts of the Law are still in effect while others are no longer in effect. And you certainly don't have the freedom to decide how you are going to obey the Law. If Congress passes a law that says you owe them a certain percentage of your income in taxes, you are not free to send them a truckload of apples in payment of the tax! If you don't do exactly what the law says, you are considered a law breaker, no matter what your intentions are. The same is true of God's Law.

Second, the laws are tied together inextricably. If you decide that you want to follow a particular law, you will have to decide what you are going to do about some of the other laws as well, because they tie into the one that you are looking at. For example, some modern groups teach that we must follow the food regulations that are given in the Law. Some foods were "unclean" to the Israelites and they weren't allowed to eat them. The problem was that this wasn't only a health issue, it was a ceremonial issue as well. Anybody who even touched one of these forbidden animals was unclean and had to undergo ceremonial washings and stay away from other people for an appointed time. Any pots that touched this food had to be destroyed. And this wasn't a small matter to God:

> Do not defile yourselves by any of these creatures. Do not make yourselves unclean by means of them or be made unclean by them. I am the LORD your God; consecrate yourselves and be holy, because I am holy. Do not make yourselves unclean by any creature that moves about on the ground. I am the LORD who brought you up out of Egypt to be your God; therefore be holy, because I am holy. (Leviticus 11:43-45)

When the Lord said something like this, you can be sure that he meant what he said — all of it — and you had better do *exactly* what he said. The problem is that if we were to take this seriously today, we may as well resign ourselves to being perpetual lawbreakers because none of us can do all that this Law requires. Not only are we not capable of doing *our* part, but the society we live in isn't going to do its part either — which means that we are being polluted against our will! The point here is that once you decide to follow any particular law, you are immediately going to run into trouble with other laws that are tied into it. And you can't get out of the dilemma by saying, "Well, I must do the right thing even if others don't." According to the Law, what others do will make *you* unclean and affect *your* relationship with God.

Third, the Law not only consists of commands about how to live life, it also makes provision for enforcing those laws — the priesthood and the Temple. The priests were the enforcers of the Law, much as policemen are enforcers of the laws of our society. They didn't perform the Law for the people; the people themselves had to follow the Law's commands and report to the priests with the results. And many of the laws had to do with the daily and special functions that went on in the Temple. None of that is in operation today; even if we wanted to follow some of the laws, there is no way we can follow through with them and complete the requirements of satisfying the priest and offering sacrifices in the Temple. All that is gone now. Even the Jews understand this problem. Their system right now is almost useless to them; they are waiting for the day when they can rebuild the Temple and put the whole system back in place. Then keeping one particular law will be meaningful because all the other related laws will be there to support it.

If someone argues that we live in a time when most of the Law is spiritualized — that is, there is a spiritual way that we obey those laws, through Christ — I would answer that you must be very careful at this point. It's true that the Law is still in effect in a spiritual sense; but it's wrong to say that we are in the same relation to the Law as the Israelites were. They were obligated to keep the Law themselves; we Christians are only to enjoy the results of what Christ did to keep the Law. When the Law entered the spiritual dimension, and the Church came into being, a new thing developed — a new way of approaching the demands of the Law. More on this later.

Israel and the Law

Go back to Exodus 20 and look carefully at what it says.

> I am the LORD *your* God, who brought *you* out of Egypt, out of the land of slavery. *You* shall have no other gods before me . . . (Exodus 20:2-3)

Notice that this Law is addressed to the Israelites. This is a very important point to get. When the Lord brought them out of Egypt, the first place he led them was to Mt. Sinai in order to receive this Law. What he was doing was forming a new nation out of these former slaves; he was placing himself at their head as their God, their King, who intended to rule over them and take care of all their needs. Israel got everything they needed here at Mt. Sinai to be a full-fledged nation complete with government.

The Lord didn't do this with any other nation. In fact, the Israelites knew how special they were, that they were the only ones who received this Law. "He has revealed his word to Jacob, his laws and decrees to Israel. He has done this for no other nation; they do not know his laws." (Psalm 147:19-20) As far as the other nations were concerned, they knew almost nothing about the true God, and they certainly didn't have the benefit of the Law to get themselves out of the moral disaster they were wallowing in.

The Law provided some precious advantages for the Israelites. **First,** we already mentioned the fact that it carefully defined what sin is. The Law not only condemns all men (because all men have sinned against God's Law) but it's the first step of salvation for those who know its doctrine. Until you know exactly what sin is, you don't know what you have done wrong — and therefore you don't know what you can do to make it right. If you don't know that you owe a particular tax, of course you are going to get caught when you don't pay it! And if you don't know what you are doing that makes God so offended with you, you have no hope of ever making it right. You will continue doing the very thing that will result in your eventual condemnation without even knowing it. So the Law informs us about what is going on in God's Kingdom.

Second, the Law carefully described how to make restitution for their sins. These are the laws concerning the sacrifices and everything that went on in the Temple. In this respect, the Law was the salvation of the Israelites. If they carefully kept the rules for sacrifice, the Lord promised to forgive their sins and not punish them. It was only a temporary measure, to be sure, since eternal, spiritual forgiveness of sins is only in Christ. But it *was* the Lord's promise, and it *did* keep the avenging angel away. The rest of the world had no advantage, no opportunity to come before God and get forgiveness. They were locked out of the Temple, so to speak, and only had the wrath of God to look forward to.

Paul confirms the fact that the Law was given only to the Israelites. In Romans 2 he says this:

> All who sin apart from the Law will also perish apart from the Law, and all who sin under the Law will be judged by the Law ... (Indeed, when Gentiles, who do not have the Law, do by nature things required by the Law, they are a law for themselves, even though they do not have the Law) ... (Romans 2:12,14)

Notice he says here that the Gentiles *did not* have the Law. Here is the situation: the Lord has a certain way of doing things, and his Kingdom (which includes all of Heaven and earth, of course) must follow his rules. He created all things to please him, including the peoples on earth. The world that he created was supposed to abide by what *he* calls righteousness. That's what is meant by "the *requirements* of the Law" – all creatures are supposed to obey the Creator; this obligation, this sense of duty, is built into our beings.

But the *giving* of the Law – the written Word given to Israel through Moses – happened when he revealed those requirements of his Kingdom to Israel. He revealed the rules of righteousness, and the procedures that deal with forgiveness of sin, only to his own people.

So the Gentiles had in their hearts the stamp of their Creator — the evidence that they are not their own, that they belong to Someone Else, that immorality doesn't fit into God's world — but they didn't have the benefit that the Israelites had of knowing the whole story of sin and salvation. Gentiles were obligated to please God; but when they didn't, there was no explanation, no merciful warning, that something was wrong, or what they could do to fix the problem.

The Israelites were supposed to take advantage of this special knowledge, but they didn't. They wasted the opportunity over and over throughout their history. And when Jesus came they missed the point again: though their own Law predicted the coming of the Perfect Man, they failed to recognize him; in fact, they hated him and killed him as if *he* were the law breaker!

They missed the biggest blessing of the Law. There is no life in the Law, of course, only the knowledge of our sin. But that knowledge is the first step in the salvation from sin! The second step is the description of the Perfect Man, someone who *could* keep the Law in all its complexity. The Law predicted the coming of Jesus Christ when it showed us the Perfect Man. "So the Law was put in charge to lead us to Christ that we might be justified by faith." (Galatians 3:24) The Law was given so that the Israelites would long for the things that *only* Christ, the

Perfect Man, can do for them. After 1500 years of struggling with a system that they could not keep, Jesus should have been a welcome sight to them! Here is someone who can solve our problem with sin and get the Law off our backs. Peter recognized this crucial truth when he said to his fellow Jewish-Christians:

> Now then, why do you try to test God by putting on the necks of the disciples a yoke that neither we nor our fathers have been able to bear? No! We believe it is through the grace of our Lord Jesus that we are saved, just as they are. (Acts 15:10-11)

Notice that he was talking about Gentiles who were already believers, and the question was whether they should be made to "obey the Law of Moses" (Acts 15:5) in one particular point only. That's exactly what modern legalists are trying to do.

Christ and the Law

Christ stands in a unique position in regard to the Law of God. He alone was able to fulfill the Law perfectly; the Law has no complaint about the character and actions of Jesus Christ. This is an amazing record, in light of how complex and demanding the Law is. But it's also understandable, since Jesus is the Son of God and could do no other than keep his own Law to the letter!

Christ related to the Law on several levels; in order to understand our own relationship with the Law, we have to distinguish each of the things that Jesus did for us:

- ***What he did with the Law:*** Christ came to earth to do more than keep the Law for his own sake. He came to solve man's problem of sin, which is *lawlessness*. The Law's complaint is with us, not with him. So here is what Jesus did: he became man, like us except for our sin, so that he could be "under the Law" and accomplish his goal. Then *as man* he fulfilled the Law completely and perfectly. When he was done, the Law was forced to admit that *a man* had kept the Law to God's satisfaction! This was the first time that such a thing had happened. Even though the Israelites had the Law for almost 1500 years, nobody had ever kept it perfectly until Jesus came.

- ***What he did for us:*** Now for the final step in God's plan of salvation. Jesus sent his Spirit and made us *one with him* — we are in him, united to him in all ways, so that whatever happens to him will also happen to us. This means several things: ***first***, since the Law is satisfied with him, it is also satisfied with us. There is nothing more to be done! This is what Hebrews means when it says that we *rest* in Christ; he rested from his labors (remember his last words on the cross? "It is finished." John 19:30) and now we rest in him. "Take my yoke upon you and learn from me, for I am gentle and humble in heart, and you will find rest for your souls." (Matthew 11:29) The work of satisfying the Law is over now, for him *and* for us. If there were any more to do on this score then salvation wouldn't be done yet!

Second, whatever rewards are in store for Christ as the perfect man, we also can expect to receive. If he was lifted on high, we will be too. (Colossians 3:1) If he sits at God's right hand, so will we. (Colossians 3:3) If he will rule over the universe, so will we. (Colossians 3:4) Since we are one with him, we will share in his glory and receive the inheritance that Jesus bought for us.

Everything that happens *to us* must go *through him* first; he put himself between us and the Law for this reason. And since he did this, we never deal with the Law directly. There is no salvation in that! Our only hope is in what Christ, as the firstborn of many brethren, achieved for us and passes on to us.

Since Christ fulfilled the Law for us, what is left for us to do? Can we sin now and not have to worry about punishment since Christ took that burden upon himself? Paul tells us that such a thing is unthinkable! "By no means! We died to sin; how can we live in it any longer?" (Romans 6:2) Remember why Jesus came: he came to save us *from* our sin, not leave us in it. "You are to give him the name Jesus, because *he will save his people from their sins.*" (Matthew 1:21)

- ***What he does in us:*** He died to save us from condemnation, but that's only one thing he wanted to do. The other was to get us out of the moral mess that resulted in our condemnation in the first place.

So, right now the Lord Jesus is busy with our sanctification — the process of making us holy and set apart for the Lord's use. He is applying *his* righteousness to *our* souls so that we look more and more like him. "And so he condemned sin in sinful man, in order that *the righteous requirements of the Law might be fully met in us*, who do not live according to the sinful nature but according to the Spirit." (Romans 8:3-4) Did you catch that phrase about the Law? The Law of God hasn't gone away; it wasn't put away permanently when Jesus fulfilled it. The Law isn't going away because the God whom it describes isn't going away. Jesus is *making* us conform to what the Law says is a righteous man; only he can do that, of course, since only he lived that righteous life. But the fact remains that the Law is still in full force; the only difference now is *who* has to keep the Law. If we do it, the outcome is in serious question; if Christ does it, it is certain to succeed.

There is a prophecy in Ezekiel that shows us what God had in mind long before Jesus came to earth, but is exactly in line with what the New Testament teaches about our present relationship with the Law.

> I will give you a new heart and put a new spirit in you; I will remove from you your heart of stone and give you a heart of flesh. And I will put my Spirit in you and *move you* to follow my decrees and be careful to keep my laws. (Ezekiel 36:26-27)

This agrees with what Paul says about the subject. The Lord will put his Spirit into us, and the Spirit will make us conform to the requirements of the Law. Before this time the Israelites were doing their best to obey the Law — and failing at it. It just couldn't be done by sinners. God finally got tired of fooling with them and predicted the time when *he* would make them righteous; instead of waiting on them to do what is right, he would change their hearts himself. When this happens, of course, he will get the credit for the job, because if the Spirit is making you conform to the requirements of the Law then *you* can't claim any credit for doing it! But that's what being part of the Church is all about; it's an entirely different thing from what the Israelites were living under.

- *What he's doing right now:* Christ is also doing something *right now* in respect to the Law. He fulfilled its requirements as far as living a righteous life; but he is also in the Heavenly Temple right now fulfilling his duties as our High Priest. The earthly Temple was a picture of the one in Heaven: if you want to know what it's like in God's eternal Temple, read the description in the Law of the Israelite Temple. You must realize, however, that none of that has disappeared from Heaven as the earthly one has. Though the Jews lost their Temple, God still lives in his! And there must still be a sacrifice on the altar to atone for the people's sins — but now it's Jesus' eternal sacrifice that was made "once for all" for our sake. (Hebrews 12:24) There must still be incense burning day and night — though in God's Temple that is the "prayers of the saints" that always go up to him. (Revelation 5:8) There must still be a Holy of Holies, because that's where God sits and rules over his people and gives them what they come to him and ask for. Now, however, the veil that used to separate us from God is torn away and the way into the Holy of Holies is open to "whosoever will." (Hebrews 10:19-22) And the High Priest still lives to intercede for the people: Christ is always presenting our requests to the Father and getting answers for us. (Romans 8:34)

So the Law hasn't gone anywhere. It's still in full force, because that is still the way that God wants to run his kingdom. The difference now is that Jesus is doing all these legal requirements for us and sending us the benefits.

The sin of legalism

Legalism ignores one thing: that only Jesus can keep the Law in a way that satisfies God. A legalist thinks that he can do what the Law commands, and usually he is satisfied in keeping only a few laws since even he knows he can't keep them all.

But the problem with that is that no man except Christ can do what the Law expects of him. The depth of the Law is like an ocean; a sinner will quickly drown in it trying to make his way through it. Our sin is so deep-rooted, even when we are supposedly believers and have the Spirit of God in us, that any Law that we try to keep will be our undoing. Jesus gave us a small sampling of the depth of the Law in Matthew 5 when he took a few examples and showed us what the Law was really after: the heart, the spiritual dimension of our lives.

A legalist won't let go and admit that only Christ can keep every law. He doesn't want God's free grace; he doesn't want Christ to do all things for him. But the Spirit is the one who must take the righteousness of Christ and mold our hearts with it. If we follow the Spirit, he will make us conform to Christ's image; if we do the Law on our own, however, we are veering away from the Spirit's leading and going on our own. *No man can succeed in righteousness without the Spirit of God.* This is what Paul meant when he rebuked the Galatians: "Are you so foolish? After beginning with the Spirit, are you now trying to attain your goal by human effort?" (Galatians 3:3)

This legalistic attitude is *a rejection of the Gospel*. The Gospel plainly states that Christ alone is our righteousness, that only he is perfect, that we get all our righteousness from him as a gift — not as a reward for our efforts at keeping the Law.

The legalist will immediately reply this way: "But I admit that we can't be considered righteous by following the Law! I believe that my only hope is in Christ's righteousness, that God accepts me on the basis of what Christ did and not my own works.

All that I'm saying is that we are not therefore free from the obligations of the Law; we must still do what the Law says."

The Scripture's answer to that is this: we are, indeed, not free from the Law's requirements. The Law still exists, because God exists. But Christ alone will see to it that the Law's requirements are met in me. He has a fail-safe way of making sure that I conform to the Law's expectations of a righteous man: through the Spirit. It's not up to me to keep the Law; rather, he will work his righteousness into my heart as I follow the Spirit.

There is *a lot* of difference between following the Spirit and keeping the Law! For one thing, if I set out to keep the Law, I will put the list of requirements in front of me and consciously watch all my actions and thoughts to make sure that I conform to its standards. One slip, however, and I'm dead — literally! The Law allows no mistakes. But if I follow the Spirit, I will open up my heart to the Lord and wait on him to do for me what I can't do. The Spirit takes from what is Christ's and puts it in me. More specifically, the Spirit does two things: he reveals the things of God so that I can see spiritual realities in Christ, and he empowers me to live in the Kingdom of God which is a spiritual kingdom. But more on the Spirit later.

The legalist insists that *we* must do what the Law says; there is his sin. But there must be no more insisting about the Law for the Christian. Since it is Christ alone who works out the requirements of the Law in us, he alone decides when and what will happen in my heart as concerning righteousness. This is his work now, not mine, this business of making me holy. I can't think of anybody I would rather have watching over me!

The sin of antinomianism

Antinomianism comes from two words: **anti,** which means *against*; and **nomos,** which means *law*. So you see that an antinomian is someone who is against the Law. This is just as much of a sin as legalism.

An antinomian teaches that we don't have to obey the Law. In fact, the Law has nothing to do with us now — Christ was "the end of the Law." The Law is our enemy; Christ put it away from us, and now we only have to deal with him. To a Christian there is only love and mercy, not Law and punishment.

This, however, is a gross misunderstanding of the purpose of the Law and what Christ came to do. When Christ came to fulfill the Law for us, he didn't do away with the Law completely. He said, "Do not think that I have come to abolish the Law or the Prophets; I have not come to abolish them but to fulfill them." (Matthew 5:17) Whoever thinks that Christ did away with the Law doesn't understand what the Law is: it's a description of the Perfect Man, and the perfect kingdom that God wants to rule. Those standards are still as much true today as when the Law was first given.

What Christ did was to fulfill the Law *in our place*. Man wasn't getting anywhere with God's exacting standards. All that the Law was doing for man was showing him how guilty and rebellious he really was. None of us had any hope of satisfying the Law's requirements. But when Christ fulfilled that Law perfectly, he became the first man to do so; when he made us one with him, he made us share in his victory.

Now, you see, since Christ is accounted perfect by the Law's own declaration, we are also accounted perfect as long as we are one with him. We also live the way the Law says to live. Or at least we will someday; the deed was done in Christ, and now he is finishing the job through the Spirit. Remember, he intends to make us conform to the Law's standards: "in order that the righteous requirements of the Law might be fully met in us." (Romans 8:4)

The point isn't that there's no more Law, but that someone else is satisfying the Law in our place. We *will*, by God's decree, conform to the Law! He will see to it, since he cannot allow any sinner to live with him in glory. We *must* look more and more like Jesus or the Father will cut us off as unfruitful branches. (John 15:2) The Law will be the eternal standard of Heaven, much to the dismay of the rebellious at heart. But the mercy of God consists in this: Christ will see to it that our hearts *change* and we please God in everything that we do. Then the Law will be describing us, as well as Christ, when it talks about a Perfect Man.

The antinomians sin against God on several counts: **first,** they are saying that God isn't holy as the Law describes (since they claim that the Law has been "set aside" and is no longer in effect). But the Law is no more and no less than a description of God's holy nature; to say that it no longer applies is to deny the glory of God's holiness. Believe me, he is still holy! **Second,** they claim that Christ "set it aside" so that it no longer has anything to do with us. That dishonors Christ, as if he would willingly do away with something that glorifies his Father. Christ *honored* the Law; he *fulfilled* the Law. He didn't destroy the very thing that defines what sin is, and what describes the Perfect Man. That would be destroying the standards! **Third,** they claim that the Law has nothing to do with us now. By saying this they are opening up the way for people to sin against God even while claiming to be his children. This is the same as what Jesus referred to when he accused the Pharisees of leading God's children astray. For such a sin, he warned, it would be better to be thrown into the depths of the ocean with a millstone around your neck! (Matthew 18:6) Never, ever tell someone that they are free from God's righteous requirements! We are not free from them; Christ is changing his people right now so that they will conform to those standards. He will not have a kingdom full of sinners! The only thing that we are free from is the burden of earning that righteousness by our own efforts. That, in fact, is what the phrase "set aside" refers to – the requirement that we have to fulfill the Law on our own.

That quote about Christ being "the end of the Law" comes from Romans: "Christ is the end of the Law so that there may be righteousness for everyone who believes." (Romans 10:4) If people are going to quote a verse from the Bible then they need to quote the whole thing! It isn't hard to see here what the word "end" means: it's something that Christ does in relation to the Law which results in *us* being righteous, without our having to obey the Law ourselves. There is only *one* thing in God's Kingdom that defines what righteousness is — that's his *Law*. "End" doesn't mean "it's gone now." It means that the final judgment has been issued, the Law is satisfied with us now, and it has nothing more to say against us. We are righteous in the eyes of the Law, something that will only happen when someone obeys the Law completely *to the end*. Of course, Christ did this impossible thing for us.

The Sabbath

One particular law that has caused a lot of concern for Christians is the Fourth Commandment:

> Remember the Sabbath day by keeping it holy. Six days you shall labor and do all your work, but the seventh day is a Sabbath to the LORD your God. On it you shall not do any work, neither you, nor your son or daughter, nor your manservant or maidservant, nor your animals, nor the alien within your gates. For in six days the LORD made the heavens and the earth, the sea, and all that is in them, but he rested on the seventh day. Therefore the LORD blessed the Sabbath day and made it holy. (Exodus 20:8-11)

The question is, are Christians obligated to keep the Sabbath? Before we answer that, let's review some of the points we looked at already. **First,** no Christian can keep the Law in a way that is pleasing to God. Israel couldn't, the Gentiles didn't even know about it, and no Christian has ever kept the Law's requirements on his own. That applies to this law as well. The point isn't whether we *should* do it, but that we *can't* do it. This means that this commandment isn't as easy as it looks! Only Christ can keep it as it should be kept.

Second, remember that it was Christ alone who kept the Law perfectly — including this Law — and now he is applying the fruits of *his* obedience to his people. That means that we are *not* to keep any of the Law ourselves; he kept it. We are only to receive from him the Spirit who leads us in the way that he already created for us. Instead of wondering how to keep this Law ourselves, we should be more concerned with how to follow the Lord in all things; he will then make sure that this law is fulfilled in us. There is a lot of difference.

The Jews themselves couldn't keep this Law, as simple as it looks. They had all sorts of ridiculous interpretations of it: by their view they couldn't do anything at all on the Sabbath that involved the simplest activities. The Law had strict regulations against any form of labor; but the Jews went even farther and created prohibitions of their own. The various applications that they came up with for this Law bordered on the absurd. Christ rebuked them on several occasions for getting it all wrong. (Matthew 12:1-13; Luke 13:10-16; John 5:5-18) And, of course, the reason they resorted to all these fanciful interpretations is that they didn't understand its fundamental meaning.

The reason we can't keep this Law on our own is that we can't possibly obey what it really means – not without Christ doing it for us. First of all, very few people even know what it really means! The Law says, if you look at it closely, only this: on the Sabbath you must *rest*. Now I'd like to make a point here that may seem picky, but when you are dealing with stubborn people who want to force others into their interpretations then you must get very serious about what the Word actually says. It does *not* say that we must go to church on the Sabbath, nor does it say that we must do anything on the Sabbath – except rest. It does say that we must "keep it holy;" but the way it reads, that simply means that we must *rest* – that's what God did on the seventh day, according to the Scriptures. (Genesis 2:2-3) It says that by resting he made it holy. And so is man to make it holy by resting. To read any more than that into these verses is not being honest and fair with the text.

Some denominations teach that this commandment says that we must worship on the Sabbath. It doesn't say any such thing. If we are going to keep the Law, then let's do exactly what the Law says to do, not what we want it to say. More wrong doctrine finds its way in between the lines of Scripture than you can imagine. If we are going to solve these difficult problems of the Bible, we must start looking at *what it says* and not jump to conclusions until we have researched the whole thing out.

We don't actually find any kind of Temple activity being done on the Sabbath until Leviticus 16:29-31 where it says that "on the tenth day of the seventh month" they must offer a sacrifice of atonement — on that particular Sabbath. Other laws follow through Leviticus and Numbers about what should happen on particular Sabbaths; in each of them, they are instructions only for the priests and the particular sacrifices they must offer. Numbers 28:9-10 mentions the sacrifice that the priests must offer on *every* Sabbath. But even though the Sabbath is mentioned many times in the Law, the only thing that the Lord tells the rest of the Israelites to do on the Sabbath is *rest*. The point is that there is no Scripture that teaches that on every Sabbath we must go to worship God, as if the *purpose* of the Sabbath was to go to worship. The only thing that the Bible says clearly must happen on every Sabbath — that is, the *point* of the Sabbath — is that we must rest. Even when Jesus went to the synagogue on the Sabbath, it only says that it "was his *custom*" (Luke 4:16). It wasn't a command from the Law of Moses, since synagogues didn't even exist until much later in Israelite history.

If someone makes the mistake of saying that the Old Testament Sabbath laws were pictures of what should happen *all the time* on the Sabbath in every age (including our own), then they have to explain a lot more than they bargained for. Those Sabbath laws included sacrifices, travel to Jerusalem for the special yearly feasts, the different taxes that the people were bound to pay, the work in the Temple and the classes of priests and Levites with their special Temple duties, and so on. As we've seen already, if you want to keep one law then you must keep them all; they are bound together so tightly that picking only one out of the bunch and ignoring the rest is capricious at best and sinful at worst.

The Sabbath, as we have seen, was kept perfectly only by Christ. None of us can do it in a way that pleases God. This should tell you something when you read the command and it seems perfectly plain to you and easy to do: evidently there is more here than meets the eye.

Now notice that in Hebrews the writer picks up on the root idea of the Sabbath — not worship, but *rest*.

> So I declared on oath in my anger, they shall never enter my rest. (Hebrews 3:11)

If you go back to see what the Lord is referring to here, it's the fact that the generation of Israelites who were brought out of Egypt didn't want to enter Canaan and get defeated by the giant natives there. They thought the Lord was crazy to send them into such a place! So because they didn't have faith in their God who does miracles, he refused to let them into the Promised Land.

The Promised Land is what is called the "rest" in this passage, because they were weary of slavery in Egypt, and wandering in the desert. For Christians, however, Heaven is our Promised Land of rest.

Then the writer says that "there remains, then, a Sabbath-rest for the people of God." (Hebrews 4:9) In other words, he makes the point that the land of Canaan couldn't have been what God had in mind about a Sabbath-rest, since the prophecy about that rest for God's people came long after the Israelites entered Canaan. (Hebrews 4:8) This Sabbath, then, is Heaven – a spiritual rest; that's the hope that believers have. It's a Sabbath for us because it will be the end of all our labors here on earth.

Do you remember what happened to Christ when he finished his work on earth? He entered the Sabbath-rest that this passage in Hebrews talks about! He ascended into Heaven, and rested from his labors on earth. There is now no more to do in regard to satisfying the Law, or gaining righteousness for his people, because he did it all — and now he rests from all that work. Just as God made the world in six days and then rested when it was done, Jesus fulfilled the Law and then rested when his work was all done.

Now Christians, being one with Christ, share in his rest. If we dare to try to grapple with any of the Laws on our own, we are saying that Christ didn't do enough and there remains more work in this area. *That's not true.* There is nothing more to be done as regards the Law. He did it all; there is nothing left for us to do. Now he rests from that labor, and we are supposed to rest with him as a testimony to his finished work. Does "resting in Christ" mean that we have to quit work on a particular day and go to worship somewhere? I think that you can see it certainly does not; such a low-level fulfillment of a precious reality in Christ would be very disappointing! Instead, study Matthew 11:29 for some insight on this. We must rest now from Law-keeping.

One last point: why do Christians worship on Sunday? I can see no other reason for it than it's simply our custom, started by the Apostles. The rest of the Church has seen no good reason to change the custom they began. But there is no Scripture that says we *must* worship on Sunday; the Bible never pushes the fact that Jesus rose from the dead on Sunday as an argument for getting together as a church on that day. For that matter, we could just as easily worship on Wednesdays or Saturdays! The problem develops when some groups insist that we must worship on a particular day in fulfillment of the Law; for that there is *no* Scripture.

Paul shows a complete indifference as to the day one worships as a church.

> Therefore do not let anyone judge you by what you eat or drink, or with regard to a religious festival, a New Moon celebration or a Sabbath day. These are a shadow of the things that were to come; the reality, however, is found in Christ. (Colossians 2:16-17)

As far as he is concerned, the Law of the Sabbath will be misleading if read by itself — as is true of any of the laws. Rather, we can only relate to the Law spiritually if we look to Jesus. The Law is designed to show us our sin, not offer a way to please God. And the Law only finds its complete fulfillment in Christ; the Lord kept that Law to a depth that we probably will never understand (but it took that kind of fulfillment to satisfy the Law!). So it's much better for us to focus on Christ and whatever he has for us, than to try to wrestle with a Law that we will never understand or fulfill. Therefore, Paul isn't concerned about whether he is keeping the letter of the Law pertaining to the Sabbath, because Christ has something far better and more meaningful for him.

Paul's argument in Galatians

The book of Galatians was written for one purpose: it was an argument against legalists in Paul's day. I cannot understand how legalists today can read his letter and miss his point. The only way I can account for such a thing is that their minds are darkened against the truth and the Spirit is not leading them into truth.

He starts out by saying that the Gospel of Christ is the supreme truth of the Church. Anybody who messes with that Gospel should be "eternally condemned!" (Galatians 1:8-9) In other words, we *must* get this thing right; we can't afford to have the least bit of doubt about it.

He then tells us why he is qualified to teach about this: he used to be an expert in the Law. In fact, for a long time he fought against the root idea of the Gospel, because *there is something in the Law that cannot exist side by side with the Gospel.* Either you live by one or by the other; you cannot have both. When he was finally enlightened about the Gospel of Christ, the rest of the Church recognized that Paul now knew the truth of the Gospel and was on their side, not on the side of the Jews. So what he says about this subject is the *last word.*

Then an occasion came up where Peter himself, one of the original disciples of Christ, had a problem about observing the Law. Paul immediately challenged him. Notice that the first thing that Paul jumped on was the fact that Peter was picking and choosing what laws to follow!

> You are a Jew, yet you live like a Gentile and not like a Jew. How is it, then, that you force Gentiles to follow Jewish customs? (Galatians 2:14)

Here is Peter, a Jew, doing away with most of the Law and living like a Gentile, not under the obligation of the Law's requirements. How, then, can he *force* the Gentiles to obey one or two laws when he himself doesn't feel the need to obey *all* of them? He just can't do that.

The Christian and the Law

Now Paul hits at the root problem behind Christians obeying the Law.

> We who are Jews by birth and not 'Gentile sinners' know that a man is not justified by observing the Law, but by faith in Jesus Christ. So we, too, have put our faith in Christ Jesus that we may be justified by faith in Christ and not by observing the Law, because by observing the Law no one will be justified. (Galatians 2:15-16)

All Christians agree with this statement, but few know how to apply it. Paul is saying that Peter is wrong in making the Gentiles obey only one or two points in the Law. He is therefore saying that *making them obey any particular law is trying to be justified by the Law instead of by faith in Christ*. He is definitely not in the mood to hear such foolishness as some people come up with, namely that once we are justified by faith in Christ then we are free to obey the Law. Dealing directly with the Law is the same thing as *turning away* from Christ, whether you do it as an unbeliever or as a believer. He calls this "setting aside the grace of God." (Galatians 2:21) Going back to the Law is "rebuilding" the Law. (Galatians 2:18) No, he says emphatically, "through the Law I died to the Law so that I might live for God." (Galatians 2:18)

He pushes this idea further on.

> I would like to learn just one thing from you: Did you receive the Spirit by observing the Law, or by believing what you heard? Are you so foolish? After beginning with the Spirit, are you now trying to attain your goal by human effort? Have you suffered so much for nothing — if it really was for nothing? Does God give you his Spirit and work miracles among you because you observe the Law, or because you believe what you heard? (Galatians 3:2-5)

Notice carefully what he says here. "After beginning with the Spirit, are you now trying to attain your goal by human effort?" In other words, a Christian is *forbidden* to return to the Law in any way! A believer should know that obeying the Law is *not* how we receive the grace of God; it can do nothing for us except confuse us and lead us in the wrong direction.

Paul has much more to say about the Law and what it can't do for Christians. But someone may wonder if the "new way" that Christ introduced is really good enough to make us holy. How can we be good unless we obey the Law? How can we please God if we don't know and follow his commands? Paul is ready for this argument too.

So I say, *live by the Spirit*, and you will not gratify the desires of the sinful nature. For the sinful nature desires what is contrary to the Spirit, and the Spirit what is contrary to the sinful nature. They are in conflict with each other, so that you do not do what you want. *But if you are led by the Spirit, you are not under Law.* (Galatians 5:16-18)

He is assuring doubtful Christians that the Spirit is fully capable of making us holy without resorting to the Law. Of course the Spirit will not introduce a righteousness into our souls that the Law doesn't recognize; remember that Paul said Christ would make sure "*the righteous requirements of the Law* would be fully met in us, who do not live according to the sinful nature but according to the Spirit." (Romans 8:4) But at no point will the Lord tell us to go back to the Law and keep it! Instead, he always tells Christians to "be led by the Spirit." There is life in that; there is only death waiting for the one who wants to do it the old way.

Our only Christian duty is this: "Since we live by the Spirit, let us *keep in step* with the Spirit." (Galatians 5:25) Doing that will keep you busy enough, without going back to the Law and trying to decide what you must do. The Spirit of God will see to it that, as you follow him, the righteousness of Christ will show up in your heart and life. If you don't know what it means to "keep in step" with the Spirit, search the Gospels and the promises that Jesus made for his followers; study the letters of Paul and see how he unfolds the life of faith. But we are never, ever told to go back to the Law for anything!

One more thing about Paul and the letter to the Galatians. This is such a strong statement about a Christian's relationship with the Law that only a blind man — spiritually blind, that is — can miss the point. He makes no bones about it: hands off the Law! We *must* get this right; we must believe this if we don't understand anything else. And, unfortunately, we *will* be confused by other issues — even in Paul's life! He continued worshipping in the Temple; he had his head shaved according to the Law; he was a Jew when among Jews, so that he wouldn't offend them. How does one explain these apparent contradictions when he came out so strongly in Galatians against us having anything to do with the Law? Well, this is what separates the good Bible students from the bad ones: we get the principles down first, *then* we deal with the exceptions. The exceptions *never* prove the rules wrong! Whatever we end up believing about Paul's personal behavior (and there are reasonable explanations for them), we must never let go of what is very clear in the Gospel.

The Christian and the Law

If you really want to do what the Law says — if you feel obligated to keep the Law in any way at all — there is nothing wrong with that. Christ did that very thing! If it was wrong to even try, then he would have been wrong for doing it. The problem is that *you would be a fool to try to keep the Law in any way at all*. The Law condemns sinners; that is its purpose. If you try to obey the Law and fail in any way at all, you are condemned as a law breaker and must be punished. When you start down that direction, you must do everything perfectly and not make a single slip or you have failed. And a sinner doesn't have the liberty to try again; there is only punishment in store for him, not mercy, when it comes to the Law.

One reason we get confused about our relationship with the Law is because we are continually enjoying the benefits of God's grace even while we struggle unsuccessfully with the Law. What I mean is this: we decide to struggle with our sin by obeying the Law; then we fail, since sinful flesh can't keep the Law to God's strict requirements; then we go to God for forgiveness in Christ (going around the Law!) and are restored to fellowship with him; then we try the Law again. We often misinterpret the spiritual success that comes by walking in faith, thinking that our success came as a result of our attempts at walking according to the Law. We need to get it straight in our minds that any spiritual success we may have comes from the mercy of God in Christ, not by our pitiful efforts at keeping the Law.

Don't underestimate the power of the Law. It looks simple enough, as if you could successfully keep it if you tried hard enough. But better men than you have tried it and failed. Remember the rich young ruler who boasted that, as concerns the Law, "all these I have kept." (Matthew 19:20) Yet he did not have eternal life because his best efforts at Law-keeping weren't good enough for Christ. There is a spiritual depth to the Law that is truly frightening, and an honest soul knows better than to take on such work alone. It's far better to let Christ do it for us.

The question often arises – what about the Ten Commandments? Aren't even Christians obligated to follow that great Law? But if you've been following the argument so far, you will know two things already: **first**, you can't obey the Ten Commandments either, not to the extent that God expects of you. Don't make the mistake that the rich young ruler made, thinking that a superficial obedience to this simple list will make you pleasing to God. Read about the true, spiritual depth of this Law in the Sermon on the Mount (Matthew 5-7) and then honestly answer whether you can do that without anybody's help!

Second, Jesus fulfilled these commands for you, and by means of his Spirit he intends to change your heart so that you will look like what the Ten Commandments expect. But the *way* to that righteousness is unexpected: it's not by tackling the Commandments directly! Jesus gave us a clue on this:

> 'Love the Lord your God with all your heart and with all your soul and with all your mind.' This is the first and greatest commandment. And the second is like it: 'Love your neighbor as yourself.' All the Law and the Prophets hang on these two commandments. (Matthew 22:37-40)

Now we reach our goal of righteousness not by obeying the Law, but by walking in the Spirit of God – the Spirit that Jesus sent us from Heaven to make us one with him. Remember that love is one of the fruit of the Spirit. There is our salvation; and there is God's solution for our problem of sin.

Should we even study the Law then? By all means, *yes!* The Law has a lot to do with you. ***First***, the Law describes what is wrong with you, the reasons that God sent a Savior to save you. If we didn't have the Law we wouldn't understand the true nature of sin and would never know the real need for a Savior. ***Second***, the Law perfectly describes Christ. Jesus is what you were never able to become on your own. If for no other reason, you need to know the Law so that you can praise your Lord for being so perfect. ***Third***, Jesus kept the Law for your sake. These requirements are still in full force, even today. God still will not accept anybody into his Kingdom who doesn't conform to the strict requirements of the Law. We shouldn't be little children in our thinking. We should know what Christ has done for us, we should know our new standing with God and how it was possible. We should also know what Christ is doing on our behalf now — he is still fulfilling the Law's requirements before the Throne of

Grace in the Temple in Heaven. All this, which is described completely in the Law, has a lot to do with our faith in Christ.

Finally, the end result is the same. The man who perfectly fulfills the Law is considered a "righteous man" in the sight of God. Only Christ has done this, however. And for the man who has faith in Christ, the Spirit will put Christ's righteousness into his life too, so that through his walk of faith, hope and love he will fulfill the righteous requirements of the Law. "Therefore love is the fulfillment of the Law." (Romans 13:10) In other words, as we follow the Lord in the Spirit, the Law is satisfied. This is a mystery, but the end result – righteousness – is the same. The difference is in *how* you go about it.

Led By The Spirit

For if you live according to the sinful nature, you will die; but if by the Spirit you put to death the misdeeds of the body, you will live, because those who are led by the Spirit of God are sons of God. (Romans 8:13-14)

The most precious gift that Christ has given his people is the Holy Spirit. Yet we know so little about him, probably because he is just *that* – Spirit – and we can't see him or sense his presence nearly so easily as the disciples did Jesus. And what we can't see, we don't concern ourselves with very much. So most of us think almost nothing about the Spirit, much to our spiritual hurt.

But the Bible tells us that the purpose of the Spirit's coming – the reason that Jesus gave him to us – is so that we might be *led by the Spirit*. Christ promised us that he isn't going to leave us alone in this world; and the Spirit is the fulfillment of that promise. There's too much that can go wrong in our lives if we don't listen to, and act on, some spiritual guidance from someone who knows the way.

Some people have formed their own opinion on what being "led" by the Spirit means. For instance, they long for the ability to have visions, or ecstatic utterances, or some sort of spiritual high during worship. Others on the other end of the spectrum want the Spirit to lead them into material wealth – they are "men of corrupt mind, who have been robbed of the truth and who think that godliness is a means to financial gain." (1 Timothy 6:5) But neither of these is what the Scripture means by being "led by the Spirit." In the first instance, *every* Christian must be led of the Spirit – but not every Christian will experience spiritual highs like the Old Testament Prophets sometimes did. In the second instance, the Spirit is leading God's people *away* from the world's riches, toward a reward that is far better than silver and gold.

The special work of the Spirit

Usually we think of the Spirit in terms of sanctification — that is, making us free from sin, or holy. "But you were washed, you were sanctified, you were justified in the name of the Lord Jesus Christ and by the Spirit of our God." (1 Corinthians 6:11) "To God's elect ... who have been chosen according to the foreknowledge of God the Father, by the sanctifying work of the Spirit, for obedience to Jesus Christ and sprinkling by his blood." (1 Peter 1:1-2)

But that's not the *primary* work of the Spirit according to the Bible. In a total of over 80 different passages that talk about what the Spirit does, I found only five places where it refers to his work of cleansing from sin, and some of those are marginal. Over half of the passages teach that the Spirit *reveals* the things of God, and the other half talk about the Spirit's *empowering* work.

- ***The Spirit reveals the world of God.*** " 'No eye has seen, no ear has heard, no mind has conceived what God has prepared for those who love him' — but God has revealed it to us by his Spirit." (1 Corinthians 2:9-10)

    If we want to know more about Heaven, the first hurdle that we have to get over is the fact that we are so earthbound. Since the day we were born, we have known only what we can see, smell, touch, taste, and hear. This world that we live in has been, to us, the *only* real world, as far as we can tell. The things that we put value on and the things that we own are in *this* world; the issues that we consider important are in *this* world; the people we respect are in *this* world; the forces that we fear are in *this* world. Most people live and die knowing nothing more than what is in this physical world, and they really don't care if there is another world — it seems like unrealistic stories anyway, myths and fairy tales.

But there is another world that's different from this one, even if we don't know anything about it: it's the world that God lives in. God is not of this world. That's a fundamental doctrine of Christianity. We have to believe that God's world is a completely different place than this world that we live in, that he can and does exist without any dependence on the physical world. He is the Creator: he made the universe, and he doesn't depend on it in the least — it depends on him. We could all snap completely out of existence and he wouldn't change in the least. He is what he is, and he will always be what he is, without our help or interference.

God's spiritual world is completely different from ours. Whereas ours is always changing, always falling apart and needing to be built up again, his is unchanging. Ours is completely physical, which means that the One who made it can unmake it just as easily (which he intends to do someday, by the way); but God's world is spiritual and therefore eternal. Our world looks good on the outside, and promises to satisfy us — but those are hollow promises, because it can't deliver on those promises (God intentionally made it unable to satisfy us); God's world doesn't look so appealing to our senses but it does satisfy the soul's deepest needs. Our world struggles under the curse of sin and death, and God has already passed judgment on it — its time will come; God's world remains untouched by that stain and therefore remains God's only choice for where spiritual life can thrive.

What about this completely "other" world that we don't know anything about? We can, and do, live our entire lives in complete ignorance that it even exists. The two worlds actually run parallel to each other, like two cities on either side of a railroad track; and if it weren't for certain historical events that forced a link between the two we would still not know how the people lived "on the other side of the tracks."

One of the most important historical events that forged a bridge between the two worlds was the giving of the Holy Spirit. The Spirit reveals, makes plain, uncovers, makes "see-able" this other world that God lives in. It's like taking the veil away from a statue so that the public can see it for the first time. It's like opening a window into Heaven so that we can see inside.

The first occasion in the Bible where we find the Spirit doing this type of work is in connection with the Tabernacle. God was concerned that Moses and the Israelites build their central place of worship in the right way; not just anything would do. So instead of running the risk that the makers of the Tabernacle would misunderstand his instructions, no matter how plain he made them, the Lord poured out his Spirit on the two men in charge of the building project:

> See, the LORD has chosen Bezalel son of Uri, the son of Hur, of the tribe of Judah, and *he has filled him with the Spirit of God*, with skill, ability and knowledge in all kinds of crafts ... And he has given both him and Oholiab son of Ahisamach, of the tribe of Dan, the ability to teach others ... so Bezalel, Oholiab and every skilled person to whom the LORD has given skill and ability to know how to carry out all the work of constructing the sanctuary are to do the work just as the LORD has commanded. (Exodus 35:30,34-35; 36:1)

And what did the Spirit show them?

> They serve at a sanctuary that is a copy and shadow of what is in Heaven. This is why Moses was warned when he was about to build the tabernacle: "See to it that you make everything according to the pattern shown you on the mountain." (Hebrews 8:5)

The Spirit showed these men what the Heavenly Tabernacle, in God's world, looked like. To what extent we don't know, but at least we know that they saw the essentials so that they could pattern the earthly tabernacle after it in a way that would satisfy God.

In Isaiah there is a prophecy of the Messiah, and it tells us that he will be filled by the Spirit:

> The Spirit of the LORD will rest upon him — the Spirit of wisdom and of understanding, the Spirit of counsel and of power, the Spirit of knowledge and of the fear of the LORD ... He will not judge by what he sees with his eyes, or decide by what he hears with his ears ... (Isaiah 11:2,3)

In other words, he won't rely on his senses to judge how to work in this world, but by what the Spirit tells him — knowledge from another world than this one.

Jesus said that when we face authorities who persecute us for our faith, the Spirit of God will give us the right words to say — words that we wouldn't ordinarily think of on our own. (Mark 13:11) He also promised to send the Spirit to us, who would "guide you into all truth." (John 16:13) The Spirit of God opened Stephen's eyes to see Christ standing at God's right hand when the Jews were stoning him. (Acts 7:55-56) The Spirit tells us what to pray for and how to pray when we don't know what to say. (Romans 8:26) The mystery of Christ "has now been revealed by the Spirit" to the Church." (Ephesians 3:5) Paul said that whoever rejects the teaching of Scripture isn't rejecting man but the Spirit, who is actually doing the teaching. (1 Thessalonians 4:8) The Spirit gives us a taste of the Heavenly gift, and enlightens us about the world of God. (Hebrews 6:4) The Prophets, Peter tells us, always spoke as they were "carried along by the Holy Spirit" — the Spirit told them what to say. (1 Peter 1:21) The Spirit testifies to the cleansing power of Christ's blood. (1 John 5:6) John the Apostle was praying in the Spirit when he had his revelation of Christ. (Revelation 1:10) The Spirit says things to the churches of Christ that they need to hear. (Revelation 2:11)

This is just a sampling from the Bible about the work of the Spirit as he reveals the world of God to our minds and souls.

- **_The Spirit gives power._** "But you will receive power when the Holy Spirit comes on you; and you will be my witnesses in Jerusalem and in all Judea and Samaria, and to the ends of the earth." (Acts 1:8)

The kind of power that this verse is talking about isn't any power that we are familiar with. Simon made that mistake when he saw the Apostles working miracles and tried to buy the power of the Spirit from them. (Acts 8:9-24) The power that the Spirit gives is a new thing, something that this world doesn't know anything about.

The first time that we find the empowering work of the Spirit in the Bible is in Genesis.

> In the beginning God created the Heavens and the earth. Now the earth was formless and empty, darkness was over the surface of the deep, and the Spirit of God was hovering over the waters. (Genesis 1:1-2)

What exactly was there at the beginning, the building blocks that God used to make the world, we don't know; we do know that it was "without form" and "without substance" (as the Hebrew words mean), which are the two necessary characteristics of matter as we know it. In other words, the Spirit brought non-existence into existence; he gave life and substance to what used to be nothing. The earth and plants and animals and man all exist because the Spirit gave us the ability to exist. Without him we would return to nothingness.

That's what happened to the world when the Spirit moved in the beginning. What happens in men's souls now? Here is where we need the Spirit most of all, because we are all dead to the world of God from our birth. (Ephesians 2:1-3) Even if we see God (the first job of the Spirit), and even if we *know* the truth about God and his world, we still can't do anything about it. God requires obedience from us — but we can't obey him because we are so bound up in our sin, and without power to obey his commands. He requires faith from us — but we can't believe in him because we are so confused, wandering in this dark world. He calls us to live in *his* world, but we can't get out of our world. At the very least we are to "love the Lord your God with all our heart and with all your soul and with all your mind" (Matthew 22:37), but unfortunately we aren't interested — there are other things that we love more.

When the Spirit works on the heart, however, that person wakes up to God's world, like opening one's eyes on a bright morning. "Wake up, O sleeper, rise from the dead, and Christ will shine on you." (Ephesians 5:14) He can see things now that he hasn't seen before. Even this dark world that we live in gets a new light: the Spirit shines on our lives, on circumstances, on other people, like a spotlight and shows us things that we couldn't see before.

The Spirit not only wakes us up to the world of God, he makes us *able* to live in God's world. "Flesh and blood cannot inherit the Kingdom of God" (1 Corinthians 15:50), simply because the conditions there would kill us. The air is different, the food is different, the light is different (I'm using symbols of the realities, you understand; "air" and "food" and "light" in Heaven are spiritual things, whereas we think of our physical world when we hear those words.) Paul said that before we can hope to rise into Heaven, some things about us have to change:

> So it will be with the resurrection of the dead. The body that is sown is perishable, it is raised imperishable; it is sown in dishonor, it is raised in glory; it is sown in weakness, it is raised in power; it is sown a natural body, it is raised a spiritual body. (1 Corinthians 15:42-44)

In order to live before God and not die, we have to change completely. Our natures as they are now can neither survive before God's glory, nor can we understand or appreciate what we would see there. Our physical senses weren't made to be aware of the things of God. Unless, of course, the Spirit gives life to our souls — our souls *were* made to be aware of God. That's why the Bible talks about having "eyes to see" and "ears to hear." The Spirit makes us alive spiritually (which Jesus called, appropriately, being "born again" — John 3:3) so that our spiritual senses can start picking up on the things of God. In order to pick up the signals from a radio station, you have to first turn the radio on. In the same way, before anybody can hope to know God, their souls must be made alive first.

    The Spirit makes it possible for us to obey God's commands; without him we could never do it. (Ezekiel 36:26-27) The Law is spiritual, Paul says (Romans 7:14), and the Spirit shows us what God means by his Law and how he will make us conform to its requirements. The Spirit of God blew over the bones in Israel and made them alive again. (Ezekiel 37:1-14) The Lord will build his Kingdom "not by might nor by power, but by my Spirit" (Zechariah 4:6); because of this, his Kingdom will be eternal and it will consist of things that will satisfy both him and us. Jesus drove out demons by the Spirit of God. (Matthew 12:28) Jesus said that, when someone has the Spirit in him, it will be a spring of water welling up inside to eternal life. (John 4:14) "The Spirit gives life, the flesh counts for nothing" (John 6:63) — and Jesus' words were Spirit because they give us spiritual life, the awareness of God and ability to live for God. Peter, the disciple whom the Jews had last seen denying the Lord, stood up at Pentecost full of the Spirit and preached the eternal Gospel to the Jews — with thousands of conversions as a result. (Acts 2) The Holy Spirit gives joy to God's people. (Romans 14:17) It's because of the Spirit's work that we have faith in Christ — a faith that comprehends the breadth and depth of Christ's person and work. (Ephesians 2:8; 3:16) The Spirit washes and renews us so that we become heirs of God's promises. (Titus 3:5)

Our journey to Heaven

You may have noticed something important in the previous discussion. The Spirit reveals – what? The world of God! He shows us the spiritual Kingdom that God lives in, the one that we've been called to live in ourselves. And the Spirit empowers us – to do what? To live in that Kingdom of Heaven! God's world is of such a nature that the Spirit has to make us *able* to come into God's presence, *able* to take advantage of the treasures that God put in Christ for us. In other words, the primary focus of the Spirit in our lives is *to make us fit to live in the Kingdom of God.*

When a person becomes a Christian, his heart changes. Jesus described it to Nicodemus (who, by the way, should have known about this already, because he was an expert in the Old Testament!).

> I tell you the truth, no one can see the Kingdom of God unless he is born again ... I tell you the truth, no one can enter the Kingdom of God unless he is born of water and the Spirit. Flesh gives birth to flesh, but the Spirit gives birth to spirit. You should not be surprised at my saying, 'You must be born again.' The wind blows wherever it pleases. You hear its sound, but you cannot tell where it comes from or where it is going. So it is with everyone born of the Spirit. (John 3:3,5-8)

Our souls, dead to God at birth and completely unable to sense his presence or feel any inclination to be interested in him, suddenly become alive to God. The Spirit blows from Heaven in a way that none of us can describe or predict and, for some reason, we are suddenly interested in the things of Heaven. We can tell now that there really is a God; we know he's there. More specifically, we find that we fear this God (which means we want to be careful how we act around him), and we hope in this God (which means that we know that he has what we need).

When this happens, we discover that we have a practical problem on our hands. It's such a precious gift to become a child of God, an heir to the eternal Kingdom, with the right to enjoy our Heavenly inheritance. But we find ourselves still on earth, with physical bodies and physical needs! We would like to leave for Heaven immediately and be done with this world! But it can't be, not yet at any rate. Even Jesus prayed about our problem:

> I have given them your Word and the world has hated them, for they are not of the world any more than I am of the world. My prayer is not that you take them out of the world but that you protect them from the evil one. They are not of the world, even as I am not of it. (John 17:14-16)

What we have here is a dual-identity problem. In Hebrews we find a description that fits all of God's children, as long as they remain here in this world:

> All these people were still living by faith when they died. They did not receive the things promised; they only saw them and welcomed them from a distance. And they admitted that they were *aliens and strangers* on earth. People who say such things show that they are looking for a country of their own. If they had been thinking of the country they had left, they would have had opportunity to return. Instead, they were longing for a better country — a Heavenly one. Therefore God is not ashamed to be called their God, for he has prepared a city for them. (Hebrews 11:13-16)

As long as we remain here, we actually have one foot on earth and one foot in Heaven. Our hearts are in another world, and our eyes are focused on the Throne of God. We know that we don't belong here anymore. We aren't supposed to love the things in this world anymore; as Jesus told us –

> Do not store up for yourselves treasures on earth, where moth and rust destroy, and where thieves break in and steal. But store up for yourselves treasures in Heaven, where moth and rust do not destroy, and where thieves do not break in and steal. For where your treasure is, there your heart will be also. (Matthew 6:19-21)

We could go on and on, listing the passages from the Bible about our new life in Christ, our new spiritual inheritance, and God's command to turn our backs on this world. It really is a new life that we've begun because of what Christ did in our hearts.

Here, now, is where the Spirit comes in. Becoming a Christian isn't just a matter of changing from the old way of life to a new way, or holding to a different set of beliefs about God. As Paul says, "If only for *this* life we have hope in Christ, we are to be pitied more than all men." (1 Corinthians 15:19) Our goal now is *Heaven*. We have begun a journey: from the moment that we woke up spiritually and saw our Savior, the rest of our lives will be a steady progress *from* earth *to* Heaven. And the Spirit is doing two things for us: leading us in the right way to Heaven, and slowly making us fit to arrive there in perfect condition and pleasing to our Master. We are making plans for *leaving* this world – and that fact should become more apparent to others as time goes on.

In the Old Testament Temple, there were certain vessels and articles that the priests used for purposes of worship only. The Law strictly forbade anybody from using these articles for common use; the priests sprinkled each article with blood and "set it aside" for this sacred use in the Temple. That's exactly what the word "sanctify" means in Hebrew – to "set aside for sacred use." Once a pot, for example, was sanctified, it couldn't be used for ordinary cooking anymore. Even if it was broken by accident, it had to be destroyed – the people were forbidden to use it for any common purpose once it had been sanctified.

That's exactly what the Spirit is doing to us. God is so holy, and the Temple in Heaven is so overwhelmingly holy, that it's forbidden that any common, ordinary, wicked sinner should ever be allowed there. Earth is full of sinners; but Heaven has, and shall have, *none*. There won't even be the hint of sin in the presence of the holy God. But you can probably see the problem here: if God calls us to come up before him, and especially to share the inheritance with Christ as God's children, what are we going to do about our sin? And even if we *were* allowed inside his Temple, what in the world would we say or do there? We know nothing about the place! So the Spirit is going to prepare us for life in Heaven. And here is how he will do it:

- *Crucify the flesh:* "Flesh and blood cannot inherit the Kingdom of God, nor does the perishable inherit the imperishable." (1 Corinthians 15:50) We like to pamper our flesh, to line our nests in this world. We want comfortable jobs, respectability in the community, plenty of friends and good times. We also like to indulge in our lusts from time to time.

  But there is nothing in Heaven for the flesh to lust for! There are no earthly pleasures, no wealth that we are familiar with, no lusts allowed – or even possible! Remember that Jesus told us that "at the resurrection people will neither marry nor be given in marriage; they will be like the angels in Heaven." (Matthew 22:30) Not too promising for anybody looking forward to pampering their flesh! The pleasures there are purely spiritual. The physical as we know it will be gone, remade, unrecognizable.

The physical has to die, like a seed, so that the spiritual can be born and live in a spiritual Heaven.

Now before we can be ready for such a strange place, and before we can even *want* to go to such a place, the Spirit has to work on us and make us into spiritual creatures who love God's spiritual Kingdom. The flesh must die.

- ***Renew the mind:*** "Do not conform any longer to the pattern of this world, but be transformed by the renewing of your mind." (Romans 12:2) Our minds are remarkable tools for enabling us to get along in this world. In fact, we pride ourselves at being "savvy" or intelligent, and we hate to play the fool and show our ignorance.

But when it comes to the world of God, we know almost nothing about it. We don't know what it looks like, we don't know much about God himself, we don't know the immense riches in Christ or how to get at them, we don't know how to act in front of God and Heaven's hosts when we pray – there is so much we don't know about God's world, that the first sight of it will surely humble us!

That's what the Spirit is going to do. He's going to renew our minds, make them able to see and understand spiritual truths and realities, and make us skilled at knowing and using Heavenly treasures.

> We have not received the spirit of the world but the Spirit who is from God, that we may *understand* what God has freely given us. This is what we speak, not in words taught us by human wisdom but in words taught by the

Spirit, expressing spiritual truths in spiritual words. (1 Corinthians 2:12-13)

- ***Fruits of righteousness:*** "But the fruit of the Spirit is love, joy, peace, patience, kindness, goodness, faithfulness, gentleness and self-control. Against such things there is no law." (Galatians 5:22-23)

What naturally comes out of a human being's heart? Read the newspapers! Earth is full of wickedness; it's been that way since the fall of Adam and Eve. None of us can claim moral perfection; even the best of us have failed God at some point in our lives.

But God can't tolerate the least trace of sin! He is so holy – Isaiah said that he is "holy, holy, holy!" (Isaiah 6:3) – that he would sooner have us all put to death than pollute his pure environment with our wickedness. Notice that he didn't have any qualms about destroying sinners in the past! Read the stories of Noah, and Korah, and the Exile, and Sodom and Gomorrah, for proof of his hatred of sinners.

But the Spirit is going to take care of this spiritual cancer in our hearts. Knowing that we can't appear before God in our own wretched rags of "morality" which haven't made us any more righteous in God's eyes, he's going to replace them with the robe of righteousness that Jesus bought for us with his obedience. Slowly, he's going to *make* us do what pleases God in our lives, day by day. Slowly but surely he's going to remake our hearts in holiness instead of leaving them in wickedness.

- ***True worship:*** "Yet a time is coming and has now come when the true worshipers will worship the Father in Spirit and truth, for they are the kind of worshipers the Father seeks." (John 4:23)

The ways that we invent to worship God in our churches and denominations can be pretty pitiful. We believe firmly that the way *we* worship God is the only right way; but, if you think about it, we can't *all* be right! We all have different versions of how to do worship. But so much of what we do is simply because of our preferences, traditions and culture.

Almost none of it, unfortunately, fits in with the way the servants of God worship him in Heaven. In fact, we probably would feel completely out of place there – we wouldn't know the first thing to do if we were presented to God in person! What would we say? What would we do? Even if we could think of what to do for the first five minutes, what would we do for the rest of the day? For a year? For eternity? Remember that the worship of God is going to be our work in Heaven *forever*. Do we have any idea of how to go about such work?

The Spirit, then, has to train us in spiritual worship. He has to show us what God likes, and what he expects from us. He has to make us skilled at saying and doing things for God that please him. He has to show us the real work going on in Heaven and what our part in it will be.

- ***Walk by faith:*** "For in the gospel a righteousness from God is revealed, a righteousness that is by faith from first to last, just as it is written: 'The righteous will live by faith.'" (Romans 1:17)

What most people mean by "faith" is a poor substitute for the tremendous spiritual gift that God has given us in true faith. Most people think it means believing in some doctrine or Biblical truth. So they think that they have faith when they, for example, believe that there is a God. James ridicules such "faith!" "You believe that there is one God. Good! Even the demons believe that – and shudder." (James 2:19)

What would happen if God would suddenly lift you up from earth and set you in Heaven? Would you recognize anything? Would everything be totally new to you? Would you be like a foreigner, lost and wandering, friendless, homeless, without a clue as to what is going on around you? If God would invite you to share in the spiritual treasures in Christ, which is your inheritance, would you even know what those treasures are? Or where to find them?

Faith is walking in the light of God's world. It's the result of the light of Christ coming down from Heaven, that the Spirit shines down on us as he reveals to us the things of God. We *know* God, we *see* God, through our faith. We see the riches in Christ; that's why we reach out to *him* when we need help. We see a world that others can't see. That "seeing" is what true faith is all about. With true faith, this physical world means little to us, and the world of God becomes our only hope. Living by faith means we conform our daily lives to spiritual realities – things that other people can't see and don't know. The Spirit, as he reveals these things to us, makes such a faith possible.

- *Hope in Heaven:* "For in this hope we were saved." (Romans 8:24) The last point leads to this one, naturally. We hope in whatever we set the greatest value on. If we love this world with all of its "riches" and "glory," and we long to fill our physical lusts with earthly pleasures, then we won't have much interest in a spiritual world where there is none of that sort of thing.

When we are brought before God's judgment seat on the Last Day, it will be plain for everyone to see what we have been putting our hope in. If our hearts have been set on things on earth, we will look with great disappointment and fear at this God that we haven't been paying any attention to. We will cringe before a Heaven without worldly pleasures. We will look back, like Lot's wife, at the earth burning behind us, destroyed by God's punishing hand, wishing that we were there instead of in this spiritual world with God and his people. What will we do if Heaven turns out to be so foreign and offensive to us?

So the Spirit is going to wean us from the world now, and set our hearts on Heavenly things. He works in us to will and do God's perfect will. He helps us pray – for spiritual treasures. He sets our eyes on Christ, seated at God's right hand, above all earthly powers and pleasures. When he gets done with us, there will be nothing on earth that we desire but God, and nothing in Heaven that so wins our hearts but God. (Psalm 73:25) The longer we live with the Spirit, the more we will *long* for Heaven.

The Spirit blows where he wills

The Israelites were bound to obey the Law that God gave them at Mt. Sinai. The Law was, simply put, a list of rules and regulations that described the government of God over his people. He expected obedience – strict obedience, upon pain of death. There was no leeway in this, either; one single broken Law and they were in trouble. The Law often required death as a punishment.

The key to understanding the Law is that *the Israelites themselves had to keep the Law.* "And if we are careful to obey all this Law before the LORD our God, as he has commanded us, *that* will be our righteousness." (Deuteronomy 6:25) They had to *do* what the Law said. When they did, God considered them righteous; if they didn't, God punished them.

The history of the Israelites is a lesson on what happens when God turns us loose with the Law: we fail miserably. None of us can keep the Law as God requires it. The Israelites couldn't. Their sin and ignorance, the temptations of the world, the deceits of the enemy, all of that conspired to trip them up in their attempted obedience to the Law. The only man who ever kept the Law completely, to God's satisfaction, was Jesus – the Son of God.

Jesus did more than keep the Law, however. He bought a righteousness for us that none of us could achieve on our own. Now he is busy applying that righteousness of his to our souls – we're getting righteous the easy way! We are reaching a spiritual level that no Israelite could do on his own. But in order to pull this off, we have to be careful and let the Spirit guide us into that righteousness.

This is a subtle point that many people often miss. Though we claim to be Christians, and we understand that nothing that we do can save us or make us righteous in God's eyes, we still try our best to follow the Law! As if we could do what the Jews couldn't do! It's so tempting to follow the Law that the Galatians fell for the mistake, and Paul had to write rough rebukes to them for attempting to do what they couldn't do and they weren't allowed, as followers of Christ, to do.

> Are you so foolish? After beginning with the Spirit, are you now trying to attain your goal by human effort? Have you suffered so much for nothing — if it really was for nothing? Does God give you his Spirit and work miracles among you because you observe the Law, or because you believe what you heard? (Galatians 3:3-5)

A Christian isn't obligated to keep the Law; he can't anyway, so it's no use trying. He has a much better approach for becoming righteous: the Spirit of God is going to do it for him. Paul describes it this way:

> For what the Law was powerless to do in that it was weakened by the sinful nature, God did by sending his own Son in the likeness of sinful man to be a sin offering. And so he condemned sin in sinful man, in order that *the righteous requirements of the Law might be fully met in us*, who do not live according to the sinful nature but according to the Spirit. (Romans 8:3-4)

In other words, follow the Spirit, wherever he leads, and you will walk right into righteousness. He will change your heart for you, in a way that you couldn't dream of doing. His whole purpose is to take the righteousness of Christ – which is perfection, something the Law can never find fault with – and shape your soul with it. You will have the heart of a righteous man, and now you will automatically do the works of a righteous man without even thinking about it – as Jesus lives in you. When the Spirit is done with you, you will shine in the image of Christ. (2 Corinthians 3:18)

So the result is the same – a righteous man – but the methods are completely different. The Law just stands coolly off to one side, arms crossed, demanding that we obey or be punished. No help, no encouragement, no hope. But the Spirit goes about it in a different way: he gives us three spiritual skills: faith, hope and love. We find these three skills listed in several places in the New Testament.

> And now these three remain: **faith**, **hope**, and **love**. But the greatest of these is love. (1 Corinthians 13:13)

> … we have heard of your **faith** in Christ Jesus and of the **love** you have for all the saints – the faith and love that spring from the **hope** that is stored up for you in Heaven … (Colossians 1:4-5)

> … your work produced by **faith**, your labor prompted by **love**, and your endurance inspired by **hope** in our Lord Jesus Christ. (1 Thessalonians 1:3)

> … he has given us new birth into a living **hope** … who through **faith** are shielded by God's power … though you have not seen him, you **love** him … (1 Peter 1:3, 5, 8)

Why are these skills so crucial for making us ready for Heaven?

- *He gives us faith.* Faith, as we have seen, is walking in the light of Heaven. By faith we are enabled to see the reality of God, the reality of the treasures of Heaven, the true nature of Christ, the true state of our souls, the true nature of the world that we live in and why we don't want to stay here. Faith opens our spiritual eyes so that we can see the truth, just as the Bible describes it. Without faith we can see nothing.

The Spirit has to open our eyes like this. And when he does, the sin, ignorance and misery that we used to live in falls away. It's the first step toward life. A person who can't see where his salvation is, will remain in darkness and die in his sins, though he might work as hard as he can at being pleasing to God. But the person who sees how to reach salvation, and where it is, can start moving in that direction.

- ***He gives us hope.*** Hope isn't just wishing that something *might* come true; it's the assurance that it *will* be true. It's what we are waiting for, not wishing for; it's been promised to us, and it's only a matter of time until we receive it. Hope, as the Spirit gives it, keeps us going even when we have no other encouragement in this world, because we know what is waiting for us at the end.

Only the Spirit can give us this kind of hope. People without hope from the Spirit have no idea how God will receive them at Judgment Day; they "hope" that he will be merciful to them, but they have no reason for their "hope." But a Christian has already heard encouraging words from his Savior. He knows that Jesus went "to prepare a place" for him in Heaven, and the Father is waiting to receive them into an eternal family. Remember, the Spirit reveals the things of God: he shows us the heart of God, the love of God, the certainty of the promises of God. He shows us Christ, who came to save sinners and restore them to a relationship with their Father. When the Spirit shows us how certain these things are, we put our sights on Heaven now instead of earth. The temptations, the sins, the darkness of this world take on their true colors and we willingly turn our backs on all of that. It's not difficult to hate what is ugly and deadly; it becomes easy to love life.

- *He gives us love.* There are different kinds of love, but the kind of love that the Spirit puts in our heart is a self-sacrificing love. The New Testament word is **agape** (pronounced, ah-GAWP-ay). John tells us what this kind of love means:

> This is how we know what love is: Jesus Christ laid down his life for us. And we ought to lay down our lives for our brothers. (1 John 3:16)
>
> Jesus said that our duty is to –
>
> 'Love the Lord your God with all your heart and with all your soul and with all your mind.' This is the first and greatest commandment. And the second is like it: 'Love your neighbor as yourself.' (Matthew 22:37-40)

A sinner isn't going to do this on his own; he sees no reason to love God whom he hates, nor love anybody else other than himself. But when the Spirit reveals the Father to us, especially the love of the Father in Christ Jesus, a love for God is born in our hearts. We love this God who first loved us. Why does this love suddenly show up in a hard heart, in a sinner who formerly didn't want anything to do with God? We can only account for such a thing by the Spirit re-making the heart and giving it the ability to love God. And because of

Led by the Spirit

our love for God, we won't settle for anything in this world – what we want is to be with *him*.

Someone who loves God will also love God's children, because they bear the image of their Father. Jesus is the oldest brother of a family, and we know that we are among our spiritual brothers and sisters. Again, this love comes because the Spirit works it into our hearts, revealing our family to us and showing us their spiritual needs that we can fulfill. And we want to fulfill those needs for them, because we want them in Heaven with us – just as Jesus wants all of us with him there. (John 17:24)

When the Spirit gives us these three skills – faith, hope, and love – we are now in the position to start walking with the Spirit and having our hearts conformed to the righteousness of Christ. Whereas someone under the Law had to try to obey the commandments, without the benefit of any outside help, a Spirit-led Christian finds himself lifted up into a spiritual world – through what he sees, hopes in, and loves. These abilities and feelings aren't natural to him – the Spirit works them into his heart – but they enable him to walk in a world of love, of wanting and living for the treasures of Heaven, of "hating even the clothing stained by corrupted flesh." (Jude 22) When we walk with God, with the help of the Spirit, the righteousness of Christ comes naturally to us. His life is the *only* life possible in Heaven! Anybody who lives completely in the world of sin and death will live as the world lives: Paul lists those sins in Galatians 5:19-21. But whoever lives in God's Kingdom will experience the life of Christ in their hearts:

Love, joy, peace, patience, kindness, goodness, gentleness, faithfulness, and self-control. Against such things there is no Law. (Galatians 5:22-23)

Problems along the way

We need to pause for a minute and take a reality check. It's nice to talk about being led by the Spirit, and we Christians claim that we *want* God to lead us, but I'm afraid that there are going to be problems along the way. Though we say that we want to go to Heaven, and be made ready to serve God forever, we find the actual process too painful to bear. Like Lot's wife, we look back longingly at the world which the Spirit is leading us away from.

- *The treasures on earth* – We love our riches, our comforts, our reputations, our good life. We panic when any of that is threatened. We think that life isn't worth living if we have to go without the good things of the world. And while we argue with God about what we get to keep and what we have to get rid of, the Spirit shows us treasures in Heaven that are overwhelmingly more valuable than the entire universe. As if gold and silver come anywhere close to the value of the spiritual riches we have in Christ! For example, the Spirit counsels us that –

> Blessed is the man who finds wisdom,
>   the man who gains understanding,
> for she is more profitable than silver
>   and yields better returns than gold.
> She is more precious than rubies;
>   nothing you desire can compare with her.
> Long life is in her right hand;
>   in her left hand are riches and honor.
> Her ways are pleasant ways,
>   and all her paths are peace.
> She is a tree of life to those who embrace her;
>   those who lay hold of her will be blessed.
>   (Proverbs 3:13-18)

Of course this makes no sense to an unspiritual person. Gold we understand, but wisdom – and that means the wisdom from God's Word – we just don't see the importance of. We tend to love what we see, not what we don't see, and we work for what we love, not for what we don't love. So we usually fight against the Spirit as he tries to lead us toward Heavenly treasures and away from earthly ones.

- *Our glory* – Glory is when we take the credit for something. Just about everything we do is for our own glory. We like to be in the limelight; we like to think that we're in control of our lives, that our successes are due to our own decisions and good judgment. When we fail, we blame others – not ourselves. Anything that puts a good light on our character, our image, our social standing, our reputation – we're in favor of that. What we don't like is to appear helpless and in need of anything or anybody.

And this is precisely what the Spirit is trying to do to our proud hearts! He wants to show us that we are spiritually helpless unless God has mercy on us. He wants to prove that, without God, we are nothing and will be nothing. "But you do not realize that you are wretched, pitiful, poor, blind and naked." (Revelation 3:17) We have no hope unless God saves us, cleans us, remakes our hearts, renews our minds, sets us in the right direction, gives us a path to walk on, gives us the strength to walk, gives us the light to see by, gives us the wisdom we need to know the truth, and guides us every step of the way. To appear so helpless in this world, in front of our friends and especially our enemies, is one of the greatest fears we have.

- *Feed the flesh* – Our well-being and contentedness comes first in life. We look out for Number One first; everyone else, including God, has to wait their turn. We listen to and feed our lusts, because pleasure is our primary reason for living. We cry when we don't get what we want, and we ignore others in their need when we are well-fed and satisfied. And we like our pleasures so much that we work to make sure that we can repeat them whenever we want; we surround ourselves with opportunities to feed our flesh with the temptations of the world.

But the Spirit knows that this is death, not life. Living for this world means that we have no concern for the next world, where the real treasures are. He knows that the only way to open our eyes to the treasures of Heaven is to cut away the flesh, to crucify the flesh, to put the flesh to death – so that when what we love is *gone*, we will then look at what Christ has for us instead. This won't be easy. The flesh and the Spirit are at war with each other. (Galatians 5:17) The Spirit is out to kill the flesh with its lusts and rebellion, because nothing short of that will prepare us for Heaven. And the flesh resists the Spirit's sanctifying work at every turn because it knows that its death is at hand.

- *Our own kingdom* – Man was born to be a ruler – God made him a ruler over the earth – but now, in his sin and death, he does things to destroy himself and the world, not to build them up. Look at the mess we've created! We are best at hatred, killing, misery and persecution, ignorance, pollution, slaughter, greed, stealing and robbery, adultery and fornication, destruction of the family – the ugly list goes on.

We have clearly demonstrated what happens when we are in control of things. Now it's time for God to rule over us, and straighten out the mess. But as the Spirit works to build God's Kingdom among us, we aren't going to want to turn control over to him. We are going to question his authority, resist his influence, ignore his commands, doubt his good intentions, speak ill of his holy character, and generally do whatever will undermine his work among us.

He knows this will happen. Bring in a new King, set up new laws and regulations, start working toward a new society, and all the rebels will rise up in protest. It's bound to happen. We are going to fight and disagree and disobey at almost every turn. We might *say* that we bow to the Lord as our King, but in our hearts we despise his rule over us.

This is ugly, but unfortunately it's too often true of us. And when we fight the very one who came to help us, it positively grieves him. He has our well-being at heart! He wants to save us. And then we respond to his love by biting him, like a dog biting the one who tries to help him get loose from a trap that's killing him. It doesn't make sense.

"And do not grieve the Holy Spirit of God, with whom you were sealed for the day of redemption." (Ephesians 4:30) The Holy Spirit sealed us to be *saved* on the Last Day; why do we fight him and run away from our salvation? As he leads us to Heaven, using methods that are designed to make us holy, why do we resist his work in us?

"Do not put out the Spirit's fire." (1 Thessalonians 5:19) The Spirit fires our hearts, burning off the chaff of sin and worldliness, purifying the gold of God's grace and righteousness in our hearts. Why do we do things that fight against that purifying process? Why do we keep dumping things back into our hearts that quench the fires, that drown our hearts in the sludge and muck of the world's pigsty? He's getting us ready for Heaven; why do we insist on letting go of our salvation and drowning in an ocean of wickedness?

Only those who persevere to the end will be saved. (Matthew 10:22) Our theology should glorify God who can save anybody, but we can't hide behind our theology and lay back unconcerned in our sin. If we resist the Spirit, what hope do we have? When he leads us in God's ways, how can we expect to be saved when we go off in our own directions? When he applies the knife to our hearts to cut out the sin and lust, why do we think we will be saved when we run away and feed those lusts again – all the while claiming to be Christians?

> It is impossible for those who have once been enlightened, who have tasted the Heavenly gift, *who have shared in the Holy Spirit*, who have tasted the goodness of the word of God and the powers of the coming age, if they fall away, to be brought back to repentance, because to their loss they are crucifying the Son of God all over again and subjecting him to public disgrace. (Hebrews 6:4-6)

It's not time for theological arrogance, but for a genuine fear of God whom we are offending with our hypocrisy! Although many Biblical scholars have debated the meaning of Hebrews 6:4-6, those who resist the Spirit's leading to life and holiness will learn its meaning all too well in the end.

How does he lead us?

Since our goal is Heaven, we have an immediate problem on our hands: how will we get there? Since Heaven is a spiritual place, there isn't anything on earth that can help us get there. In fact, most religions don't even pretend to deal with Heaven now, since we can't see it or feel it or know for sure that it even exists. Some of them promise Heaven in the end, but nobody knows for certain that such a place is real. Least of all do they offer us a way to get there *now*, before we die.

That's where the Spirit of God comes in for Christians. He does two things for us: *first*, he shows us that Heaven is very real; he lets us taste the fruits of that Promised Land before we arrive there. **Second**, he leads the way along certain prescribed paths; he shows us the way to Heaven.

Those paths to Heaven are well known to most people. Of course, many people make up their own roads to Heaven, claiming that they can reach God in any way that they please. They're wrong, and they will find out how wrong they were on Judgment Day when they stand face to face with a God they never knew! Their paths led them to their own gods, not to the God of the Bible. But many other people have heard about the true roads to Heaven, and have been taking those roads for a long time.

But it's entirely possible – in fact, it usually happens – that most people try to travel on these roads to Heaven *without* the Spirit leading them. One may as well try to drive on a road in pitch-black darkness! It's possible to try that, but it's impossible to arrive safely at your destination if you do. The Spirit has to show us the way as we travel that road; he sheds just enough light to show us the road at our feet, so that we know where to go next. Without him we will head off in the wrong direction, run into things that stop us, get into trouble, and get hopelessly lost.

These five roads lead to Heaven. Just remember two things: we have to take the right road, and the Spirit has to lead us on that road. We must at least get on these roads if we hope to see God, because no other roads will lead to him. But keep in mind that as we travel these roads, we have to keep tuned to the Spirit and let *him* do the driving!

- *The Word of God* – Man is a rational creature, the only one on the planet. And when God created Adam and Eve, he gave them a unique job: to rule over the creatures on earth in his place, in his Name. In order to do this, they had to have a mind capable of understanding God, the world, and what God wanted done in his new world. As they ruled the earth, they were to get their instructions and goals from the King of kings and see to it that God's wishes were carried out on earth.

  Adam and Eve fell into sin and created a gigantic mess as far as their original responsibilities were concerned. But now Christians have a second chance. They too are called by God to a special job: this time, they are lifted up higher than Adam and Eve and made kings and priests in God's spiritual Kingdom. (Revelation 20:6) Their calling is to help expand and rule over God's spiritual Kingdom (which is done this time by serving others, as Jesus pointed out – see Matthew 20:25-28).

  Again, in order to do this job, we need *information.* We need to know the mind of God, his instructions and will, his purposes, his likes and dislikes. We need to know what the seat of the Kingdom is like (Heaven), and we need to know the ways we can carry out his will on earth. There is a tremendous amount of information that we need if we are to do our jobs well.

This information comes from the Bible, the Word of God. That's the reason that God gave us this book: so that we will know what his will is, what his Kingdom is like, what our place is in his plans, what our resources are, what we are called to do, and what only God can do.

> "No eye has seen, no ear has heard, no mind has conceived what God has prepared for those who love him"— but God has revealed it to us by his Spirit. The Spirit searches all things, even the deep things of God. For who among men knows the thoughts of a man except the man's spirit within him? In the same way no one knows the thoughts of God except the Spirit of God. We have not received the spirit of the world but the Spirit who is from God, *that we may understand what God has freely given us.* This is what we speak, not in words taught us by human wisdom but in words taught by the Spirit, expressing spiritual truths in spiritual words. (1 Corinthians 2:9-13)

The Spirit shows us the truth, which men have searched for throughout history and never found. Here, though, in the Bible, we find out what is really going on – God reveals the truth about ourselves, our world, about himself. We also see that other religions and philosophies have been deceiving us! This may sound narrow-minded, but it was Jesus himself who put us on to this idea: *"Your Word* is truth." (John 17:17)

So, if you want to see God, study the Bible. Spend time in it; learn it; meditate on it; master it; use it. Here is the information you need to fulfill your destiny as king and priest in God's Kingdom. You can't do your job to God's satisfaction without it. For example, here are a few passages that show how important it is to get God's wisdom: "I have hidden your Word in my heart that I might not sin against you." (Psalm 119:11) "Give me wisdom and knowledge, that I may lead this people, for who is able to govern this great people of yours?" (2 Chronicles 1:10) "My people are destroyed from lack of knowledge. Because you have rejected knowledge, I also reject you as my priests." (Hosea 4:6) "If you remain in me and *my words* remain in you, ask whatever you wish, and it will be given you." (John 15:17)

If you "meditate" on the Word of God, "by day and night" (Psalm 1:2), then expect to find the Spirit of God there. This is his testimony to you about the spiritual world of God. He is behind all the Bible, behind everything that every writer wrote and what every person saw and heard about God. The Spirit of God is the primary "eyewitness" to the reality of God, and he helps all of us to see and know God – from the Apostle Paul to the least saint in Christ's Church. He lives in this Book. He is ready to help you see God in it, if you come to him in the right way.

But remember that we *could* take matters in our own hands and try to drive this road without the help of the Spirit. Most people, sad to say, do this very thing. They know the Scriptures by heart; they know doctrine and theology; they can quote chapter and verse. Many of them are masters of the Bible. The trouble is, they have no spiritual understanding of any of it – and you can tell, because they aren't any closer to Heaven or more skillful in spiritual duties for all their knowledge. They aren't being made to look like Christ.

The Jews in Jesus' day were famous for this. Jesus uncovered their problem in a revealing condemnation:

> You have never heard his voice nor seen his form, nor does his word dwell in you, for you do not believe the one he sent. You diligently study the Scriptures because you think that by them you possess eternal life. These are the Scriptures that testify about me, yet you refuse to come to me to have life. (John 5:37-40)

They knew the Old Testament far better than we know our New Testaments today! But they were driving down the road of Scripture by themselves; turning their backs on the Spirit, they could only see what they wanted to see – not what God wanted to show them in the Bible. So for all their Biblical knowledge, they actually got farther away from Heaven!

We do this all the time, each in our own way. We are blind to certain subjects in the Bible, because we don't want to think about them or we were deceived about them by others. We form our own opinions that take the place of what the Bible teaches – so that instead of getting our knowledge about God from the Bible, we simply make up what we want our God to be instead. Or we will get off-balance, emphasizing one idea in the Bible so much that we ignore other important ideas that we also ought to be studying. And we often find ourselves reading the Bible for the wrong reasons: instead of coming to listen to God and receive whatever he says to us there, we search through it for support for our own special purposes, things that the Bible was *not* written for.

But in order to be led of the Spirit when we read the Bible, we must come humbly, ready to listen and learn, ready to throw out what we thought we knew and replace it all with new information – *his* information. When we come like this, the Spirit will do something for us that we could have never done on our own: he will make the world of God real, so much so that we will know the *certainty* of what we read about. He will let us taste the fruit of Heaven, and see the treasures waiting for us that Jesus talked about. We will see who Jesus really is – not a dead, historical figure that only exists in a dusty Bible, but a living Savior that is ready to do for us everything that we read about in the Biblical account of him. The Spirit makes this world of God come alive for us. When we read the Bible in the Spirit, we *know* (we can't prove it to anybody, but that doesn't make it any less real!) that there is a God and that it pays to live for him. (Hebrews 11:6)

And when we study the Bible in the Spirit, ready to be led and taught by him, he will show us what God thinks is important for us to know, not what many people *think* is important to know. For example, many people think that it's important to know one's system of doctrine, according to the denomination or local church or traditions handed down to them from the past. But the Bible tells us plainly that there are certain things that we *must* know in order to please God and be able to serve him faithfully – and usually these things aren't often taught in the local church! For a start, look at Psalm

105:1-11. This says that we must know about his Name, his works, his covenant with Abraham, his judgments, his miracles, and true worship. You will find that these are *not* topics in a standard theology textbook! And for that reason, very few people know much about these topics. But in order to please God, according to this passage, we must know a great deal about *these* subjects. Do you?

- ***Prayer and Worship*** – Obviously, if we want to get in touch with God, one of the primary ways of doing that is through prayer and worship. Now there are two ways to pray: you could either stay here on earth and try sending a message Heavenward, hoping that it gets there somehow; or you could deliver the message in person – right into the presence of God.

Ordinarily, people don't understand the second approach. Prayer to them means saying a formula, or even pouring out their heart with deep meaning and feeling – by *long distance*. They hope that their prayer reaches Heaven; but they don't know for certain that it does. But it really doesn't matter, because they are so used to praying in this way that they don't know that there is another way.

This is what I meant by driving by yourself. Many people pray, because they instinctively know that prayer is one of the roads to Heaven. What they don't know, however, is that in order to get there they have to turn control over to the Spirit and let him take them there.

This is so important that Paul counsels us –

Led by the Spirit

> Pray *in the Spirit* on all occasions with all kinds of prayers and requests. (Ephesians 6:18)

He knew that we can't hope to reach God in prayer without the Spirit leading us there.

"Praying in the Spirit" is a highly charged subject today due to the charismatic movement. We are not defining it here, though, as many do – visions, ecstatic utterances, prayer languages, etc. The answer is very straightforward and simple – we do it exactly as the Bible says. When you pray in the Spirit, this is what will happen: you will come into the presence of God. You won't be stuck on earth anymore; spiritually you will be lifted up and brought before God. You will see the Temple in Heaven, and the saints gathered there. You will hear continuous worship from the multitudes which surround God's throne.

> But you have come to Mount Zion, to the Heavenly Jerusalem, the city of the living God. You have come to thousands upon thousands of angels in joyful assembly, to the church of the firstborn, whose names are written in Heaven. You have come to God, the judge of all men, to the spirits of righteous men made perfect, to Jesus the mediator of a new covenant, and to the sprinkled blood that speaks a better word than the blood of Abel. (Hebrews 12:22-24)

Isaiah saw this. When the Spirit enabled him to enter Heaven, this is what he saw:

> In the year that King Uzziah died, I saw the LORD seated on a throne, high and

exalted, and the train of his robe filled the temple. Above him were seraphs, each with six wings: With two wings they covered their faces, with two they covered their feet, and with two they were flying. And they were calling to one another: "Holy, holy, holy is the LORD Almighty; the whole earth is full of his glory." At the sound of their voices the doorposts and thresholds shook and the temple was filled with smoke. "Woe to me!" I cried. "I am ruined! For I am a man of unclean lips, and I live among a people of unclean lips, and my eyes have seen the King, the LORD Almighty." (Isaiah 6:1-5)

The Apostle John was in the Spirit, we are told, when he saw Jesus in his glory:

On the Lord's Day I was in the Spirit ... I turned around to see the voice that was speaking to me. And when I turned I saw seven golden lampstands, and among the lampstands was someone "like a son of man." (Revelation 1:10, 12-13)

I hope you realize that you will experience the reality of Heaven only as you read his Word. The two go hand in hand. You can't see the true Heaven apart from the only revelation of Heaven; you can only hear God speak to you when you open the book in which he spoke to you. And it's not as if we must get a full-scale vision like the old prophets did; the Spirit stands ready to take *any* believer to Heaven, through the Word, and enlighten their minds and understanding with its reality. We *all* must worship this way. Jesus put it in a nutshell:

> Yet a time is coming and has now come when the true worshipers will worship the Father *in Spirit and truth*, for they are the kind of worshipers the Father seeks. God is Spirit, and his worshipers must worship *in Spirit* and *in truth*. (John 4:23-24)

We aren't prone to do things this way; we would rather pray and worship under our own power. What we usually do, therefore, since we can't see God or any part of his spiritual Kingdom, is focus on ourselves in prayer. (This is inevitable when we won't use the Bible as our prayer book.) We want God to come down to *us*. This comes out most clearly in our "Christmas lists" that we haul out during prayer. We naturally have our own interests at heart, and we want God to get started working on certain things in order to please us. In other words, we tell him what *we* want! We come up with the answers and expect him to get busy filling our list. This is always wrong. God is the Lord, we are his servants. If the Spirit were really leading us in prayer, we would come in humility before the King who is waiting for us to listen to *him* and be ready to do what he wants. Solomon taught us how to worship like this:

> Guard your steps when you go to the house of God. Go near to listen rather than to offer the sacrifice of fools, who do not know that they do wrong. Do not be quick with your mouth, do not be hasty in your heart to utter anything before God. God is in Heaven and you are on earth, so let your words be few. As a dream comes when there are many cares, so the speech of a fool when there are many words. (Ecclesiastes 5:1-3)

Another way we end up driving prayer and worship on our own is by insisting on certain rules and traditions made by men, as if "true worship" has to be done according to methods that *we* approve. This is obviously ridiculous. If there are a million churches in the world, and if we think that just *our* church is worshipping God in the only correct way, then 999,999 churches are doing false worship! That's not true. The rules of worship are made in Heaven, not on earth, and only the Spirit can show us what those rules are and enable us to follow them in a spiritual way. It's closer to the truth to say that a little of true worship happens in many churches around the world – usually in spite of man's traditions and efforts! We will discover that the outward practices that we've invented in our forms of worship do us little good in the spiritual court of Heaven, where flesh and blood can't go, and where all creatures must worship God *in Spirit*.

And we also show that we are doing the driving when we worship false gods. None of us in our Christian circles would claim to do such a thing, of course; we all take the name of Christ upon us and claim to be worshipping the one God. But think of this: if we say that our God is like such and such, but the Bible's description of him is different than what we say he is, how can we claim to be worshipping the Bible's God? Many people worship a "God" who allows sin, who doesn't do miracles for his people, who "helps those who helps themselves," who doesn't require a sacrifice for sin. This is *not* the Bible's God – therefore we can assume that the Spirit is *not* leading them in their prayers.

When the Spirit leads us in prayer and worship, we *see* what we hope in – the one true God. We can also expect to get answers. Those treasures in Heaven that we see through the Spirit are for us. Those are the answers for our prayers, waiting to be given out. Praying in the Spirit means that we get close enough to God to take what he has given us in Jesus. In other words, prayer done in the Spirit *will* get answers from Heaven, because that's what true prayer is all about.

In case you're worried about whether you *can* pray in the Spirit, God has that problem covered too. Of course we can't simply press a button that instantly turns our prayer into a spiritual success. Often when we pray, we feel anything but successful – we wonder if we're getting through to God at all. But if you come to him prepared to let him lead, prepared for what he has in store for you, then rest assured that he *will* make it work. Even if we don't know what to do, he will get us to Heaven and train us in how to act in God's presence:

> The Spirit helps us in our weakness. We do not know what we ought to pray for, but the Spirit himself intercedes for us with groans that words cannot express. And he who searches our hearts knows the mind of the Spirit, because the Spirit intercedes for the saints in accordance with God's will. (Romans 8:26-27)

- ***Walking in Faith*** – Christians are people of faith. One of the best known passages concerning this life of faith is found in Romans:

> For in the Gospel a righteousness from God is revealed, a righteousness that is by faith from first to last, just as it is written: "The righteous will *live by faith*." (Romans 1:17)

What isn't so obvious is what this means. Faith isn't just believing in a set of doctrines, or holding onto your religious beliefs with all your heart. If this is faith, then just about everyone would have faith – and be headed to Heaven! But we know that's not true.

Faith is living in the light of God's world. Until we have faith, we have no idea of the true nature of this world, or of our hearts, or even who God really is. We are blind and spiritually in the dark. But when God makes us alive in Christ, he makes our formerly-dead souls alive spiritually so that we can see now. We can see him, we can hear him, we know when he touches us. Spiritual things aren't hearsay for us anymore, but realities. We can't prove them to others who are still blind, but we know, nevertheless, that they are real.

> Faith is *being sure* of what we hope for, and *certain* of what we do not see. (Hebrews 11:1)

That is, we don't see them with our physical eyes, but with our new spiritual eyes. We see these things because the Spirit shines his light down from Heaven all around us. We are living in light, and we can see what is around us now. Now when we walk around, we know what dangers to avoid – we can see that they *are* dangerous and what they will do to us. We can see our spiritual brothers and sisters and pick them out from among the people we know. We know what they need, and we know that we can and ought to help them. We can see Jesus for what he is, and we know why we need him for all of our spiritual needs. We can see that God filled Jesus with treasures of Heaven. We can hear God speak to us in his Word – "The sheep ... know his voice." (John 10:4)

Walking by faith, in other words, is living according to certain spiritual realities that *you* can see, but others can't see. They are going to think you're crazy for being a Christian! It's because they don't have that faith, that ability to see God and his Kingdom, so naturally they will live in a different way. They are on the road to death and they don't know it. You are on the road to life and, by the mercy of God, you know that you are.

Again, I hope you realize that this can't happen unless you study God's Word (where that spiritual world is laid out before you) and are led by the Spirit (who reveals all spiritual realities to God's people). We keep coming back to this, don't we?

But there is a way of having "faith" without the Spirit's help; most people have this kind of "faith." They hold to a set of "beliefs" that they feel describe what they need to know to get along in life. They might have gotten it from their ancestors – a set of traditions, in other words – or they got it from their culture, or they came up with it on their own. Wherever they got it, they hold to it as Gospel truth. They think that if they faithfully stick to these beliefs then everything will turn out all right for them in the end.

That's not what the Bible describes as true faith, however. We know this because these people keep saying things that directly contradict what the Bible teaches! For instance, these misguided people feel very comfortable in this world, and have found ways to rely on the world in many ways and look to the world to fulfill their needs. But the Bible warns us with a revelation about the world:

> Do not love the world or anything in the world. If anyone loves the world, the love of the Father is not in him. For everything in the world — the cravings of sinful man, the lust of his eyes and the boasting of what he has and does — comes not from the Father but from the world. The world and its desires pass away, but the man who does the will of God lives forever. (1 John 2:15-17)

God has plans to destroy the world. There is nothing in the world that can help our souls, or even fulfill the great spiritual needs in our hearts. The world is full of darkness, deceit, wickedness, violence, death, destruction, failure and hopelessness. The world is enemy territory – God's people don't belong here! We are actually "aliens and strangers" as long as we are still in this world! (Hebrews 11:13; 1 Peter 2:11) Our home is Heaven, where Jesus has gone to prepare a place for us. (John 14:1-4) Only someone who lives by faith will see this.

Another way we turn our backs on the Spirit is when we try to control our own destiny, when we dream up what *we* want to do and then demand that God go along with our plans. We piously call this "living by faith" – meaning that we are going to believe, with all our hearts, that God will do what *we* want. But that isn't living by faith. "In his heart a man plans his course, but the LORD determines his steps." (Proverbs 16:9) The Spirit must lead us through life, putting us through trials and troubles that God has determined is for our good. He teaches us in his Word the things we are responsible to do, and gives us strength from Heaven to perform those duties faithfully. Only as we go where *he* tells us to go in life will he bless us with success.

The key to living by faith is to take advantage of what the Spirit has put at our disposal. Through the Word, and because of his promise to take us there, we are to –

> … set your hearts on things above, where Christ is seated at the right hand of God. Set your minds on things above, not on earthly things. For you died, and your life is now hidden with Christ in God. (Colossians 3:1-3)

When we have our eyes set on the things in Heaven, naturally our hearts will follow after. We will be working toward that, instead of things on earth. And that's what we want: there is life there with God, and only death here on earth.

You prove that your faith is genuine when you follow Christ's advice:

> Do not store up for yourselves treasures on earth, where moth and rust destroy, and where thieves break in and steal. But store up for yourselves treasures in Heaven, where moth and rust do not destroy, and where thieves do not break in and steal. For where

your treasure is, there your heart will be also. (Matthew 6:19-21)

This makes no sense to someone who can't see those treasures. And for those who like the sound of it, but still can't see it, they won't have any *certainty* that they are really doing the right thing and they might think longingly on the pleasures that they could have had from the world. But those who live by the Spirit can easily see what is in store for them in Heaven, and their walk through life (which often means doing without the pleasures of earth) is much easier in that light.

Walking by the faith that the Spirit gives means that we don't go by outward appearances. This world looks too good to pass up; its temptations are tempting, its treasures look valuable, its dangers appear frightening. But when we get true faith, we see that the world's treasures and temptations are empty promises that don't fulfill us. We see that dangers are toothless monsters that can do nothing to those protected by God. Paul describes it this way: "We live by faith, not by sight." (2 Corinthians 5:7) We don't go by what our physical senses tell us, but by what our spiritual senses tell us – since we are now spiritually aware of God's world.

- ***The Church*** – Amazingly, through good times and bad, there has always been a true Church. Tyrants have been unable to destroy it, and power and prosperity have been unable to permanently corrupt it. Not that the Church has always been in good spiritual health – it usually isn't – but its persistence is impressive proof of its divine birth.

Let's define our terms at the beginning, however, before we get confused. By the "Church" I mean the body of Christ, the true believers who have found eternal life in him. They are adopted children of God, marked out to be "kings and priests" in his Kingdom, and appointed to receive the inheritance of Heaven waiting for them. They were once like all wicked people, living in darkness and sin and death; but Christ saved them from that moral and spiritual disaster and, through the Spirit, is making them fit for eternal life in the presence of the holy God.

This isn't the same as the "churches" that we go to on Sundays. Members of the true Church attend these services, and sit next to people who aren't part of the true Church. What people mistakenly call "church" is usually a social event, or religious meeting, at which little if anything spiritual actually goes on.

This may sound harsh, but history bears out the picture. It's awful what has happened in the name of Christ's Church throughout history. True believers would never claim the ridiculous and painful episodes of churches doing what God never told them to do.

When a person becomes a Christian, he automatically becomes part of the Church of Christ – no matter where or when he lives in the world, no matter what his culture or race or sex or political stripe. And with that "membership" comes certain spiritual privileges: he is heir to God's promises, he is part of the family of God (with Jesus as our elder brother), he is marked to escape the destruction coming on the world, his sins are put away "as far as the east is from the west," and many more privileges.

But though these things are automatic, *living* in the Church isn't. It really takes a spiritual maturity to live with others who are in that same fellowship, which is one of the ironies of Christianity. Though we are new creatures, brothers and sisters under one Father, possessed of one Spirit and one faith, we can't seem to get along with each other! Where there ought to be peace, there is usually war and division. Often one has more enemies *in* the Church than outside of it!

The Bible says that God intends us to be *one body*. In Christ he united both Jew and Gentile to make one man. (Ephesians 2:14-18) As you would expect, then, Jesus told us to live as if we were one family: "My command is this: love each other as I have loved you." (John 15:12) And since God is love, "whoever does not love does not know God, for God is love." (1 John 4:8)

The trouble is that we can't possibly do this without the Spirit of God. So, to make the impossible happen, God sent his Spirit to dwell among us. It's *in the Church* that the Spirit lives and works among us. In one of the most beautiful images of the Old Testament, we see how God works on us:

> How good and pleasant it is
>   when brothers live together in unity!
> It is like precious oil poured on the head,
>   running down on the beard,
> running down on Aaron's beard,
>   down upon the collar of his robes.

> It is as if the dew of Hermon
>   were falling on Mount Zion.
> For *there* the LORD bestows his blessing,
>   even life forevermore. (Psalm 133:1-3)

Oil was a symbol of the Spirit, and Aaron represents the high priest – who is, for us, Jesus. The Spirit comes down on us from the Head, who is Christ. But look at what he says about eternal life – it will be found *in the body of Christ*, as the Spirit works among us. In other words, we can't continue to be loners, not if we want to get to Heaven. The road to eternal life is by way of the Church of Christ.

One of the most powerful ways that the Spirit works on us in the Church is through the spiritual gifts. They are listed for us in several places; here is one list:

> But to each one of us grace has been given as Christ apportioned it. This is why it says: "When he ascended on high, he led captives in his train and gave gifts to men." … It was he who gave some to be Apostles, some to be prophets, some to be evangelists, and some to be pastors and teachers, to prepare God's people for works of service, so that the body of Christ may be built up until we all reach unity in the faith and in the knowledge of the Son of God and become mature, attaining to the whole measure of the fullness of Christ. (Ephesians 4:7-13)

This passage also shows us *why* the Spirit gives gifts in the Church: to "prepare God's people for works of service." Do you remember that we were given a job to do in God's Kingdom? Here is how you will be trained to do that job! As others do their job for your spiritual benefit, you will grow enough to start doing your job for the benefit of others. It was for good reason that the Bible likens it to a living body: each part does its job for the benefit of the whole.

But the reason that this doesn't often happen in a local church is that people don't want to follow the Spirit when they "do church." They immediately take control away from the Spirit and do things their own way. Instead of listening to the Head of the Body – that is, Christ – and letting him run things, they assume that things won't get done unless *they* do it. So they volunteer for jobs that they have no spiritual skill for. They decide what the worship service will be like, even though little of it focuses on God or directs people toward him. They draw attention to themselves. They get followings, and they criticize everyone who won't join willingly in *their* program. They try to do the church's work in the ways that the world would go about things, instead of the ways that God likes to work.

They obviously don't have any trust at all that the Spirit knows how to run the Church! If they would do things God's way, and wait on God to provide what they need in a local church, much of the sin, ignorance and failure in our churches today wouldn't be happening. When God does things, they work; when *we* are running the show, however, nothing works – at least in a spiritual sense. For a while it may appear that we are achieving our purposes in our church programs, but it's only a superficial success and time will show how empty and powerless they were.

One of the surest ways to grieve the Spirit in the life of the Church is to say almost nothing about God and Christ in the service. For some reason, this spiritual shortsightedness seems to be rampant in today's churches. Take notes during a service and you will see what I mean. God's name is used a lot, but almost nothing is said *about* him. The emphasis is almost always, "*We* must do this, *we* must be this way, *we* must avoid sin, *we* must have faith, *we* must carry the cross, *we* must pray, *we* must persevere, *we* must trust in God." As you can see, the content of the message is *man*, not God. There is no salvation in that! When we worship, supposedly we are come together to meet *him* and to see *him*. The teaching, the preaching, the hymns, the testimony, the encouragement – all of it is supposed to uncover and reveal our God so that we can all see him more clearly. When that happens, then we see him well enough to know him and put our trust in him. That's what the Spirit does: he reveals God, and Christ our Savior. Without this revelation in church, we have no God and therefore no hope for our lives.

Jesus said that to *know God* is eternal life. (John 17:3) So tell me about him! What is he like? What does he do? What are his ways? What is his Kingdom like? When I learn something about God, *then* I know where I fit into his world. For example, if Paul would have written Ephesians 4-6 (our spiritual responsibilities) without first writing Ephesians 1-3 (knowledge about God in Christ) it would have made no sense, and we would have no hope of ever achieving such an impossible lifestyle.

One other way that people "do church" without the Spirit is to turn the whole thing into a social affair. They know down inside that they need "religion" in some form, and "religion" happens at church, so they go to church to get some "religion." But since true religion doesn't get into us this way, what results is just a time for gossip and play and politicking and conversations about everything under the sun except spiritual matters! This doesn't help us to grow spiritually, obviously, so we can assume that the Spirit has nothing to do with church meetings like this.

When Christians rely on the Spirit to make the Church work for them, spiritual impossibilities happen. People learn about God there; they see him at work there. They get trained in spiritual skills and go out into the world ready to work. They share God's concern for a lost and dying world. They hear about Heaven and see others living for the treasures of Heaven, and so are encouraged to do the same. They learn to love each other, they see precious children of God in each other, and they gladly do things for each other that may even cost them something. They get strong there – there is strength in unity – and successfully frustrate the work of the enemy, both in the Church and in the world where they live and work. And they become shining lights in the darkness, living witnesses to the power of God in a holy life.

A church led by the Spirit *works*. There isn't spiritual failure there, but success. It looks like this:

> As a prisoner for the Lord, then, I urge you to live a life worthy of the calling you have received. Be completely humble and

> gentle; be patient, bearing with one another in love. Make every effort to keep the unity of the Spirit through the bond of peace. There is one body and one Spirit — just as you were called to one hope when you were called — one Lord, one faith, one baptism; one God and Father of all, who is over all and through all and in all. (Ephesians 4:1-6)

If a church doesn't look like this, and *stay* like this, then the Spirit isn't leading them.

- **The Cross** – Now for the fatal flaw of our human nature. When we think that we have Heaven wrapped up, that we can have anything there that we want, that God will just let us cruise painlessly into his Kingdom without giving up anything along the way, along comes Paul with some bad news:

> I declare to you, brothers, that flesh and blood cannot inherit the Kingdom of God, nor does the perishable inherit the imperishable. (1 Corinthians 15:50)

God is Spirit, and whoever worships him must do it in Spirit and in Truth. (John 4:24) Heaven is spiritual, and all the inhabitants there are spiritual. Physical things can't exist in such a rarefied atmosphere; we would die from the lack of a physical framework to support us.

There's an additional problem. We were born into sin, so much so that we naturally follow the lusts of our flesh for everything we want. We are slaves to the temptations of the world, which deceive us and lead us into finding ways of fulfilling those lusts. But we were not originally designed to live like this! God made us to control the inclinations of our bodies and follow his instructions only, enjoying the physical world only within the limitations of his Law. But ever since Adam made the fateful decision to be ruled by his own feelings, desires and opinions, we turned our backs, collectively as a human race, on God and his will. Living according to what we want and feel has resulted in the misery and wickedness and death that constantly surrounds us.

Paul tells us plainly what our flesh leads us into:

> For the sinful nature desires what is contrary to the Spirit, and the Spirit what is contrary to the sinful nature. They are in conflict with each other, so that you do not do what you want ... The acts of the sinful nature are obvious: sexual immorality, impurity and debauchery; idolatry and witchcraft; hatred, discord, jealousy, fits of rage, selfish ambition, dissensions, factions and envy; drunkenness, orgies, and the like. I warn you, as I did before, that those who live like this will not inherit the Kingdom of God. (Galatians 5:17,19-21)

The solution is to crucify the flesh. This isn't good news; it means pain, suffering, trials, discipline, hard times. It means doing without what our flesh desperately wants. It means traveling a lonely road when others do exactly what they please, and putting up with their mocking. It means walking with Jesus, who suffered for his faith, and parting company with those who refuse to go to God for life.

Someone once described the flesh as being like a vicious dog. Feed it, and it will get stronger and meaner. But starve it, and it will grow weaker and eventually die – and cease to be a problem! That's what Paul meant when he said, "So I say, live by the Spirit, and you will not gratify the desires of the sinful nature." (Galatians 5:16) Quit feeding the flesh with the temptations that it wants, and it will lose the strength and power that it once had. Then the soul, fed by the Spirit from the Master's table in Heaven, will daily grow in strength to the point that we will be able and willing to live by God's will instead.

Many people know about the "cross" in life, but they are mistaken as to what it really means. They think that they have to take care of this matter of crucifying the flesh themselves – without God's help. You probably have heard about those who invent crosses to carry: they beat themselves, they give up something for Lent, they deny themselves legitimate blessings in life, they become hermits, they create new rules and conform to outward customs and traditions to set themselves apart from the world, and so on. But none of this works – it doesn't really please God, because it's all on the outside and does nothing to change our souls into the righteous person that he requires.

> Since you died with Christ to the basic principles of this world, why, as though you still belonged to it, do you submit to its rules: "Do not handle! Do not taste! Do not touch!"? These are all destined to perish with use, because they are based on human commands and teachings. Such regulations indeed have an appearance of wisdom, with

their self-imposed worship, their false humility and their harsh treatment of the body, but they lack any value in restraining sensual indulgence. (Colossians 2:20-23)

But when the Spirit is free to determine what our cross will be, it changes our souls. I like the image in Isaiah that talks about this:

> My loved one had a vineyard on a fertile hillside. He dug it up and cleared it of stones and planted it with the choicest vines. He built a watchtower in it and cut out a winepress as well. Then he looked for a crop of good grapes, but it yielded only bad fruit. (Isaiah 5:1-2)

God plants us as vines, in the soil of this world, and tends us as a gardener. He clears our hearts of the stones of sin and hardness to him. He builds a winepress – trials and troubles designed to squeeze our hearts – so that he can get good juice out of us (the fruit of the Spirit). Those troubles, in other words, are crosses that are specially designed to determine what we really are inside, spiritually. If we fail our test, we fail him. And unfortunately this is precisely where we often fail God – in how we handle the hardships of life that he takes us through.

We don't like to think that our problems are due to God's testing us, but it's true. We are his children! And in order to make us fit to live in his house, he has to trim the old nature from us, and clothe us in the righteousness of Christ. The writer of Hebrews puts the thing into perspective for us.

> Endure hardship as discipline; God is treating you as sons. For what son is not disciplined by his father? If you are not disciplined (and everyone undergoes discipline), then you are illegitimate children and not true sons. Moreover, we have all had human fathers who disciplined us and we respected them for it. How much more should we submit to the Father of our spirits and live! Our fathers disciplined us for a little while as they thought best; but God disciplines us for our good, that we may share in his holiness. No discipline seems pleasant at the time, but painful. Later on, however, it produces a harvest of righteousness and peace for those who have been trained by it. (Hebrews 12:7-11)

Paul tells us that "we know that in all things God works for the good of those who love him, who have been called according to his purpose." (Romans 8:28) It's a beautiful sight to see a Christian accepting the Spirit's leading and shouldering the cross that God provides. Someone who willingly and cheerfully accepts hardships as opportunities for spiritual growth is a wise Christian. They resemble Paul, who said –

> To keep me from becoming conceited because of these surpassingly great revelations, there was given me a thorn in my flesh, a messenger of Satan, to torment me. Three times I pleaded with the Lord to take it away from me. But he said to me, "My grace is sufficient for you, for my power is made perfect in weakness." Therefore I will boast all the more gladly about my weaknesses, so that

Christ's power may rest on me. That is why, for Christ's sake, I delight in weaknesses, in insults, in hardships, in persecutions, in difficulties. For when I am weak, then I am strong. (2 Corinthians 12:7-10)

However, you will often find that those who rely the most on their own outward signs of their religion will fall the hardest when God puts *his* crosses on them. Putting your trust in your own crosses will turn you into a spiritual wimp; naturally you will go easy on yourself, especially in those areas where you want the least interference. But that's the target that the Spirit aims for, and when he hits you with a cross that crucifies your favorite area you are really going to hurt! That's what separates the sheep from the goats.

You don't always have to get hit so hard, however – if you are used to following the Spirit, that is. If you already know that he wants you to put away a certain sin, then you can work *with* him in this instead of against him. If you fight him, he's going to come back with discipline and *make* you conform to God's righteous standards. But if you walk *with* him, then you'll know not to stray into areas that he doesn't approve.

> Dear friends, I urge you, as aliens and strangers in the world, to abstain from sinful desires, which war against your soul. Live such good lives among the pagans that, though they accuse you of doing wrong, they may see your good deeds and glorify God on the day he visits us. (1 Peter 2:11-12)

Just say no! You can avoid a lot of trouble from sin that way, and you'll avoid getting into trouble with God too. That's what Paul meant by "keeping in step with the Spirit." (Galatians 5:25)

Led by the Spirit?

To sum up, it's entirely possible *to try* to get to Heaven on your own. Many people try it, and fail. The reason they fail is because they reject the means of getting there, which God has graciously provided for us in the Spirit.

The Spirit knows how to get us to Heaven, and he is capable of getting us there safely and ready to enjoy the new world of God. He also knows that you must *change*: and there is a lot of work to be done on your soul before you are ready for Heaven. You aren't going to particularly like the ways he prepares you, but you have to submit yourself to his leading, wherever that takes you, knowing that God has your good at heart.

But for those who give up trying to get there on their own goodness and works, and give up trying to keep the Law on their own, living in the power and revelation of the Spirit is a refreshing change. Things work when he leads us.

The Church

For where two or three come together in my name, there am I with them. (Matthew 18:20)

In our day the concept of church means many things to many people. For example, church can mean a denomination – a collection of many congregations who all believe the same set of doctrines and think that other "assemblies" aren't real churches, or at least aren't functioning as God wants them to. To others, church means the local body of believers that meets together at stated times to worship God. The gathering itself, in other words, is the church coming together. To others, the church is the building where people meet to worship. Some have defined a church as any place where the Word is preached and the sacraments (baptism and the Lord's Supper) are observed.

And there are many reasons that people "go to church." Many go for the social interaction, the "fellowship" with other people – where they share either their spiritual experiences or (what's more likely) socialize around purely physical functions, like bingo or a bazaar. Others go because it's the tradition; the family that they grew up in always went to church, so they keep up the tradition in their own family. Others go because they have work to do there. Some go because it's a learning experience that they look forward to. Some like the ceremony at church – the acts of prayer, singing, and other ceremonies in the service make them feel closer to God. And there are some who get a "spiritual high" by being at church; they feel spiritually refreshed and ready to attack a new week out in the world.

If a person does "go to church," he must have some reason for doing it. It must fulfil some need in his life or he wouldn't bother doing it. In other words, the church experience, whatever it is, touches a deep felt need in the human heart.

There's the other side of the coin too. The church is full of problems, unfortunately. People will refuse to go to a particular church because it doesn't believe the right things. Or perhaps the church is cold and lifeless, and those looking for spiritual zeal and life are disappointed and leave empty. Another problem that ought not to be is the endless divisions and arguments that go on in just about every congregation; though Jesus said that the world would know us by our love, it seems that we are best known for our hatred and jealousy and anger and back-stabbing instead!

The Apostolic Church

Is there such a thing as a "perfect church?" Many people think not; they believe that there have to be many different kinds of churches, even churches that believe contradictory doctrines, to fill the needs of all kinds of people. The solution, they say, is to just move around from church to church until you find one that best suits your needs. And always remember that even *that* church won't be perfect.

That "solution" has never convinced me. Instead of promoting unity, we've come up with excuses for division. What we have now in our denominations and church splits is separation. This isn't what Paul told us to do:

> If you have any encouragement from being united with Christ, if any comfort from his love, if any fellowship with the Spirit, if any tenderness and compassion, then make my joy complete by being *like-minded*, having the same love, being *one* in spirit and purpose. (Philippians 2:1-2)

The Church

The early church knew nothing of denominations; in fact, there was basically only one "denomination" for more than a thousand years of church history. For all the problems that the Catholic Church had (and it had many!), it understood the importance of unity in the cause. At the very least, the Apostles certainly didn't promote the kind of division in the ranks of Christians that we have now. Our present state reflects the problem that was in the Corinthian Church, the "divisions" that Paul was concerned about:

> I appeal to you, brothers, in the name of our Lord Jesus Christ, that all of you agree with one another so that there may be no divisions among you and that you may be perfectly united in mind and thought. My brothers, some from Chloe's household have informed me that there are quarrels among you. What I mean is this: One of you says, "I follow Paul"; another, "I follow Apollos"; another, "I follow Cephas"; still another, "I follow Christ." (1 Corinthians 1:10-12)

It may sound simplistic to some, but the pattern for everything that God wants for his children is to be found in the Bible. Therefore it should be no surprise to us that **the Bible describes the normal church**. If, as we claim, the Bible is our infallible guide for faith and practice, then we must be willing to be taught how to carry on church. Just as the Bible teaches us how to walk in faith, or how to pray, or how to fight the enemy, it also teaches us what our churches should look like.

Many people object to using the Bible as the model for a church. They claim that it was an ideal, an extraordinary time in church history when the Spirit of God was working on earth setting up the church. Because it was a period of special activity, we shouldn't expect that this is the way church should always operate. In our day, they say, we shouldn't expect extraordinary things to happen.

But this ignores several facts: the people in the early church were flesh and blood just as we are. They were sinners like us. They weren't any more holy, or any less sinful, than we are. They were just as human and spiritually helpless as we are. They also had the Spirit of God given to them, but so do we – the same Spirit fills our hearts, and the same Spirit teaches us the same wisdom that they were taught.

Therefore, if they could have a powerful and living church, then I argue that we can too. There are going to be some differences – we don't have the Apostles around anymore, so some things aren't going to happen that could only occur in the presence of Apostles. But the purpose of the account of the church in the New Testament is to teach us what a real church ought, and in fact can, look like. If we have the same Spirit that the early Christians had, then this is not beyond our grasp – it's the promise of God to all his children.

To see the church as it ought to be, all we have to do is look in the book of Acts. There we find the new believers gathering together and doing these things:

> They devoted themselves to the Apostles' teaching and to the fellowship, to the breaking of bread and to prayer. Everyone was filled with awe, and many wonders and miraculous signs were done by the Apostles. All the believers were together and had everything in common. Selling their possessions and goods, they gave to anyone as he had need. Every day they continued to meet together in the temple courts. They broke bread in their homes and ate together with glad and sincere hearts, praising God and enjoying the favor of all the people. And the Lord added to their number daily those who were being saved. (Acts 2:42-47)

The Church

Now let's set these two churches – Apostolic and Modern – side by side so that we can easily compare the activities of the two.

Our church	**Apostolic church**
Social interaction, functions	Teach/Learn
Tradition	Fellowship (praising God)
To work/to learn	every day
Ceremony	Prayer
Get a spiritual high	Wonders/signs
	Break bread together every day
	Always together
	Had everything in common
	Sold land, property for needs
	Every day they met to worship
	New converts every day

Not all of us would admit to the fact that the left column describes *our* church completely, but still I think you can see a major problem shaping up here. Our church looks pretty tame compared to the Apostles' church. We try to pump up people's interest, and get them involved in church activities; the Apostles and their followers, however, were seized with the thrill and excitement of being involved in the greatest event of history. We are trying to revive interest in old stories; they were part of the story.

There have been times in history since the days of the Apostles when a church or several churches were caught up in a new excitement – we call this a "revival" – that resembled the experiences of the Apostolic church. They found something vital that changed their whole outlook on life, that gave them a new perspective on God and themselves. They discovered a spiritual reality that, until that point, people had only been talking about. When people suddenly meet God face to face, instead of sitting around and talking *about* God, they are no longer the same.

The Church

Suddenly they feel the overwhelming need to please God in all that they do; life will never be the same for them.

Those times of revival are what I call the "normal" church. Believers live in God's presence, and they take advantage of the open access to God through the Spirit. The church experiences that most of us go through, however, aren't "normal" any more than a starvation diet is normal. Our lack of faith, of zeal, of "good works prompted by love" is a sickness of the soul, a sign that we don't know what we're doing spiritually. In other words, if our church doesn't look like the Apostolic model, there is something dreadfully wrong with us. And to defend such a sad state in our churches is only confirming our sickness.

This means, then, that if our churches aren't operating according to the New Testament model, the problem *isn't* that it can't be done – it's because we *don't want* to do it that way. God has given us all the resources to have a church like theirs. If you think about how the early church did things, modern Christians probably would have problems in these areas:

- **We would have to give up too much.** The disciples willingly gave up houses, land, property, time (lots of it – they met daily with each other!) and who knows what else to make the church work. On the other hand, even though we're some of the richest people who ever lived in history, we often are the stingiest – we hate to give up even $10 for the collection plate!

- **We don't trust the Lord to make it work.** Jesus takes a personal interest in living churches. In Revelation we read that he watches over his churches, purges them of sin, teaches them the right things to do, gives his gifts to individual members for the benefit of the entire congregation, leads the group in certain directions by making known his will, and so on. We're not used to turning over control of church functions like that to someone else – not even to the Lord himself. We would rather run the church ourselves, according to our own opinions on what a church ought to be. This means, of course, that Jesus isn't the Lord in our churches – *we* are.

- **We don't want to make that kind of commitment to each other.** The early Christians *loved* each other. That's what motivated them to commit themselves totally to the church. They did this not only because the Lord expected them to, but because they loved each other so much that no amount of effort was too costly. Anything less than a deep commitment to each other can't produce a living, working, God-honoring church. But what is our usual attitude? We're only too glad that we don't have to spend more than an hour or two a week with each other!

The church that's described in the New Testament is a pattern for the rest of history. In other words, we ought to be able to have the same kind of church in our day. Many people think that this is an impossible dream. But I feel that we won't truly honor God, and we won't really get our needs met and our problems solved, nor will we be able to struggle against the world and win, unless we get our act together and have a church patterned after the original in the New Testament.

There's no reason in the world we can't have the same kind of church that the early Christians had. We have the same Lord, the same Spirit, the same Word of God, and we live in the same household of faith. (Hebrews 3:6) We are part of the same Body that they were part of.

> Make every effort to keep the unity of the Spirit through the bond of peace. There is one body and one Spirit — just as you were called to one hope when you were called — one Lord, one faith, one baptism; one God and Father of all, who is over all and through all and in all. (Ephesians 4:3-6)

The key to a vital, powerful church is this: **first** we need to learn what a church is. **Second**, we have to reorganize things in our churches so that the light from Heaven can shine through unobstructed. What seems impossible for us to do is possible with God.

What is the Church?

First we have to find out what a church really is. This will help us understand its workings, and what its goals really are, and how it will reach those goals.

The Old Testament, true to form, shows us the church in graphic reality. When Solomon built the Temple, he was building a replacement for the Tabernacle that the Israelites used to carry around with them during their wanderings in the desert. The Temple was the place where sinners could bring their animal sacrifices before God and be forgiven of their sins. It was also here that the priests would receive blessings and instructions from God and hand them on to the Israelites.

What made this system work, however, was that *God was there* in the Temple. They weren't praying to a God far away who couldn't hear what they were saying to him. God literally took up residence in the Temple:

> The LORD has said that he would dwell in a dark cloud; I have built a magnificent temple for you, a place for you to dwell forever. (2 Chronicles 6:1-2)

Of course Solomon understood that the Creator of the universe couldn't be contained by a little Temple on earth!

> But will God really dwell on earth with men? The heavens, even the highest heavens, cannot contain you. How much less this temple I have built! Yet give attention to your servant's prayer and his plea for mercy, O LORD my God. Hear the cry and the prayer that your servant is praying in your presence. May your eyes be open toward this temple day and night, ***this place of which you said you would put your Name there***. May you hear the prayer your servant prays toward this place. Hear the supplications of your servant and of your people Israel when they pray toward this place. Hear from Heaven, your dwelling place; and when you hear, forgive. (2 Chronicles 6:18-21)

By putting his Name in the Temple, he would – in the Spirit – be able to hear anybody who *called* on his Name. It was important, therefore, to the Israelites to turn to this Temple when they needed help from their God; that's where they could find him.

One more point about the Temple. Inside the heart of the Temple, in a special room (called the "holy of holies") sealed off by a heavy curtain, was the **ark of the covenant**. It was a gold-plated wooden chest that contained the original stone tablets that God first wrote the Law on and gave to Moses at Mt. Sinai. There were two golden statues of angels fastened at the two sides of the chest. Between the angels was the place where God sat. In other words, the ark was the throne of God as he sat among his subjects, in his Kingdom of Israel. Here is where all the sacrifices and prayers focused – at the throne of God on earth.

This entire picture that we have in the Old Testament was a symbol of the reality that we now have in New Testament times. The point is this: *God lives among his people.* They knew God was there, on his throne, ruling and blessing them. When the priests entered the Temple in Solomon's day, God made it known to them that he was really there:

> Then the temple of the LORD was filled with a cloud, and the priests could not perform their service because of the cloud, for the glory of the LORD filled the temple of God. (2 Chronicles 5:13-14)

When the Israelites left Egypt, Moses told them that it was God who was leading them through the wilderness. If they were like us, they probably wondered at times whether it wasn't just Moses' imagination that God was really there with them – especially when they wandered through a desert with no food or water! It was for that reason that God proved to them that he was there:

> After leaving Succoth they camped at Etham on the edge of the desert. By day the LORD went ahead of them in a pillar of cloud to guide them on their way and by night in a pillar of fire to give them light, so that they could travel by day or night. Neither the pillar of cloud by day nor the pillar of fire by night left its place in front of the people. (Exodus 13:20-22)

When God got disgusted with the Israelites and their many sins, he sometimes did what he knew would be the worst thing that could ever happen to the people of God: *he left them.* For example, when he decided to send his people off to Babylon in exile, he revealed to the prophet Ezekiel the real tragedy of the Israelites – his Presence left the Temple, in fact left the entire city of Jerusalem. To a discerning Jew it was a terrible punishment: since the Lord was no longer in the Temple, there could be no forgiveness of sin, no blessings for the people, no direction or Word from God. Since the Lord even left the city, the people of God were left defenseless before the invading Babylonian army.

The Church

You can read about the gradual withdrawal of the Presence of God in Ezekiel 1-11.

One more example: once when the Israelites had again angered God, he let the Philistines defeat them in battle. The loss was so great that the enemy even captured the ark of God, which was the heart of the Israelite religion. The wife of one of the sons of Eli heard about the terrible defeat; even though she had just lost her husband in battle, and the Israelites had lost the fight, she realized the true magnitude of what happened. She gave her newborn son this name:

> She named the boy Ichabod, saying, "The glory has departed from Israel"— because of the capture of the ark of God and the deaths of her father-in-law and her husband. She said, "The glory has departed from Israel, for the ark of God has been captured." (1 Samuel 4:21-22)

In our day, however, God doesn't sit on a physical throne. God is in Heaven, because his spiritual Temple where we worship now is in Heaven. But when we worship God, we find ourselves in the presence of God. The church service itself becomes an open door into God's throne room. God himself comes among us, just as real as when he sat on his throne among the Israelites.

> For where two or three come together in my
> name, there am I with them. (Matthew 18:20)

Worship brings us into the throne room of God where we can see him, hear him, and be transformed by his touch. Hebrews describes what happens to us every time we worship him as a church:

> But you have come to Mount Zion, to the Heavenly Jerusalem, the city of the living God. You have come to thousands upon thousands of angels in joyful assembly, to the church of the firstborn, whose names are written in

Heaven. You have come to God, the judge of all men, to
the spirits of righteous men made perfect, to Jesus the
mediator of a new covenant, and to the sprinkled blood
that speaks a better word than the blood of Abel.
(Hebrews 12:22-24)

Do you see these things when you are in a church service? Whether you do or not, it's happening – if you "worship by the Spirit of God." (Philippians 3:3) It *has* to happen if you hope to present your requests to him, or get anything from him.

And just as in the Old Testament, Jesus thinks that the worst thing that could possibly happen to a church is if *he left them*. He threatens to do that to churches that aren't listening to him.

Repent and do the things you did at first. If you do
not repent, I will come to you and remove your
lampstand from its place. (Revelation 2:5)

We can summarize all of this by saying that –

The Church is where God lives and rules among his people.

Now if God is at our church, we ought to be able to see evidence of that. He isn't our imagination, and he isn't just a story. He's a *living* God who insists on changing our world and us. There ought to be things happening in a church that can't be accounted for in any other way except God is there doing the things that only God can do.

The reason this is such a radical way of understanding what a church really is, is because we are so used to defining a church around what *we* do, not what God does. If we gather together, we call that a church; if we preach and teach and offer the sacraments, we call that a church; if we worship, we call that a church. But really a church is a spiritual meeting between God and his people. We don't (or shouldn't!) do these things in order to *find* God; these church functions happen *because* God is there. Our man-centered definition of a church hopes that God will be there, but can't guarantee it; that's why it often doesn't work. A God-centered definition of a church expects great things to happen because the Creator and Redeemer has called together his people for the purpose of doing great things among them. There's a lot of difference.

The Body of Christ

Let's dig deeper into Scripture to see how the presence of God transforms an ordinary social event into a dynamic encounter with God. The place to start, of course, is with the Lord Jesus Christ.

Paul develops this idea the most clearly for us. He states that the Church is literally the body of Christ, and he is the Head of the Church:

> Now you are the body of Christ, and each one of
> you is a part of it. (1 Corinthians 12:27)

> And he is the head of the body, the church; he is the beginning and the firstborn from among the dead, so that in everything he might have the supremacy. (Colossians 1:18)

This means, of course, that we are **one** people – not many. Jesus pulls us together to make us all one. The life we have from Christ comes by way of the Holy Spirit, which all Christians have. It's a way that the Lord "standardizes" all Christians, so to speak; he stamps us with the same mold. That's why you will often find that, when you meet strangers and find out they are Christians, you immediately feel one with them and you know that you both share a common life in the Lord.

Our union with him is *mystical* – meaning that extraordinary things happen to us because we are literally one with him, even though it appears on the surface that he's far away and we're still alone in this world. Whatever Jesus lived through, we also experience. For example, he lived such a righteous life that the Law could say nothing against him: he was the perfect man as the Law understands it. Now we share his righteousness because he made us one with him. Another point: he was crucified on the cross for our sins, and God released him from the burden of that sin in his death. Now we, because we are one with Christ, find our own burden and yoke of sin broken from our necks – we don't have to serve sin anymore because we also have been crucified to sin. One more point: Jesus was raised from the dead and he ascended to Heaven, to sit at God's right hand. Now we, because we are one with him, find ourselves (in the Spirit) able to rise above this world and see God. Nothing can hold us back from him.

This unity with the Son of God can happen because we are a *new creation*:

> Therefore, if anyone is in Christ, he is a new creation; the old has gone, the new has come! (2 Corinthians 5:17)

We should expect new and exciting things to happen because of our rebirth into Christ. From now on, the kind of life that one would ordinarily only see in the rarified atmosphere of Heaven will fill the church and make it an unearthly place – a "new Jerusalem" that comes out of Heaven to rest on earth. "The Kingdom of God is near!" (Mark 1:15)

But a body needs a head to manage things. The Church – no matter where on earth we find it – has only one Head: Jesus Christ. He's the Master, the Lord, the King of kings, the one to whom God the Father has given all authority and power. He manages his church the way he wishes. And that leads us to an extremely important point about how a local church operates: if Christ really is the Head of the church, *that should be easy to see*. People won't be making the important decisions, and people won't be doing the important work. Those are things that the Lord reserves to himself alone.

For example, who is responsible for deciding who the teachers in a church will be?

> But to each one of us grace has been given as *Christ* apportioned it ... It was *he* who gave some to be Apostles, some to be prophets, some to be evangelists, and some to be pastors and teachers. (Ephesians 4:7,11)

In other words, he chooses his own workers; he doesn't leave that decision up to us. As Head he reserves full responsibility for the work that goes on in his church. So how do we honor his authority in this matter? Too often we call for volunteers! As if such important work can be given to anybody, skilled or unskilled. Or we pick the person we like the best, or whoever is most popular, or (worse yet) a leader in the affairs of the world. This dishonors our Head because we're taking his responsibilities away from him and running the church the way we see fit. Instead, what we ought to do is find out who the Lord *already* gave those gifts to – in other words, find out those who are already using those gifts to some degree – and recognize the Lord's calling on them by making them our teachers. In this way we *follow* the Lord's leading instead of grabbing the reins out of his hands.

The early church understood this principle. When the church at Antioch needed missionaries, they didn't immediately select some of their members and send them out. They went to God and asked him for *his* will:

> While they were worshiping the Lord and fasting, the Holy Spirit said, "Set apart for me Barnabas and Saul for

the work to which I have called them." So after they had fasted and prayed, they placed their hands on them and sent them off. (Acts 13:2-3)

In other words, when the church put their hands on Barnabas and Saul (or Paul), it was recognizing what the Lord himself had *already* decided. For all we know, these two men would not have been the first choice of Antioch's elders!

Another example: often when preachers and teachers present the claims of God to church members, they "browbeat" the people into submission. They shame people, and belittle them, and threaten them with punishment from God if they don't obey. The leaders who do this are actually taking over the church as their little domain, over which they are responsible. They are "micro-managing" people's lives. The people end up fearing the leader instead of God. It's easy for this to happen when the leader has a strong, domineering personality, and the people are like sheep in his hand. He ends up ruling over them as much as any king might do in a kingdom.

The problem with that is that only Jesus is Lord in the church. People have no business fearing man; they must obey Christ and his commands. The leaders are charged with carrying Christ's word to his people and then leaving it at that. No browbeating, no threats – just present it and then *back off*. The reason is simple: these Christians belong to Jesus, not to them. If they obey or if they don't obey, it's the Lord's business alone. The leader is only responsible for the part that Christ has given him. And if people don't listen, the leader's *only* option under God is to be patient and try again. Notice Paul's attitude toward those who may not agree with his teaching – even though he has the authority of an Apostle!

All of us who are mature should take such a view of things. And if on some point you think differently, that too God will make clear to you. Only let us live up to what we have already attained. (Philippians 3:15)

The situation becomes even plainer when we read in Scripture that the Church is actually the bride of Christ:

> To this John replied, "A man can receive only what is given him from Heaven. You yourselves can testify that I said, 'I am not the Christ but am sent ahead of him.' The bride belongs to the bridegroom. The friend who attends the bridegroom waits and listens for him, and is full of joy when he hears the bridegroom's voice. That joy is mine, and it is now complete. He must become greater; I must become less." (John 3:27-30)

A husband is jealous for his wife. He may want a friend of his to deliver a message to his wife, and the message may even be a solemn warning. But woe to that friend who makes the mistake of taking that man's wife in hand and beating her! The husband in his rage will not listen to him, no matter what excuses he gives. So it is with Christ and his bride. Conviction for sin, the need for repentance, the motivation to love God and be holy before him – all this comes by the work of the Holy Spirit upon a sinner's heart. No preacher or teacher has the right or the ability – or the calling – to force that conviction to happen. It's true that wayward Christians will pay dearly for disobedience, but they aren't going to answer to church leaders for their sins – only to God.

> The man who eats everything must not look down on him who does not, and the man who does not eat everything must not condemn the man who does, for God has accepted him. *Who are you to judge someone else's servant?* To his own master he stands or falls. And he will stand, for the Lord is able to make him stand. (Romans 14:3-4)

These are a couple of examples of taking seriously the presence of the Lord among us; we could list many more. Jesus isn't an irresponsible leader; he's going to lead us in real ways. The wise among us will see him leading his people, and give him room to do just that. If we can learn the difference between his work and our work, that gives tremendous freedom to the Spirit to operate among us. And of course when we don't learn that, we are always getting in his way, trying to do his work for him (which of course we can't do successfully, only he can!) and the church fails.

The purpose of a Church

When we know what the church *is*, we can then know what the church is supposed to *do*. And when we know what it's supposed to do, we can set up a way of measuring whether it's actually doing it. In other words, we can tell the difference between a successful church and a failure by the results.

We saw that the church is where God lives among his people. His presence there makes it special from any other type of organization or movement. His works add a miraculous, Heavenly touch to the life of the church; things happen in church that can't be accounted for in any way except that God did them. God, in other words, is on center stage, so to speak, as the first and key figure; what happens in the church is primarily his work. We are only providing support services as his servants.

This truth helps us to see what *must happen* in a church:

- **God must get glory** – The word "glory" means this: who gets the credit? In other words, when something happens, who was responsible? Who was the one behind the scenes who made it happen?

    The unique kinds of things that happen in a church, that make it a powerful force in people's lives, have to come from God's hand alone. He converts people, he saves them from their sins, he opens their eyes to the realities of Heaven, he makes them holy, he leads them along the right ways to Heaven, he heals their diseases and makes them whole inside, he protects them from the enemy, he gives them spiritual weapons and trains them in their use, as well as many other things. God is behind every event of importance that happens in the church.

But does God get credit for any of this? Do the people even know that these kinds of things are going on in the church? Usually certain people get credit for things, even in church – and that's because it's often the case that the Lord isn't doing much in their church anyway – they won't let him. And when God does do something, it usually isn't published or made known; many churches have no effective way of getting that news out to the congregation.

There are ways of getting this news of God's work out among the people. Just as a business needs to advertise its products, so in the church we have methods of letting people know what God has done. For example, the **songs and hymns** that we sing are usually full of praise for specific acts that God does for us. In fact, even if the preaching and teaching ministry is woefully lacking on giving God credit for anything, the hymns almost always display God prominently to everyone. Next time you sing a hymn, notice *what* it talks about: you will almost always find it teaching and explaining something about God to you.

Prayer is another way of giving God glory, of putting him on center stage, so to speak. Whoever prays – if he prays in a way to honor God – will call on God by Name, because the name describes what God is and does. He wants a specific God who does specific things. He has heard from Scripture what God will do for his people, so he prays for that. In other words, he is lifting up his hands helplessly to God who alone can do what we need, as a child turns to a Father for help.

Sermons and Bible lessons – here's an area that churches are typically weak in. Let's be as simple and plain as we can be here: the point of the ministry of a church is to *glorify God*. In other words, what people need to hear in a sermon or Bible lesson is who God is and what he does. This is information that leads to life. When people hear something about God that they need, that makes them respond in hope (they turn to God and ask for it!) and faith (they trust God to keep his promises). Giving God glory works the same way as advertising: people want what they hear about, when it promises to fulfill their needs.

What too often happens, however, is that preachers and teachers talk about everything but God! They talk about man, about our responsibilities, about our duties, about our needs, about our opportunities – and little or nothing about God. They use his name frequently in their lessons, but there's little hard information about him for us to go on. *There's no life in a ministry like that.* What people need to hear is news about their God, about what *he* can and will do for them.

Some churches have an opportunity for giving **personal testimonies**. Testimonies are powerful tools for glorifying God, but again only if the focus is on what *God* has done. A witness (which in Greek is from the same word that "testimony" comes from) tells what he has seen or heard. The witness was there when something happened; his testimony, therefore, isn't a doctrinal treatise or book analysis; it doesn't require great learning. He simply tells us what he saw God do. This also convinces people that there really is a God and they can go to him for the same things. And that's the reason for giving God glory: he wants the news about him to spread around, to draw more sinners to him for salvation, and saints to him for spiritual life.

Another testimony that we make to the world as well as to the community are the **sacraments** – that is, baptism and the Lord's Supper. However your church carries out these ceremonies isn't important here; the point is that they are specially designed to be public statements of spiritual realities. Baptism symbolizes our union with Christ, being dead to the world and alive to God through the washing and indwelling of the Holy Spirit. Communion symbolizes our eating the Bread from Heaven and drinking the wine of the blood of Christ for our cleansing from sin. These are sermons in themselves, speaking volumes about what we believe about Christ's work for us with hardly a word being spoken.

- *We are witnesses* – One of the jobs that God has called us to do is to be his witnesses among the nations. (Acts 1:8) As we said above, a witness testifies to the reality of God and his work on our behalf. But not only do we testify to God's power and wisdom by our *words*, we are living witnesses to his reality by our *lives*. In other words, when God does powerful things for us and solves our problems, the rest of the world sits up and takes notice: they've never seen a God who does things like that for his people.

For example, the first and greatest miracle in a person's life is **conversion**. At first Christians start out like everyone else – they are dead to God, dead to righteousness, slaves of sin, filled with ignorance, and helplessly led around by the Enemy. But when Jesus breaks the bonds of death on their lives, they are transformed into new living creatures. Suddenly, with apparently no explanation, they know God. They can see him and his glory. They love God so much that they willingly leave their life of sin behind to pursue his righteousness. They aren't slaves to sin anymore; they are free now to serve God alone. The transformation is so amazing that people who knew them before their conversion are left wondering how in the world such a change could come over them. *That's* a testimony: God did something that everyone can see.

> You yourselves are our letter, written on our hearts, known and read by everybody. You show that you are a letter from Christ, the result of our ministry, written not with ink but with the Spirit of the living God, not on tablets of stone but on tablets of human hearts. (2 Corinthians 3:2)

Another testimony is when God answers our **prayers**. Unbelievers think that there is no God who can help us, and weak Christians think God could but won't help us. Then along comes a

Christian of faith who lays firm hold on what he sees in Jesus – and he won't let go until the Lord blesses him. God honors faith like that; he will give that person whatever he asks of him. Then when the answer comes, everyone is surprised and suddenly interested in a God who apparently answers prayer! *That's* a testimony: God listens to his children's pleas and gives them concrete answers to their needs. Answers to prayer are often more powerful testimonies to God's reality than the most eloquent arguments; after all, who can argue against real results?

Another powerful testimony to the reality of God in a church are the **fruits of the Spirit**. In Galatians, Paul lists the characteristics of typical sinners and then of real Christians:

> The acts of the sinful nature are obvious: sexual immorality, impurity and debauchery; idolatry and witchcraft; hatred, discord, jealousy, fits of rage, selfish ambition, dissensions, factions and envy; drunkenness, orgies, and the like. (Galatians 5:19-21)

Unfortunately this kind of behavior comes naturally to people; you will find them everywhere you go in this world. But in the church, because the Spirit is there in people's hearts transforming them to look like Christ, you find these behaviors instead:

> But the fruit of the Spirit is love, joy, peace, patience, kindness, goodness, faithfulness, gentleness and self-control. (Galatians 5:22-23)

When people who used to do nothing but fight among themselves actually love each other, and give of themselves for the benefit of others, that's something to sit up and take notice of! It's a testimony to the reality of the Spirit working among the people of God.

- ***God wages war against the world*** – Another thing that *must* happen in a church – if God really is in it – is war against the world.

In order to understand this, we have to clearly define our terms. God made the world and everything in it; and as its Creator he naturally takes a special interest in how well everything is working. He loves his creatures – the Scripture tells us that he provides for the needs of his creatures daily. (Psalm 145:15-16)

But man the sinner has taken God's creation and twisted it to his own ends. Instead of accepting the way God has made things, and ruling over the world to maintain God's created order (the charge that God gave man in the beginning), man immediately set about to change the world to suit his own perverted desires instead. Now what we have is a world full of rebellion, ignorance, wickedness, suffering, and death. The world that we've formed for ourselves is the opposite of what God intended in Creation. It's this world that God hates, the creation of Satan and man who work in cooperation to remove God's rule from the earth. (1 John 2:15-17)

Naturally God isn't going to let this challenge to his authority and wisdom go unnoticed. He first gathers warriors together (his church) and arms them for conflict: he delivers them from the world – by taking away their love for it, and putting a love for God's Kingdom in their hearts. Now they will fight for eternal treasures instead of earthly ones. Then he gives them weapons that the enemy doesn't have: love, the Bible, righteousness, peace, all the pieces of armor that are listed in Ephesians 6. Last, he makes them skilled in fighting the enemy: he trains them in the ways of the enemy and how to "demolish strongholds." (2 Corinthians 10:4)

Then the fight begins. God's warriors go out into the world and, one by one, win enemies over to God's side. Evangelism, good works, witnessing, preaching the truth, prayer – in the hands of God's people, all these weapons and skills force the Enemy to yield ground and lose his slaves to the Kingdom of Light. The growth of the church over the centuries has been irresistible. In spite of the enemies of God and all their assaults on God and his Word, Christianity has grown and prospered – it always will.

- ***We are Priests in God's Temple*** – One of the responsibilities that God has laid on each of us in the church is to take care of the others in the group. All of us, even though we are now converted and in God's Kingdom, continue to suffer with burdens, temptations and many needs both physical and spiritual. And instead of having to deal with all of these problems alone, the Lord graciously gave us each other to help bear these burdens together.

People already know that cooperation and working together make things go a lot easier. "Many hands make light work." "Two heads are better than one." But for some reason, when it comes to the church, people are reluctant to get involved with each other. Maybe it's because it requires time and money; or it will mean getting emotionally involved with people who are hurting, when we can hardly handle the stresses of our own lives.

In the church, however, we have a situation that's surprising. In order to understand it, we have to look back at the Old Testament system with its priests. The priest served God in the Temple. His job was to bring the sacrifices of the people to the throne of God to get God's forgiveness for the sins of the people. Then he would take God's blessings (that is, the very things that he asked for) from the Throne of Grace back to the people.

We in the church have been formally called to be priests for God's people:

> To him who loves us and has freed us from our sins by his blood, and has made us to be a kingdom and *priests* to serve his God and Father. (Revelation 1:5-6)

This is our calling as Christians, as members of the congregation of Christ. Our job is to carry the needs of our brothers and sisters to the Throne of Grace and intercede for them. We are required to "carry each others' burdens" because our brothers and sisters need that help. (Galatians 6:2) God helps them *through us*; our ministry, even when giving a cup of cold water in Jesus' Name, is the very hand of Christ touching the lives of his people. (Matthew 10:42) We could quote passage after passage about our duty to love each other and help each other; we all know our duty. What we may not have seen yet is that God *expects* us to show up with these concerns at his Throne; he's waiting to honor our requests that we make on behalf of others. We are his official priests assigned to work for the well-being of our brothers and sisters in the faith.

Here is the source of answered prayer! When we take our jobs seriously and "look to the interests of others" (Philippians 2:4) then God is pleased to give us what we ask for.

How the Church works

If you've followed the point up to now, you can see that there are certain things that *must* happen in a church in order to fulfill its calling:

- **We must be able to see God**
- **Christians must help each other**
- **We must be fortified against the enemy**

How do we go about making sure that these things happen in a church? Fortunately we don't have to wonder about it; God in his wisdom has already drawn up blueprints for a successful church. Not only has he drawn up the blueprints, but he insists on setting up the system himself so that he can make sure it will work to his satisfaction. Our responsibility is to stay out the way as he sets it up – he doesn't want us to mess things up with our opinions, solutions, skills or vain works. Once he has it set up the way he likes, he wants us to take our places and work *within* the system he made. If we do that, we acknowledge that *he* is the Lord and *he* must keep the church running, not we. We only support him as he calls us to serve him in various capacities. And that's as it should be in a Kingdom.

How does the Lord structure the church to make it work?

- ***The Holy Spirit*** – Jesus took care of his disciples while he was on the earth, but he knew that they would still need help after he was raised from the dead and returned to Heaven. So the first thing he did when he ascended to the Throne in Heaven was to send them the Spirit (which he had promised them earlier – see John 14:16-18). At Pentecost, when they were in a room together worshiping, the Spirit came on them in power:

> When the day of Pentecost came, they were all together in one place. Suddenly a sound like the blowing of a violent wind came from Heaven and filled the whole house where they were sitting. They saw what seemed to be tongues of fire that separated and came to rest on each of them. All of them were filled with the Holy Spirit and began to speak in other tongues as the Spirit enabled them. (Acts 2:1-4)

The reason he sent his Spirit to the church was to take care of them with the resources of Heaven. From now on, Christians can tap into Heaven's power, Heaven's wisdom, and Heaven's righteousness. It's important that we are able to do this, because we have nothing in this world that can enable us to please God or build his Kingdom. We literally need help from God's throne in order to carry out our calling as God's people.

Remember that the demands on individual Christians, and the church as a whole, are greater than we can handle on our own. We have a skilled and treacherous Enemy who can easily destroy us if we don't turn to God for help against him. We have a task of working on an eternal

Temple, making it out of the lives of God's people – and it has to last forever. How can we do such a thing without wisdom from God? For that matter, we've been called to be citizens of Heaven, who look forward to living there forever. How do we find our way there? What should we do to prepare our hearts for that kind of life?

So the Lord sent us the Spirit so that we can overcome all of our problems, easily defeat the enemy, crucify the sin in our hearts once and for all, learn the ways of God so that we can be pleasing to a perfect Judge, and in wisdom and understanding build up the Kingdom of God to the Lord's exacting specifications. Without the Spirit we could never do anything the Lord expects of us; with the Spirit, we can't fail.

- ***Spiritual gifts*** – As we have already seen, God expects us to help each other in the church. But how do we help others when we don't even know how to help ourselves? How can I do more than God can do for them? Shouldn't church members be turning to God for help? What use is it to turn to weak and sinful men?

But we mustn't forget the Spirit of God, who was sent to the church to enable people to do the impossible. Jesus told his disciples that they would be able to do amazing things through the Spirit:

> I tell you the truth, anyone who has faith in me will do what I have been doing. He will do even greater things than these, because I am going to the Father. (John 14:12)

That statement "because I am going to the Father" refers to the fact that, once on the Throne of Heaven, he would send out his Spirit – the Spirit of power and wisdom, the very Spirit of Christ himself.

What this means is that ordinary men and women would suddenly find themselves capable of doing extraordinary acts. The disciples found that they could preach and get thousands of converts! They touched the sick and they were healed. They formed churches, they turned pagans back to their Creator, they resisted the enemy and threw him back in defeat. Ordinary, unlettered fishermen suddenly knew strange languages and could pin experts in the Law to the wall with the claims of the Gospel. Others who knew what these men really were, were amazed – they said of them, just as they did their Master, "where did these men get their learning?" The world didn't know what to do with these miraculous works.

The entire church is designed this way, however. The early church wasn't the ideal; rather it was the picture of the *normal* church. Jesus also sends us the Spirit so that *we* can do extraordinary works. Each believer is given a spiritual gift that enables him or her to build the spiritual Kingdom of God on earth.

> I tell you the truth, anyone who has faith in me will do what I have been doing. He will do even greater things than these, because I am going to the Father. (John 14:12)

> But to each one of us grace has been given as Christ apportioned it. This is why it says: "When he ascended on high, he led captives in his train and gave gifts to men" ... It was he who gave some to be Apostles, some to be prophets, some to be evangelists, and some to be pastors and teachers, to prepare God's people for works of service, so that the body of Christ may be built up until we all reach unity in the faith and in the knowledge of the Son of God and become mature, attaining to the whole measure of the fullness of Christ. (Ephesians 4:7-8,11-13)

You can find what those gifts are by studying the following passages: Romans 12:6-8; 1 Corinthians 12:7-11; Ephesians 4:11; 1 Peter 4:10-11.

- *Fellowship* – Most people like to socialize; in fact, that's why many people like to go to church – to socialize with other Christians. But we have to be careful here, lest we confuse "fellowship" with "socializing." The two aren't the same.

Fellowship is spending time with each other to share the spiritual treasures we have in Christ. It's like socializing, with one important difference: instead of talking about families and ball games and politics and business, we talk about Scripture and God's Names and the promises of God and the Kingdom. Instead of putting our eyes on "things below," we look together at "things above." (Colossians 3:1-2)

The Church

I liken it to sitting down together at a feast. God has already laid the feast out for us – the treasures in Heaven, the fullness of the Godhead in Christ, the rich Names of Jesus throughout the Bible – it's endless, the table that God has laid out for us in this wilderness world. When Christians gather around this table to worship and pray and discuss the spiritual Kingdom, the possibilities that the Spirit of God has to build us up in the faith are enormous!

But we won't benefit from these treasures unless we come to the feast. Jesus told the story about those who were invited to God's feast – but they had all sorts of excuses why they couldn't come! Strange as it may seem, they didn't want what God offered them. So, Jesus says, "not one of those men who were invited will get a taste of my banquet." (Luke 14:24)

God intends to bless the assembly, in ways that individuals won't be able to experience on their own. The Old Testament has a beautiful picture of what God does in the midst of his people when they come together in his Name:

> How good and pleasant it is
>   when brothers live together in unity!
> It is like precious oil poured on the head,
>   running down on the beard,
> running down on Aaron's beard,
>   down upon the collar of his robes.
> It is as if the dew of Hermon
>   were falling on Mount Zion.
> For *there* the LORD bestows his blessing,
>   even life forevermore. (Psalm 133)

Notice that the passage says the Lord will pour out his blessings on the church – through the gifts of the Spirit, of course. Anybody who wants to taste the spiritual blessings of God must come together with the church of Christ.

The point of all this is that God wisely set up the church in such a way that, if we cooperate with him, it *has* to succeed. If we work along with him, and take advantage of the way he structured the church, it can't fail. God will be free to work among us, so powerfully that it will be obvious to everyone who it is that is really at work.

And what are his works? What will we see God do in a successful church? He will prepare us for Heaven by making us holy and putting our hearts and minds on the treasures in Christ that are waiting for us. He will reveal himself so clearly to us that we will fear him, we will love him for what he is, we will obey him in whatever he tells us, and we will serve him. He will issue orders to us – he has a kingdom to build and the enemy to defeat, and he wants us to get skilled in his ways and covered with his armor. He will open the field of labor to us, showing us the "fields white for harvest," and give us fruit for our labor. All these things and more happen in a church whose front door opens into the throne room of grace.

Church administration

A word here about church organization. The Bible teaches two lines of organization in the local assembly: gifts and offices. The gifts we've already looked at. The offices are only two – elders and deacons. However your church chooses to call these offices or what they're responsible for, the only thing we wish to add here is to look again carefully at what exactly the Bible says about this subject.

The Church

Believe it or not, the pastor is not an office in the church! "Pastor" shows up in the list of spiritual gifts, not offices:

> It was he who gave some to be Apostles, some to be prophets, some to be evangelists, and some to be **pastors** and teachers ... (Ephesians 4:11)

Our practice of hiring pastors adds a great deal of confusion to an already ailing system. Technically, we can't "hire" a pastor any more than we can "hire" someone who speaks in tongues! Someone who has a spiritual gift can't turn it off and on at will, nor is it something that should be bought or sold with a paycheck. On the other hand, our modern idea of the "pastorate" is a career choice in our day; it certainly doesn't fit the pattern of the early church.

When we "hire" a person to lead the church, what we're really doing is assigning the duties of administration to someone. We also want him to do all the preaching, and visitation, and much of the teaching (at least church-wide) – jobs that actually require spiritual skills. But the more duties we give him, the less we expect of others in the church – as if the "pastor" is going to be the only one who can do any of this with the necessary skill.

The point we are making is this: our pastors are not the only ones who have been given gifts to exercise in the church. The pastor is only one – and certainly not the most important or crucial – gift among many in the church. To honor one man, and a hired one at that, as being the head and center of all church activity is throwing away the model and changing the way the church works to suit ourselves. Someone who has a spiritual gift has been called by God, not by man; he must do what the Lord called him to do, whether or not people "honor" him with a paycheck or a formal job in the church. So a pastor will be doing the work of the pastor even before the church would formally recognize his ability; he does it not for money, but for the welfare of the church and to obey his Master.

How should we organize the church, then, if the "pastor" is a spiritual gift and not an administrative position? The answer is in the elders and deacons: these are not spiritual gifts, but offices in the church. And as offices, they assume the leadership in the church in this sense: they guide the life of the church, making sure that the gifts are operating, and that the members of the church are open and free to the work of the Spirit as he uses his people to grow the church. They are, as Jesus called them, servants – not lords and masters. (Matthew 20:24-28) They are facilitators: they see to it that the church takes every advantage of the spiritual life offered her in the Lord Jesus. Only the elders and deacons have jobs that can be "assigned" to them – since they aren't spiritual gifts, the church can decide whether to have someone assume the role of administrative leadership or not. This of course shouldn't get in the way of them exercising whatever spiritual gifts that they have received.

I know that this kind of thinking is radical, but again we can't very well expect the Lord to bless our churches if we deliberately ignore his model in the Bible. There are reasons that we're ignoring it, reasons we can easily change if we wanted to – it's just that none of us wants to change. If this is the case, we at least ought to know why the Lord will refuse to make our churches successful.

Where we go wrong

It should be no secret to you that churches generally fail this high standard that Scripture shows us. Although the example of the early church in Acts is a description of the normal church (not the impossible church, as many believe!), there aren't many congregations in our day which fit that description. Unfortunately there are many things we can do to foul up the works. When we don't know what the Lord wants of us, or we don't want to do what the Lord tells us to do, then our church will fail. As much as we might want spiritual answers from Heaven, and spiritual life in our congregation, we may be our own worst enemy: the way we insist on running our churches is the very reason God isn't interested in blessing us. He knows it can't be done the way we're trying to do it.

There are many circumstances in a church that make it difficult to keep a high level of spiritual activity. One type of difficulty is the awkward position that our conversion has put us in! God saved us, remade us, and set us in a new spiritual world. That solves a lot of problems that we used to have, but it raises a whole new set of problems that now we have to deal with.

For one thing, everyone is still a sinner. Even the best Christians do things that offend God and hurt other people.

> There is not a righteous man on earth
> who does what is right and never sins.
> (Ecclesiastes 7:20)

When you get a roomful of sinners together, their best efforts at cooperation and love will fail sometime, somehow. It's something we must expect and make plans to deal with when it arises. The Bible tells us how to deal with sin when it shows up in the lives of Christians.

Another problem is that there are all levels of spiritual maturity in a church. Some Christians are brand new to the faith, others have been Christians for a few years and have some experience, while others have walked with the Lord for many years and have a great deal of experience and wisdom. You would think that the younger ones would willingly learn from the older ones, but that doesn't usually happen: people like to think what they want and do what they want without consulting those with wisdom and experience first. So the leaders of the church have a big job on their hands trying to minister on all spiritual levels.

Another problem is that we are all aliens and strangers in this world. Jesus himself said that we Christians don't really belong here – our bodies may be here, but our hearts are already in Heaven:

> I have given them your Word and the world has hated them, for they are not of the world any more than I am of the world. My prayer is not that you take them out of the world but that you protect them from the evil one. They are not of the world, even as I am not of it. (John 17:14-16)

> All these people were still living by faith when they died. They did not receive the things promised; they only saw them and welcomed them from a distance. And they admitted that they were aliens and strangers on earth. People who say such things show that they are looking for a country of their own. If they had been thinking of the country they had left, they would have had opportunity to return. Instead, they were longing for a better country — a Heavenly one. Therefore God is not ashamed to be called their God, for he has prepared a city for them. (Hebrews 11:13-16)

We don't really fit in with our surroundings here in this world. We live here, we have to work and eat and rub shoulders with everyone else, but our hearts aren't here. We don't really want what this world has to offer; we've decided to wait for Heavenly treasures. Even our lives are of less value than what we have been promised in Christ. At least this is the way it should be! Not everyone is so eager to give up the old way of life. This makes for interesting arguments during business meetings in the church!

In addition to the predicament we find ourselves in because of conversion, there are other reasons that our churches fail. We *purposely* do things that make it difficult if not impossible to please God in the way we do church.

First, it must be said that many Christians simply don't want the kind of church that's described in Acts. It would mean spending a great deal of time with each other, fellowshipping over spiritual issues – we don't have the time nor are we all that interested in perpetual Bible studies or prayer meetings. It would mean giving up possessions and money (significant amounts of it!) to help others who are in need. It would mean changing our schedules around completely to give priority to the work of the church. We are too comfortable with our lifestyles the way they are; we would lose too much of this world's benefits if we put the church's life at the center of our lives. And sad to say, many church leaders don't want their churches to be like the model either – they have worked hard to build up their little kingdoms where they rule over people's lives. They stand to lose too much if they turn over the rule of the church to the Lord. Church leaders don't always do their work from altruistic motives.

Second, we structure the church the way *we* want it, which stifles and chokes any spiritual life from getting through from Heaven. One way that many churches do this is to hire a pastor to do all the work for them. He's a paid employee, in other words, who does everything that the church members would be doing if they were taking their spiritual gifts seriously. In a church like that, we can't expect God to bless his people when they have rejected God's system of running a church.

Third, we base much of the church's work on volunteers, not spiritually gifted workers. We have no good way of finding those people who have been given spiritual gifts from God. The leaders of the church just assume that things don't work that way, that the only way the work of the church can go on is if someone volunteers for the job. But God can't afford to give this precious work to volunteers! The person may be genuinely interested in helping, but that doesn't mean that he/she knows how to do the job. In the physical world we all know that we can't give a skilled job to a common laborer; we'd end up with disaster as a result. But we do that all the time in the church, because we are too afraid to insist on excellence and wisdom from Heaven and the sign of the presence of the Spirit in the work of our church help. We therefore willingly accept the services of anybody who offers, even if it's a bad idea. This, by the way, is why Paul counseled not to accept the zealous but ignorant services of the newly converted: since they don't really know what they're doing, they will soon get filled with a false sense of pride in their position – when really they can do nothing useful for, and often will hurt, the church as a result. See his counsel about this in 1 Timothy 3:6.

Fourth, we lack community. Modern American culture has trained us to be individuals, rebels and loners. We don't like to spend time with each other in the church, especially when we're married and have jobs and struggle with overwhelming schedules. All we want to do is come home and crash at the end of the day! The eight-to-five career mentality that most Americans have is killing the life of the church: we simply don't have the time nor the interest to fit the church into our busy lives. But the church can't survive without being a strong community; most of its functions only happen in the context of community. And an hour or two on Sundays doesn't make it happen!

Fifth, and this is a fundamental problem, we aren't focusing on God himself. We discussed this already, but it bears repeating. Unless we turn our attention away from ourselves for a change and start looking at God, and what he is and does, we have no hope of having a living, vital church. A church lives because it comes in contact with the living God:

> Now this is eternal life: that they may know you, the only true God, and Jesus Christ, whom you have sent. (John 17:3)

If we turn our attention away from God – if we focus on the world, or ourselves, instead of intently gazing on the glory of the Lord and never leaving his presence – our churches will die. If you step away from the fire, you will get cold; if you take your eyes off the quarry, you'll lose it. If God is no longer the center of your attention, then spiritually you will begin to experience what the wicked will discover throughout eternity: "without hope and without God." (Ephesians 2:12)

What should we do?

Unfortunately it's not easy to change the way an established church works. The leaders may not be in favor of change, the people may just like the way things are now, people get set in their ways and resist change, and other circumstances can be used for excuses. Each church has its problems, and the solution will be different according to the unique situation of each church.

Without being specific about how to go about changing a church to fit the New Testament model, we can lay out some general guidelines according to the principles we've already seen:

First, we have to stop doing what gets in the way of the Spirit's work in the church. If our ideas of what a church should be and how it should run aren't the same as God's ideas, then whenever we do what we want instead of what God said to do, it's like clogging up the plumbing with debris. The water has no chance to get through the pipes. We have to be willing to set aside our opinions and listen to the Lord for a change; we have to be willing to change the way we do things so that the Spirit has a chance to get through to his people and bless them with the presence and power of God. In other words, we have to learn how God designed the system to work; and then work along with, instead of work against, his system.

Second, we have to put ourselves close to the Throne of God. If we have been so far away from him that nobody can remember the last great spiritual work of God among us, then it's time we returned to him. There is no life apart from him. To be so long away from our life and light and spiritual food is certain to have adverse results on our spiritual health. The angels, the Bible says, stand around his throne continually; so do the elders and the living creatures. There's a good reason for that: only God can provide them with what they need. The church has such special needs that this world can't provide them for us; we have to learn the art of waiting on the Lord for his powerful treasures.

Third, we have to wait on him to do his part. This is the critical step. For a while we may be willing to try the experiment and do things in God's way. But after a while, when nothing seems to be happening, we begin to panic – like Abraham did when no son was forthcoming, even though God had promised him. (Genesis 16-17) We tend to take matters in our own hands when we don't see God stepping in to do his part. *We must resist this temptation with our whole hearts and minds.* God will keep his promises; if he waits, he only wants to know how serious we are about inviting him into our church to do his special work. By waiting on him to do his part, we honor him and show him that we believe he really is the Lord of the Church. None of *us* want to replace him!

If we find ways to put this plan into action, we will discover the secret to a successful church: instead of trying our creative best to force a church to conform to the New Testament standard – and failing because of problems and people who won't cooperate – the church will start working out all on its own. Instead of struggling to make it work, it will automatically happen. When *we* struggle to make a church, it never works out well; but when we back away and let the Lord make his church his way, it comes together so easily that it's nothing short of a miracle.

> Unless the LORD builds the house,
> its builders labor in vain.
> Unless the LORD watches over the city,
> the watchmen stand guard in vain.
> (Psalm 127:1)

Judgment Day

For we must all appear before the judgment seat of Christ, that each one may receive what is due him for the things done while in the body, whether good or bad. (2 Corinthians 5:10)

Ultimately, God seeks glory in all that he does. And the universe is a particularly effective platform for getting him glory. This was no accident: just as a master craftsman makes furniture in a way that will show off his skills to his customers, the Lord made the universe in such a way that it's hard to miss the point of his wisdom and power. Only the Almighty could have done such a thing in such a way.

Not only can we see how capable and wise he is in making the physical world, it's truly awesome to see how he could interweave the lives of men and nations in such a way as to perfectly fulfill his spiritual purposes too. We are often dumbfounded when we try to imagine how God will get glory out of the complicated, entangled disaster that we have made of things. And how could he possibly be in control over the seemingly random and rebellious acts of human beings who are determined to do the *opposite* of his will? For example, look at the massive scale of destruction of the devil, and the darkness and deceit of the world system – this doesn't give us much hope that God is really the Master of all the earth.

Judgment Day

Nevertheless he *is* in complete control, there will be no surprises for him, and everything will turn out in the end exactly as he planned – which will bring him everlasting glory when he shows us how he could do such a thing. Somehow he will straighten everything out: the wicked will get exactly what they deserve, and the righteous will get what they deserve, and nobody will be treated the least bit unfairly. It's going to take an infinite wisdom to do that.

The Last Day will be one of the most crucial events in God's timetable for the world. It's then that he will unveil the secrets behind the control and power that he exerted over the entire world all through history. There before his judgment seat we will hear the explanation for everything that has happened; there we will see the mysteries uncovered, and then we will all know what's going on just as he *now* knows. This is the idea of Judgment Day.

And this means that we are *all* going to be there. Many Christians think that, since they've been made clean by the blood of Christ, there's no need to appear before God's judgment throne. But that's not true: it's extremely important that we are all there. It will be a day of glory not only for the Lord, but for all his people as well. The only ones who need fear Judgment Day are those who have reason to fear the outcome!

His honor rests on his ability and wisdom to judge everything in righteousness; it should be no surprise, then, that we find him hard at work even now on this matter of judgment. If we can't appreciate the full scope of his work in this area now, we will at the end of the world. Like waiting on an artist to unveil his work at the pre-appointed time, we will become witnesses of his amazing work on Judgment Day.

What is Judgment?

The concept of judgment is often misunderstood. When we think of "judgment" we usually think of getting into trouble for something. And people often confuse it with the act of passing a sentence on a convicted criminal. But there's something much more important that has to happen before the court reaches that stage of passing out the sentence.

You probably noticed that, when accused of a crime, most people rarely tell the truth about themselves, especially if there's a possibility that they will be punished. Usually the defendant will plead "not guilty;" and if we simply accepted the bare statement of many defendants, we would let most if not all of the criminals in our justice system go free! Everyone has a "good" excuse for what happened, nobody is responsible (or so they claim), and it's always someone else's fault. So we have to have a better way of coming to some sort of decision than believing the accused; we have good reason to believe that many of them will lie about what they did or didn't do in order to stay out of trouble.

So, we have a judge. He listens to the arguments for the prosecution and for the defense, he listens to the witnesses, he examines the evidence, and then pronounces his impersonal judgment on the case. In a court setting, the judge is the person who determines the answer to the question: *what really happened?* When he's satisfied that he has heard everything, he then gives a ruling: this, in my judgment, is what really happened.

His assessment is what the court officially records to be the truth, and any further actions of the court will be based on his assessment. For example, if the judge finds that a man is guilty, the police will take him off to prison and be perfectly in the right for doing so – the judge *declared* him guilty, so nobody can legally argue about what the authorities proceed to do with him.

The Bible tells us plainly that God is the Judge over all the earth. The reason is this: the Lord is capable, in a way that no human judge can hope to claim, of discerning the true state of a person's heart. "Man looks at the outward appearance, but the Lord looks at the heart." (1 Samuel 16:7) Jesus, it was said, "did not need man's testimony about man, for he knew what was in a man." (John 2:25)

And the reason the world needs a Judge is because of the situation that things are in right now. Man is a criminal; he is guilty of crimes against the King and he must be brought to justice. We don't like to think of ourselves in this light, but when we think about what the Bible says about us, we have to agree – it does describe us perfectly.

- *Man has rebelled against his original calling.* When God first made man, he gave him a specific job to do:

    > "Let us make man in our image, in our likeness, and let them rule over the fish of the sea and the birds of the air, over the livestock, over all the earth, and over all the creatures that move along the ground." So God created man in his own image, in the image of God he created him; male and female he created them. (Genesis 1:26-27)

    In other words, man was to be the vice-regent of the earth: ruling in God's Name, carrying out God's orders, caring for God's creatures. But right away Adam and Eve turned their backs on their calling; although people *are* subduing the earth now, it's not for God's glory nor is it done to carry out God's will.

- *Man ruined God's Creation.* Sin and death entered the world by means of Adam's sin, and that means the world fell into pain, suffering, and destruction as a result. (Romans 8:21) Thanks to us, the world that was supposed to be a beautiful reflection of God's goodness is a terrible scene of wicked men and women ruining and destroying the world instead.

- ***Man rebelled against God's Law.*** The Law of God is good: it's a description of a perfect man, and the kind of Kingdom that God wants set up here on earth. But instead of living that kind of life, man has thrown off God's Law and chosen to live in filth and wickedness. We make our own laws now – laws that will allow us the freedom to live in sin. In making our own rules we will inevitably break God's rules; the two systems of morality don't match. God is after holiness, we are after our own glory, comfort, and pleasure. Sinners in God's world are punished; sinners in our world go free. There is no justice or righteousness – as God defines those words – in the world of our making.

- ***Man honors the Enemy.*** We were supposed to give God all glory, and carry out his orders in his creation. Instead we've chosen to follow Satan; Eve opened up her mind and heart to the lies of the Enemy, and we her children have learned to do the same. Satan will give us our heart's desire – pleasure without responsibility – as long as we willingly turn our backs on God's Word. He knows that following God's Truth builds God's Kingdom, and following lies will destroy God's Kingdom. We are so well trained now in the Enemy's ways that Paul describes us in this way:

    > You were dead in your transgressions and sins, in which you used to live when you followed the ways of this world and of the ruler of the kingdom of the air, the spirit who is now at work in those who are disobedient. All of us also lived among them at one time, gratifying the cravings of our sinful nature and following

its desires and thoughts. Like the rest, we were by nature objects of wrath. (Ephesians 2:1-3)

- ***Man built a new world.*** God made a *good* world (Genesis 1:31), and God loves the world that he made (John 3:16). But we have rejected the world that he made and are remaking it to suit our own purposes. Our world, as a result, dishonors God, breaks his rules, exalts us instead of him, and invites sinners to rebel against the Lord – in many creative and powerful ways. As a result, of course, the world of our making is full of frustration, suffering, crime, and death. *Our* world is what the Apostles warned us against:

    > Do not love the world or anything in the world. If anyone loves the world, the love of the Father is not in him. For everything in the world — the cravings of sinful man, the lust of his eyes and the boasting of what he has and does — comes not from the Father but from the world. The world and its desires pass away, but the man who does the will of God lives forever. (1 John 2:15-17)

    In our world, we change the rules and pervert the structure of things to suit ourselves. People have twisted what ought to be obvious and just and right and good; they've made horrible perversions out of the good things of life. Anything that is good and holy and pure, they've turned into sin and suffering and death. The Garden of Eden has been changed into a barren wasteland. We can imagine a little bit of God's disgust with what we've done when we read about his terrible wrath against sinners – for example, the wholesale destruction of the world during Noah's day.

It's bad enough to have a beautiful creation turned into a disaster, but man adds insult to injury when he won't admit his guilt! We have talked ourselves into thinking that we've done nothing wrong:

> This is the way of an adulteress: She eats and wipes
> her mouth and says, 'I've done nothing wrong.'
> (Proverbs 30:20)

We are incurable liars; we've learned the lesson well from our master the devil – who is the father of lies. (John 8:44) If we are accused of being sinners, we deny it; if we're faced with proof of our sin, we have "good" excuses why we did it. And if there's any way to avoid the subject, we will. So instead of taking responsibility for our actions, we harden our hearts and deny that we have done anything wrong. All of us think well of ourselves, and certainly none of us agree with the Bible's harsh indictment of us.

The problem is that *we* are to blame for the state the world is in – not God! God knows exactly what we've done wrong, even though we don't want to look at it. This is his Creation and we're ruining it. We *are* responsible for our actions – and in God's Kingdom the criminal *will* be brought to trial. The Lord certainly isn't going to let us run free! And since we are such stubborn liars (even the gentlest human soul will deny guilt at some point or another), God will bring out the truth about us in ways that we can't avoid the truth anymore. (Romans 3:4) Someone has to take the blame. God is going to do this in such a way that our sinful hearts will be made bare and open for all to see, and even we ourselves will be forced to admit that we are as guilty as God's Law says we are. God the Judge will successfully prosecute this case and convict the sinner to the satisfaction of all concerned.

The Judge of all the earth

God is the supreme Judge over all of creation – he's the only one who *can* be the Judge. None of us could possibly pass judgment on the hearts of men and women and be fair about it. When we do, we inevitably run into serious problems.

> Do not judge, and you will not be judged. Do not condemn, and you will not be condemned. (Luke 6:37)

For one thing, there are usually extenuating circumstances: the person we hate, or the person we want to blame for doing something wrong, often isn't to blame – they may be innocent victims of misunderstandings. Also, we are quick to judge others of sins that we ourselves are guilty of, if we're honest enough to admit it; how can a sinner judge a sinner? Finally, we don't fully understand the complex and limitless standards that God would use when he judges someone. Since we weren't there at Creation, and since this Kingdom that we live in is God's and not ours, we naturally don't know the full depth of the Law as God knows it and can apply it. So our judgment is pretty much useless.

Anybody who judges the human heart has to have the necessary qualifications for the job. Otherwise people would have reason to doubt the wisdom of his judgment, or reject it as unjust. This is why God is the only just judge by *right* and by *ability*:

- **By right** – because the Lord made this world and it all belongs to him. Everyone must play by his rules because we are in his court. The one who creates has the right to make the rules; he has right of ownership because he made all things. The Bible never questions God's right to rule over us. In fact, this is one of the reasons that the Bible starts out with the Creation account – to show us who's really in charge. Not only do we learn from the Creation account that God made us and the world, we also learn that we belong to him – that he *commanded* Creation to exist. This immediately sets the stage for a Master-servant relationship between God and man.

- *By ability* – because only he can fully know the complete situation of every creature in the world. Only he can decide what will be the fate of every creature. The Creator knows how things work because he made them; who else could better judge the worth of a thing than the one who made it? He not only knows how it was made, he gave everything a purpose at the beginning – and he can tell if it's measuring up to its purpose. He has inside knowledge of its inward structure, a point of view that no creature could possibly have. And he also has the power to destroy those who have rebelled against his authority, even against his original design for them, and can reward those who cooperate with him. Neither his threats nor his promises are empty.

Because God has the right and ability to judge us, *his judgments are final*. There can be no appeals. If he owns us, then he has the right to dispose of us as he wishes. And if he knows what we are better than anybody else does, to whom would we appeal over his wisdom? And if rewards from the Master are far better than anything we could get from other sources, his word of commendation is more precious to us than anybody else's. So is his word of condemnation a powerful reality: those who are doomed to hear that from the Master will learn what misery really means!

From the first day until now, the Lord has the world continuously under examination. When Adam and Eve – the first criminals – tried to hide from God in their sin and shame, he immediately went to work uncovering what really happened, and only after the facts were laid out in the open did he issue his judgment and condemnation.

> Then the man and his wife heard the sound of the LORD God as he was walking in the garden in the cool of the day, and they hid from the LORD God among the trees of the garden. But the LORD God called to the man, "Where are you?" He answered, "I heard you in the garden, and I was afraid because I was naked; so I hid." And he said, "Who told you that you were naked? Have you eaten from the tree that I commanded you not to eat from?" (Genesis 3:8-11)

In Genesis 6 we read of another example:

> The LORD saw how great man's wickedness on the earth had become, and that every inclination of the thoughts of his heart was only evil all the time. (Genesis 6:5)

After making this judgment of the human situation, God thought it proper and necessary to destroy the earth and start all over again. He spared only Noah and his family, and used them to begin the family tree again. This destruction on such a massive scale may seem to us to be overkill, but God evidently felt that it was the only just way to solve the problem.

Throughout the history of Israel, God was about the business of judging the hearts and actions of his people. Since they usually tried to cover up their sin, he first had to expose it to full view so that everybody could see what was really in their hearts; *then* he issued his sentence based on the facts. This is what a Judge does: when he brings out all the truth so that everyone can see it, and nobody can deny it, then God hands down his verdict.

For example, he had a long-standing feud with the Israelites about their worship of idols. For centuries he sent Prophets and warnings to them to throw their idols away; but they wouldn't listen to him. Idolatry became big business in Israel: they started out secretly worshiping false gods at their pagan neighbors' houses, then went to a full-scale idolatry from the king's palace on down! After hundreds of years of this, and millions of people taking part in it, and scores of prophets and hundreds of prophecies sent to warn them, it shouldn't be any surprise that the Lord finally drew the line and sent terrible punishment upon Israel. He is a long-suffering God, willing to forgive anybody who admits his guilt and comes to him to be saved. But when, after his repeated efforts to be reconciled to his people, they continue to sin against him in even greater ways, nobody can blame him for carrying out his punishment on them. When God finally did send disaster, nobody could argue with the fact that he had been more than patient in the face of their rebellion and wickedness. The facts were too obvious to ignore.

Much of the work of the Prophets centered on exposing the secret sins of the Israelites to public view. For example, the Lord showed Ezekiel what was really going on in the Temple away from public view. The priests were supposed to be presenting sacrifices to their God; but what were they actually doing there in secret in the back rooms of the Temple?

> Then he brought me to the entrance to the court. I looked, and I saw a hole in the wall. He said to me, "Son of man, now dig into the wall." So I dug into the wall and saw a doorway there.
>
> And he said to me, "Go in and see the wicked and detestable things they are doing here." So I went in and looked, and I saw portrayed all over the walls all kinds of crawling things and detestable animals and all the idols of the house of Israel.

Judgment Day

In front of them stood seventy elders of the house of Israel, and Jaazaniah son of Shaphan was standing among them. Each had a censer in his hand, and a fragrant cloud of incense was rising.

He said to me, "Son of man, have you seen what the elders of the house of Israel are doing in the darkness, each at the shrine of his own idol? They say, 'The LORD does not see us; the LORD has forsaken the land.'" Again, he said, "You will see them doing things that are even more detestable."

Then he brought me to the entrance to the north gate of the house of the LORD, and I saw women sitting there, mourning for Tammuz. He said to me, "Do you see this, son of man? You will see things that are even more detestable than this."

He then brought me into the inner court of the house of the LORD, and there at the entrance to the temple, between the portico and the altar, were about twenty-five men. With their backs toward the temple of the LORD and their faces toward the east, they were bowing down to the sun in the east.

He said to me, "Have you seen this, son of man? Is it a trivial matter for the house of Judah to do the detestable things they are doing here? Must they also fill the land with violence and continually provoke me to anger? Look at them putting the branch to their nose! Therefore I will deal with them in anger; I will not look on them with pity or spare them. Although they shout in my ears, I will not listen to them." (Ezekiel 8:7-18)

We might have wondered if the *way* that the Lord dealt with his people – sending the Babylonians to kill hundreds of thousands of Israelites, destroying the city and the Temple, dragging the survivors back to Babylon in slavery – was too harsh a punishment. But when we see what the Jewish leaders were really doing in the back rooms of the Temple, we begin wondering instead why God didn't do something sooner than he did! So, the Judge is careful to uncover the truth first, then we can better appreciate his sentence on the criminal.

Judgment Day

Jesus often uncovered the hearts of men. The Pharisees, the woman at the well, Peter's heart, Nathanael, the rich young ruler, Paul the persecutor – all these people tried to hide their hearts from God, but Jesus easily stripped away the veil and exposed what they really were inside. For example, he knew what the Pharisees were thinking about him, even though they thought they were keeping their thoughts to themselves:

> Now some teachers of the law were sitting there, thinking to themselves, "Why does this fellow talk like that? He's blaspheming! Who can forgive sins but God alone?" Immediately Jesus knew in his spirit that this was what they were thinking in their hearts, and he said to them, "Why are you thinking these things?" (Mark 2:6-8)

When the Romans took Jesus away for his trial, Peter and the other disciples followed but not too closely. Some people accused Peter of being one of Jesus' followers, a charge that Peter denied vehemently. Supposedly Peter thought that Jesus would never hear about his denials! But as he denied for the third time that he even knew Jesus, Christ looked across the courtyard with a look that withered Peter's heart:

> About an hour later another asserted, "Certainly this fellow was with him, for he is a Galilean." Peter replied, "Man, I don't know what you're talking about!" Just as he was speaking, the rooster crowed. The Lord turned and looked straight at Peter. Then Peter remembered the word the Lord had spoken to him: "Before the rooster crows today, you will disown me three times." And he went outside and wept bitterly. (Luke 22:59-62)

What made this worse was that Jesus predicted that Peter would do this! Peter thought he was a sufficient judge of his own heart; when Jesus told him that one day he would turn his back on Jesus, Peter refused to believe it:

> "Simon, Simon, Satan has asked to sift you as wheat. But I have prayed for you, Simon, that your faith may not fail. And when you have turned back, strengthen your brothers." But he replied, "Lord, I am ready to go with you to prison and to death." Jesus answered, "I tell you, Peter, before the rooster crows today, you will deny three times that you know me." (Luke 22:31-34)

Obviously the Lord's ability to judge our hearts far exceeds our own; we should get used to listening to what he has to say about us and acting on that instead of our own exalted opinions of ourselves.

You will also remember, from what the Lord told us, that *only he* is able to judge aright. He told us, "do not judge, or you too will be judged" (Matthew 7:1), simply because we often jump to conclusions based on insufficient data – or more often, according to our sinful hearts. Only the Lord knows the full situation, and only he can see what is invisible to man. "He knew what was in a man" (John 2:25); therefore he takes the necessary steps to deal with man justly.

How much does he know about us? He knows our hearts – he knows how we feel, what we think, what we like and what we don't like. He knows what's inside us, whereas others only know what they see on the outside. We show other people only what we want them to know about us, because we can control (usually!) what others see of us. But we can't hide anything from God. He sees our guilt, our stricken conscience, our lusts, our hatreds and loves; he knows what we live for, why we don't like his ways, and what we work for. He also knows where we fall short – since he knows what it takes to get into his Kingdom, he knows what we're missing and why we wouldn't fit in there. He has such an encyclopedic knowledge of us that we wonder why he's so interested in us!

> What is man that you are mindful of him,
> the son of man that you care for him? (Psalm 8:4)

Another aspect of God's judgment of us is that it's the basis of all his acts toward us. Whatever he does to or for us, is based on his judgment of what we are and need from him. For example, in Genesis 6:5 we are told that "the Lord saw how great man's wickedness on the earth had become, and that every inclination of the thoughts of his heart was only evil all the time." *Therefore*, it says, based on this judgment of the situation, "I will wipe mankind ... from the face of the earth." (Genesis 6:7) His actions are based on his judgments.

We often wonder why God does what he does. But if we could see the circumstances as he sees them and know the full story as he knows it, then we wouldn't wonder anymore; his acts would seem entirely fitting to the case. In fact, when we get to Heaven we will spend a lot of time reviewing what he did in our lives and praising him for his remarkable discernment and wisdom. His judgment of us is so exact and correct that his solutions answer our needs perfectly, whether any of us understand what he's doing or not. For example, we hate the trials of life – the circumstances that make life difficult or painful. Yet in God's hands these trials are shaping our characters so that we become more holy and pleasing to him:

> And we know that in all things God works for the
> good of those who love him, who have been called
> according to his purpose. (Romans 8:28)

Though a problem of life is painful, who can doubt God's wisdom behind it when it gives us more faith, or repentance for our sin, or more courage to face the enemy? Pain in God's hands is a useful way of shaping our souls. This shows his unerring judgment of what it takes to make us look more like Jesus.

> The Word of God is living and active. Sharper than any double-edged sword, it penetrates even to dividing soul and spirit, joints and marrow; it judges the thoughts and attitudes of the heart. (Hebrews 4:12)

This is probably the first thing that hits people when they come into God's immediate presence. His eyes penetrate into and through us so that we feel quite naked in front of him – not only physically but naked of soul as well. We simply can't hide a thing from him! Saints and sinners alike must bow down in fear in front of him who sees to the bottom of their hearts.

Adam and Eve (Genesis 3:8) cowered in the brush when God came walking in the garden; they feared his penetrating looks and questions. They knew that they wouldn't pass the test. Isaiah (Isaiah 6:5) cried out in anguish when the Lord looked at him, because he knew he had sin stains upon him just like the other Israelites had. Peter (Luke 22:61) caught a single look from the Lord Jesus, on the night he betrayed him, and spent the rest of the night weeping bitterly because of the pain of that judgment. John, the Apostle whom the Lord loved, fell down on his face "as though dead" when Jesus turned his "eyes like blazing fire" upon him. (Revelation 1:17) You can find many, many more examples of people in the Bible who felt stripped and bare in God's presence and didn't like the feeling a bit.

The truth of the matter is that God is always watching us like that; we just aren't aware of it all the time. If we were, then we wouldn't get a thing done! We would be afraid to move for fear of offending him. But even when we can't sense his presence, that shouldn't make us feel like we finally got away from him.

> Where can I go from your Spirit?
> Where can I flee from your presence?
> If I go up to the heavens, you are there;
> if I make my bed in the depths, you are there.
> If I rise on the wings of the dawn,
> if I settle on the far side of the sea,
> even there your hand will guide me,
> your right hand will hold me fast.
>
> If I say, "Surely the darkness will hide me
> and the light become night around me,"
> even the darkness will not be dark to you;
> the night will shine like the day,
> > for darkness is as light to you. (Psalm 139:7-12)

You are on center stage: the spotlights of Heaven are aimed at you and every whisper that you utter echoes through the halls of the King of glory. Your actions are studied, your thoughts are studied, your likes and dislikes are analyzed, your attitudes about everything are made the topic of divine discussion. You are like a medical specimen on the operating table that the doctor knows like the back of his hand – a spiritual autopsy. You have no privacy at all; even the angels know all about you, because God opens up your heart for all to see.

Why judgment is necessary

There is a reason why the Lord judges everything in the world: he wants everything to conform to his will, exactly, to the last detail. In all things he "works out everything in conformity with the purpose of his will." (Ephesians 1:11) It won't do at all to have a single thing out of line and ruining his long range plans. So he examines every single piece of the puzzle to make sure that it will stand the test of his standards. Everything that survives the coming day of fire *will* be pure and holy and upright and will reflect God's glory perfectly. Even our work – or should we say, especially our work! – he will put to the test to see if it passes muster:

> But each one should be careful how he builds. For no one can lay any foundation other than the one already laid, which is Jesus Christ. If any man builds on this foundation using gold, silver, costly stones, wood, hay or straw, his work will be shown for what it is, because the Day will bring it to light. It will be revealed with fire, and the fire will test the quality of each man's work. If what he has built survives, he will receive his reward. If it is burned up, he will suffer loss; he himself will be saved but only as one escaping through the flames. (1 Corinthians 3:10-15)

The Lord won't allow you to have any privacy. It might seem unfair that everything you do is put to extreme scrutiny like this; but you have to understand where he is coming from. You are the one thing in creation that has the ability – in fact, you've already done it to some extent – to foul up the works. You are a loose nut in the machinery of the world. Your potential for evil and destruction is enormous, and the fact that you were created in God's image means that you, of all his creatures, can do the most damage to his cause. He's got to keep an eye on you! If for no other reason than to protect everything and everyone around you from your wickedness. To take his eyes off you is like turning one's back on a drunk; one may very well be responsible for what the drunk ends up doing if one lets him go.

But it isn't only a negative reason that God keeps us constantly in his sight. He studies our motives and thoughts in order to sanctify us too. This also is a full-time job, because thoughts run through our brains like a wildfire through dry brush. Paul said that "we take captive every thought to make it obedient to Christ." (2 Corinthians 10:5) Where does Paul hope to get the insight on what to take captive, and how to take it captive, and what to do with it once he's got it captive? He has to get this wisdom from God who knows all of Paul's shortcomings and weakness.

We little realize *how much* God wants to judge everything in this world. Judgment Day is an event that the Lord has been looking forward to for a long time. We can even see his anticipation designed into the physical world itself. Scientists often speak of the "arrow of time" – that characteristic of the universe that makes it run only in one direction, time-wise. In other words, we aren't comfortable with a world that runs backwards, like a comic film sequence played backwards to make impossible things happen. A broken jar can't put itself back together, or jump back up on the table from which it fell. Neither can the universe itself "rewind;" it *must* proceed forward along the time line. So far the scientists haven't discovered why this is true about the physical world. They have most other things about the world figured out, but the "arrow of time" is still a mystery.

It has never been a mystery, however, that the all of Creation is headed toward Judgment Day. That's the driving principle behind the "arrow of time." Judgment Day *must* happen, because God must get full glory for all of his works. There has to be a final explanation for everything that has happened in history.

There may be a physical law behind the "arrow of time" that scientists will one day discover, but the main *spiritual* reason for that inexorable march to the end is this: **God must finish his works**. He must be revealed *fully*. It must be made plain that the entire universe and its history really were the work of his hand. Right now we can only guess at a few of the reasons why he works the way he does in history and the events of men and nations. But on the Last Day we will finally learn that he knew exactly what he was doing, and it will be obvious that he knew very well how to deal with us.

When the universe finally reaches the *end* of its journey, that will be the signal for the greatest revelation of God. We were all designed to meet him there for judgment, and meet him we will; hence the "arrow of time." We are being dragged forward to that Throne.

How God judges

Because God is the ultimate Judge – because he always knows what's going on in his world (he *has* to know as he performs his work as King over his Creation), Judgment Day was a foregone conclusion from the first day of Creation. He made all things with that day in mind; it was over the horizon at the first dawn. We can see the first traces of his judgment in his pronouncement about the world that he had just made:

> God saw all that he had made, and it was *very good*.
> (Genesis 1:31)

The point is that his world must measure up, it must meet his expectations, or it's no good to him. Either it brings him glory by being and doing what he told it to do, or he will do away with it as worthless to him. Therefore everything stands under his constant scrutiny; he has been judging it from the very beginning.

We can expect that this exacting perfectionist would use a standard on us far beyond what we would use on ourselves. And he is going to judge us in such a way that we won't even know that he's looking at us. A child who knows he's being watched is on his best behavior; but watch him when he thinks he's alone, and you will see the way he really is.

> ***He judges by the standard*** – "He will judge the world in righteousness; he will govern the peoples with justice." (Psalm 9:8) The standard that God uses to judge us is his Law. You will not find a

fairer piece of legislation by which to rule a kingdom. It perfectly glorifies God and his nature in its requirements, it demands no more and no less from us than what is our duty as God's creatures, and the penalties and rewards that it lays out are entirely fitting to each case.

You know the feeling when you see a judge in a courtroom giving out an unjust judgment. If he allows a criminal to go free, the community cries out in protest! And if the innocent is condemned, the wheels of justice are set in motion to overturn the bad decision in higher courts. We have these strong feelings about the judge's judgements because *we measure his decision against a standard to see if he did justice by that standard.* If a judge openly defies a standard that we all accept, then something has to change – either the judge has to go or he must be made to change his decision. We will not give up our standards; our lives are based on certain values and we all must conform to those values. The judge is the highest appeal to those values, and the courtroom is the place where things will be put to right and the values will be upheld. "When the righteous prosper, the city rejoices; when the wicked perish, there are shouts of joy." (Proverbs 11:10) This is because the people can see their values at work providing justice and protecting them from the wicked.

You've probably seen how a plumb line works. A builder hangs a weight on the end of a string and lines it up along the wall that he is building. Since gravity pulls the plumb straight down, he can tell if his wall is straight – he simply compares the wall with the string. He *knows* the string is right, and therefore he can judge if his wall is straight too.

The Lord judges the world by his Law because his Law is *right*. He simply compares our hearts and our actions with the straight Law. Since he knows that the Law describes only what is good and holy and true, he can easily see – and so can we! – if we measure up to the "righteous requirements of the Law." (Romans 8:4)

The reason he's so interested in the Law, by the way, is because it's the perfect and complete description *of his own nature*. The Law is simply a description of God and his Kingdom. This explains why the Law is so high, so perfect, so unattainable for us sinners. When Jesus told us to "be perfect, as your Heavenly Father is perfect" (Matthew 5:48) he was pointing us to the matchless perfection of God for our standard. No other standard will suffice; man's rules and regulations are not enough to satisfy God's tough requirements.

Think of it this way: the Lord is very particular about his environment; he likes things just so. He is offended by sinners; their unholy ways are repulsive to him. Whereas we can live in a moral pigsty and not seem to mind at all, he can't tolerate the atmosphere of sin. "Your eyes are too pure to look on evil; you cannot tolerate wrong." (Habakkuk 1:13) "Such people are a smoke in my nostrils, a fire that keeps burning all day." (Isaiah 65:5) Whatever God wants and does and thinks and says is the only standard of excellence – all of creation either must conform to his holy nature or be destroyed as so much worthless trash. That's hard for us to think about, especially since we value ourselves so highly and we consider whatever we do as valuable. But we've already proven how poorly things turn out when *we* are running things – with sin and death as a result! – so now it's God's turn to apply *his* standard to our lives and get what he wants – justice and life and peace and holiness.

He works on the conscience – "At this, those who heard began to go away one at a time, the older ones first, until only Jesus was left, with the woman still standing there." (John 8:9) This story tells us that Jesus bent down and began writing in the dust. It doesn't tell us what he wrote, but he never did anything that was pointless. There is a Scripture that may very well give us a clue of what Christ was writing:

> O LORD, the hope of Israel, all who forsake you will be put to shame. Those who turn away from you will be *written in the dust* because they have forsaken the Lord, the spring of living water. (Jeremiah 17:13)

If this is what Jesus was doing, evidently he penetrated the heart of every man there when he wrote their names in the dust. They knew their Scriptures; they couldn't bear up under the shame that they felt in front of him. Their own hearts convicted them without Christ having to utter a word. He – and they – both knew their past histories, their own times of sin and rebellion towards God. They had no right to condemn this woman in light of their own sins against God.

Conscience is the inner knowledge of what is right; it's the moral counterpart of instinct in animals. God burned it into our souls so that it would always be there, guiding us in his ways according to his truth. Remember that it's *his truth* that is right, not our own opinions. We have minds that can work out solutions to problems, but we need the Divine programming in our consciences to guide us in the direction of the Law to tell us when our actions are right or wrong. Paul tells us that every human being was made with the Law of God etched in the heart: "the requirements of the Law are written on their hearts, their consciences also bearing witness, and their thoughts now accusing, now even defending them." (Romans 2:15) It may be that a person turns a deaf ear to his conscience or, what is worse, he will deceive himself intentionally so that he can silence his conscience. So he will ignore what little guidance is able to seep through to his heart. The Bible calls this the "searing" of the conscience – deceiving oneself so that one no longer hears the truth from inside the heart.

Conscience can be a terrible master. God wisely made us with this very human characteristic because it will often keep us in line when nothing else will. We find ourselves doing what is right even when nobody is looking – why? Simply because it's what we *should* do! But if we sin against our conscience then the hard part comes. Our conscience won't let us alone; the awful deed stains us like blood on our hands, and we feel like everyone knows what we did, or at least they will soon know. A man can live with all sorts of physical punishments better than he can live with the terror of the conscience. "A rebuke impresses a man of discernment more than a hundred lashes a fool." (Proverbs 17:10)

Most people live within a few seconds of the lashings of an offended conscience. You don't have to speak to them much about God, and about their past history of sin, before they begin to wilt inside. They try to avoid the subject of their own sinful hearts and they move on to other safe subjects. That's the conscience at work. Just a whisper from God's Law and they run like hunted criminals. "I will make their hearts so fearful in the lands of their enemies that the sound of a wind-blown leaf will put them to flight ... because of their sins." (Leviticus 26:36,39)

People often take God to task for his seemingly severe approach to sin. Can the Lord really be concerned with every little detail of our lives like this? Is he really offended with the smallest sins? Isn't it contrary to his basic nature of love to get so angry when we commit a little sin – a "venial" sin as they call it? But they are ignoring one big reality when they question God like this: they have already committed enough sin to sink a battleship. It's not the case that someone has only done one little sin; rather he has added a new sin (little or big) to a lifetime of rebellion and willfulness and immorality. We're looking at a single rotten tree and wondering why God takes notice, when he's looking at the whole forest sitting there in ruins.

When the Last Day comes and God summons each of us before him to give an account, it's this *lifetime* of sin that will be staring us in the face. Right now we have a little memory problem; we don't remember *everything* we ever did that God might have taken offence at. But on that Last Day the Lord will take the blinders off our eyes and we will be able to see, just as clearly as he can see, the whole embarrassing mess in our hearts and minds. We will be struck dumb; we won't have anything to say. Our own conscience will testify to us that God was right all along, that we are just as bad as he told us we were, that we did indeed ignore many chances to change our ways, that when he came close to us in our lives we simply tuned him out, and many more things that we don't want to think about right now. And he will say to us, "I told you about all this before now."

> Now we know that whatever the Law says, it says to those who are under the Law, so that every mouth may be silenced and the whole world held accountable to God. (Romans 3:19)

He judges by means of Creation itself – We mustn't miss the importance of the connection between the Judge and the Creator. The One who *made* all things, has the power and authority to *judge* all things. He alone "knows how we are formed." (Psalm 103:14) The Designer knows best whether his Creation meets the specifications.

But not only *can* he judge us, not only does he have the ability to uncover our hearts, he fully *intends* to expose what we are. The Lord didn't make the world simply to exist, but to be a showcase for himself and his abilities, a platform to reveal who he is and how he works through us, and a kingdom in which all his subjects obey him willingly and completely. We are foolish if we think we will escape his notice. He promised us many times that he's watching us and is planning to uncover what we are before the entire world:

> No one lights a lamp and hides it in a jar or puts it under a bed. Instead, he puts it on a stand, so that those who come in can see the light. For there is nothing hidden that will not be disclosed, and nothing concealed that will not be known or brought out into the open. Therefore consider carefully how you listen. (Luke 8:16-18)

So, he will always be testing us to see if we measure up to his standards.

This brings out an interesting characteristic of God's Creation. Since we are always to be under his judgment to see if we meet his specifications, God designed the world in such a way as to easily reveal the true state of our hearts. Whether we know it or not (and usually we don't) we show the world *by our actions* what we really are inside. This wasn't by accident but by design of the Creator. The process of judgment has already started, from the beginning of the world. Just by living, we show God and everyone what we are. This shows an amazing wisdom behind the way that God made the world, and how we so easily and yet unknowingly reveal what we really are. Judgment Day will be only the final wrap-up of the process that started in the Garden of Eden.

Jesus revealed this aspect of Creation's design in several passages:

> By their fruit you will recognize them. Do people pick grapes from thornbushes, or

figs from thistles? Likewise every good tree bears good fruit, but a bad tree bears bad fruit. A good tree cannot bear bad fruit, and a bad tree cannot bear good fruit. Every tree that does not bear good fruit is cut down and thrown into the fire. Thus, by their fruit you will recognize them. (Matthew 7:16-20)

You brood of vipers, how can you who are evil say anything good? For out of the overflow of the heart the mouth speaks. The good man brings good things out of the good stored up in him, and the evil man brings evil things out of the evil stored up in him. But I tell you that men will have to give account on the day of judgment for every careless word they have spoken. For by your words you will be acquitted, and by your words you will be condemned. (Matthew 12:34-37)

But the things that come out of the mouth come from the heart, and these make a man 'unclean.' For out of the heart come evil thoughts, murder, adultery, sexual immorality, theft, false testimony, slander. (Matthew 15:18-19)

The good man brings good things out of the good stored up in his heart, and the evil man brings evil things out of the evil stored up in his heart. For out of the overflow of his heart his mouth speaks. (Luke 6:45)

In other words, right at Creation the Judge made us in such a way that we *will* tell the truth in our actions even if we lie with our mouths. What profound wisdom behind the design of Creation – the Judge is always at work in us.

> His eyes are on the ways of men; he sees their every step. There is no dark place, no deep shadow, where evildoers can hide. God has no need to examine men further, that they should come before him for judgment. *Without inquiry* he shatters the mighty and sets up others in their place. Because he takes note of their *deeds*, he overthrows them in the night and they are crushed. (Job 34:21-25)

Let's step back now and look at the entire Creation from the point of view of Judgment Day. By designing the universe – and us – in such a way that it would be continuously displaying its true character and usefulness to its Creator, God ordained that the very structure of the world will be moral and spiritual, not solely physical. In other words, it's true that we have bodies, and we live in time and space in a material world. But time and space are only the means for a higher purpose: they provide a "stage," so to speak, for a moral existence. God is primarily interested not in how the laws of physics work, but in whether his creatures glorify him.

Man in particular has a body which he uses either to glorify his Creator or dishonor him. We can't help it, because our mouths were made to praise *him* and our hands were made to build *his* kingdom on earth. A mouth that doesn't praise God is dead, void of spiritual life and purpose. It's only fit to be thrown away – it isn't doing what it was designed to do. (Matthew 5:29-30) Hands that don't build God's kingdom on earth are dead, spreading destruction and misery among God's creatures instead of handing out the treasures of Heaven among God's subjects. In other words, we fulfill our purpose if we use our physical bodies to build a spiritual kingdom. God intends to judge us by our actions done while *in the body*, because we were given bodies specially designed to glorify him by our actions:

> For we must all appear before the judgment seat of Christ, that each one may receive what is due him for the things done *while in the body*, whether good or bad. (2 Corinthians 5:10)

So, Judgment Day tests the worth of the original Creation. The two events are linked together, like two knots at either end of the same rope. It is one continuous story, from beginning to end. Whatever Creation started, God intends to test and finish up at the end of time.

He has always been judging his creation, and he will continue to do so right up to the end. The Scriptures teach us that he works constantly at judging, and his work is so subtle and so extensive and so complex that we can only be amazed at how well he does the job.

God will use his Word to judge us – Many people may think that the Bible is simply an old book that we can safely ignore. But for those who have dared to open its pages, unbeliever and Christian alike, it's the judgment of God that penetrates our hearts. Its words pin us to the wall with the truth about us, like no other book can. I know of non-Christians who are afraid to read the Bible – they know that when they read it, it will convict their hearts of something and they don't want to go through that experience. It describes man's heart so well! It calls a spade a spade; it opens our hearts and minds and describes what is there, for all the world to see. Some people can't sit through a sermon for that reason: the Word of God is so penetrating, so potentially embarrassing, that they often feel the preacher is talking about them!

But for us who are being saved, it's the wisdom of God and the power of God. The Word will tell us what we need to know about ourselves, and what God intends to do in order to save us. We should *want* to know the truth! We should want a right judgment about ourselves. That's why the Word is so precious to us; it's our salvation. It shows us where we are going wrong, why we are going wrong, what it will take to heal us, how we can better relate to others and to God – isn't that what we want to hear? "Come, see a man who told me everything I ever did. Could this be the Christ?" (John 4:29) Thank God for his judgment of me! That means that salvation also stands at the door.

The smart thing to do would be to use the Bible now as a guidebook, to prepare ourselves for Judgment Day before it comes. We already know his standards, we can easily learn what he'll be looking for, and it will tell us how to get ready for what's to come. Since there won't be an opportunity to work on this on Judgment Day itself, it makes sense to get busy now on it. What a precious gift that God has given us in his Word – the very blueprint of what he wants us to be!

Armed with this knowledge, we can be prepared for what's to come.

The goal of Judgment Day: God's glory

On Judgment Day the work will be finished. Jesus Christ will then dominate all of Heaven and earth, the new Kingdom will be ready for unveiling, the old kingdom will be ripe for destruction, and eternity will begin. A new chapter in the history of the world will start. The Judge will then "open the books" and examine the entire situation before him. Since he has already designed the system to reveal its true nature on its own, it will simply be a matter of looking at each creature under Heaven and pronouncing its destiny according to its developed character. In other words, how did it turn out? Whatever fits in with the new spiritual Kingdom will be kept, and whatever doesn't fit will be destroyed. By then every detail of every part of this world will be obvious to everybody.

> At that time his voice shook the earth, but now he has promised, "Once more I will shake not only the earth but also the heavens." The words "once more" indicate the removing of what can be shaken — that is, created things — so that what cannot be shaken may remain. Therefore, since we are receiving a kingdom that cannot be shaken, let us be thankful, and so worship God acceptably with reverence and awe, for our "God is a consuming fire." (Hebrews 12:26-29)

> As the weeds are pulled up and burned in the fire, so it will be at the end of the age. The Son of Man will send out his angels, and they will weed out of his kingdom everything that causes sin and all who do evil. They will throw them into the fiery furnace, where there will be weeping and gnashing

of teeth. Then the righteous will shine like the sun
in the kingdom of their Father. He who has ears, let
him hear. (Matthew 13:40-43)

If you think about it, you would realize that only by finishing in this way will God get the full glory that he deserves. If there will be no Judgment Day, there would be too many questions left hanging. We have already been asking those questions ourselves: for example, why is there evil? What was accomplished by having millions die in ignorance of Christ? What about the "innocents?" Is it really important to be so careful about how one lives? If these questions were left unanswered, God's character would be forever in doubt. People would think that he wasn't fair with us, that he was expecting more of us than we could reasonably do. But God *is* just, and he does all things *well*. Therefore, Judgment Day is going to clear his character in such a way that even the most rebellious and hard-hearted of the wicked will have to admit that God is just.

> The righteous will be glad when they are avenged, when they bathe their feet in the blood of the wicked. Then men will say, "Surely the righteous still are rewarded; surely there is a God who judges the earth." (Psalm 58:10-11)

One surprising aspect about God's judgment is that there are witnesses. "On the testimony of two or three witnesses a man shall be put to death, but no one shall be put to death on the testimony of only one witness." (Deuteronomy 17:6) This is straight from God's Law, and we can certainly expect the Lord to follow that Law himself. And when we stand before his judgment seat at the end of time, he will bring out witnesses who will testify for or against us.

God is sufficient witness in himself for anything that happens. We want more than one witness in our courts of law, because one witness may have the story wrong or he may even be trying to deceive the court. But two (independent) witnesses make a strong case; if they both agree on what happened, then we can be pretty certain that it happened that way. But who can see all things like God? How can thousands of witnesses add anything to the testimony of God? His is the perfect testimony that nobody can improve on.

But he is going to have witnesses anyway. Judgment is a serious matter with him; if we're going to face an accusation of having sinned against the Lord of Heaven and earth, then he is going to have other witnesses there at our trial. It's very uncomfortable how he brings witnesses out of the woodwork like this! People we know and people we don't know are going to testify that yes, they saw us do such and such sin; and yes, they have their own gripe against us for the way we treated them (or ignored them, whatever the case may be). As the trial goes on we are going to realize, perhaps for the first time, that the life that God gave us affected many others, and there were people who depended on us for important things, and we failed them as well as God. The enormity of our responsibility is going to hit us between the eyes when God calls all these witnesses against us. Even the earth and the heavens will mount the witness stand: "This day I call Heaven and earth as witnesses against you that I have set before you life and death, blessings and curses." (Deuteronomy 30:19)

This examination reminds us of our first duty that God gave us – to fill the earth, subdue it, and rule over it in God's Name with his image on our persons. Where does it stop? How much am I responsible to do in my life? Who is my brother, that I have been accountable to him? Was my every step, my every word, a burden to others, a cross in their lives, that I was never aware of? How much of this would I have avoided if I had taken God more seriously in life?

The role of witnesses in God's judgment is a very serious matter to him. He is busy collecting all the evidence that will relate to each one of our cases. In Revelation 6:9-11 we read about the witnesses who have been killed for the Lord's sake – and God has them under the altar in Heaven, waiting until the time is right to bring all the details out in the open. Notice that the testimony will work two ways: these witnesses will testify against those who had them executed, and their executioners will be forced to witness in their favor to exonerate their names. We know this last fact will occur by what another passage tells us:

> Live such good lives among the pagans that, though they accuse you of doing wrong, they may see your good deeds and glorify God on the day he visits us. (1 Peter 2:12)

Judgment is a very public affair; God isn't the only one who is interested in the results. Just as we haven't lived in a vacuum all of our lives, we will have to answer to more than God at the end of time. What we have done and said, even though in secrecy, "will be proclaimed from the housetops" (Luke 12:3) so that all the universe will know. So it's a very involved, complex affair that God is preparing as the Judge of all men; that last day will show how well-organized and prepared the Lord is for uncovering the truth about everyone.

Heaven and Hell

When most people think of Judgment Day, they think of Heaven and Hell first – in other words, the rewards and punishments. I hope that you see by now the difference between judgment and reward – there first has to be a thorough judgment, an assessment of the situation, before a proper sentence can be given. If any of the details of the case are overlooked, people are going to wonder if the sentence was really just. So the Lord will examine everything about us so that, when he does give his sentence about us, everyone will be in complete agreement with it. Everyone will and must know how proper God's treatment of us is – it brings him glory as the perfect, just, all-knowing God that he is.

Another fact about judgment is that it will be basically done *before* Judgment Day arrives. Remember the ways he uncovers our hearts: through Creation, through the Word, by examining our actions in life. We bear fruit according to the way our hearts are already made. We will have displayed before God's eyes what we are inside by the time we die; then on Judgment Day he will hold us up before everyone else and show *them*.

This is why so many people are going to have a shock on the Last Day. They've been planning on a defense for that day; they intend to offer reasons that God should go easy on them. It will be a surprise to them when God doesn't even allow them to speak before his Throne! The Bible says that "the dead" will rise on the last day; and dead men can't talk. As far as he's concerned, they've been telling him their entire lives what's inside their hearts; there won't be need for any more explanations. The *only* thing that will happen on that day is that God will raise them from the dead, display them to the entire Creation for what they are, and pass his sentence on them. There will be no discussion, no appeal, no pleading – none of that will be necessary.

> ***Fitting reward, fitting punishment*** – "Your eyes are open to all the ways of men; you reward everyone according to his conduct and as his deeds deserve." (Jeremiah 32:19) Man has always known, deep down, that this is a "do good and you will live" system he lives in. The social scientists make fun of primitive societies that try to appease their gods with sacrifices and other such "useless" activities; but those primitive peoples are simply addressing the pain of conscience (just as we moderns do in our own ways) and trying to buy

righteousness for themselves. They know that there is good and bad waiting for us all, and this life is the door into reward or punishment.

God does have good and bad waiting for us. He told us clearly what those options are in the Bible and in the history of his special people Israel; he expects us to take all this seriously because *he* takes it all very seriously. He has been busy preparing the full extent of those options ever since the world began, and we will finally see his work at the end of time when he calls us to one or the other. Why don't we take it just as seriously? We seem to forget that there is another world, even when we claim to have an interest in the matter. This world takes up so much of our time and energy that thinking about what is to come next seems like being "too Heavenly minded to be of any earthly good!" But this is a poor excuse for Christians, for a people who have been called into God's Kingdom. "No eye has seen, no ear has heard, no mind has conceived what God has prepared for those who love him." (1 Corinthians 2:9) We should be fascinated with the subject.

You'll remember that God is building a house to live in, which will be fully manifest only at the end of the world. (Revelation 21:2-4) He is busy working now, laying stone upon stone, life upon life, testimony upon testimony, in order to have a people all of his own. When it's done then the old earth and the old heavens will pass away and the great preparations that God has been making for the eternal joy and peace of his people will finally be made plain. This will be the final reward of the saints: they will be so close to God that he will live *in them* as in a Temple.

Jesus reminded his disciples that he wasn't going back to Heaven to relax now that his suffering was over; he was going back to work on *their* reward. "I am going there to prepare a place for you." (John 14:2) What he is doing, and why it takes all this time to prepare, we can't possibly imagine. But perhaps this will help: remember when your parents or someone close to you would make you wait for a present? The longer it took, the worse was the waiting! But when they finally brought it out to you, you could see that the extra time was necessary – they put a lot of effort into making it something that you would be happy with. That, dear Christian, is what Jesus is up to right now. Imagine the infinite power and wisdom of Christ applied to the task of coming up with a reward that will make you happy! Can you conceive of what the Lord of Glory will come up with if it took him these 2000 years to create it?

The Lord is also busy preparing the just reward of the wicked, only that won't make them at all happy. Does the Lord prepare disaster for the wicked? He organizes and plans even this to the smallest detail!

> The LORD works out everything for his own ends — even the wicked for a day of disaster. (Proverbs 16:4)

To some, unfortunately, he is going to say "Depart from me, you who are cursed, into the eternal fire *prepared* for the devil and his angels." (Matthew 25:41) What, do you think, did he prepare for the devil and his angels? An unquenchable fire, a worm that doesn't die, torment to cause weeping and gnashing of teeth. We don't know much more than that (and who would *want* to look inside?) but again we have to realize that Hell must be an awesome place because it took someone with no less wisdom and power than God to come up with it.

The Bible gave us hints all along that God was working on something in eternity. The symbolism of the Temple, for example, wasn't meant to confuse the Israelites; they weren't supposed to look at the blood of bulls and goats and think that this animal sacrifice would really cleanse their hearts from sin. The picture pointed to the reality that God was putting together in the Heavenly Temple. Just about everything in Israelite history points to a spiritual, eternal reality that God was building. Did they inherit the Promised Land? Canaan was only a symbol of the Promised Land that God was preparing – "for he has prepared a city for them." (Hebrews 11:16)

Finally, the Lord will give to each of us no more and no less than what we wanted from him anyway. It's characteristic of the Lord to work out things so that we get what we asked for. The pagans will get what they ask for and no more; they didn't want God in the first place, and that's precisely what they are going to end up with: *no God*. The problem is that they didn't anticipate how terrible that would be! They built for themselves a life that leaves God out of the picture, and at the Last Day the Lord is going to take the final step back and leave them to themselves in misery. Only then will they discover that, through what they valued as "personal freedom," God gave them the rope to hang themselves.

Christians, on the other hand, will find that their works preceded them into Heaven. If they've taken their responsibilities seriously (not all of them do!) then they will find treasures there with their own names on them. They will be given crowns. The Lord will give them "cities" to rule over, as a reward for a job well done. They will be made judges over the angels. They will sit with Christ at the right hand of God and rule over God's Kingdom with Christ. And this is a fitting end to a life lived in the service to the King: his Kingdom, his righteousness, his honor and glory, were the only things that were important to them in this world; so in the next world he will give them an unlimited supply of what they loved.

Do all things with that day in view

The Bible says that at the end of time, whenever God decides to wrap things up, the earth will be destroyed by a great cataclysm. He will have accomplished his purposes for it; he won't need it anymore, since a physical earth that was corrupted with sin and death will be useless to him for creating a spiritual reward for his people. Just as a wrecked car can only be taken to the junkyard and scrapped, so the Lord will do away with his first creation.

People in our scientific age don't think that such a thing can happen, but their disbelief doesn't make the Bible's testimony false. There was one other time in history that God showed us the power of his wrath!

But they deliberately forget that long ago by God's Word the heavens existed and the earth was formed out of water and by water. By these waters also the world of that time was deluged and destroyed. By the same Word the present heavens and earth are reserved for fire, being kept for the day of judgment and destruction of ungodly men. (2 Peter 3:5-7)

But the day of the Lord will come like a thief. The heavens will disappear with a roar; the elements will be destroyed by fire, and the earth and everything in it will be laid bare. (2 Peter 3:10)

If God intends to destroy the earth, how then should we live? What should we be doing to get ready for that day?

Since everything will be destroyed in this way, what kind of people ought you to be? You ought to live holy and godly lives as you look forward to the day of God and speed its coming. (2 Peter 3:11-12)

The point is to get ready now, *before* Judgment Day. If you've been paying attention, you will know that the Lord will give us no chance to present any appeals, requests, denials, opinions, problems, hostility, frustration or prayers on that day. His judgment of us will be already complete; the only thing left for him to do will be to reveal our hearts to everyone else before he hands down his sentence. It will be a spiritual autopsy; there will be no chance to make any changes then.

This means that *now* is the day of salvation. If we want a favorable judgment, we have to get busy now so that we can show up on Judgment Day dressed in robes of righteousness. We have to work on holiness, and faith, and love for God and his children, and all the other graces of a Christian heart. We have to get rid of the slander, murder, thievery, lies, hatred and adultery that fill our hearts. We've got to do what Paul counseled us:

> Put to death, therefore, whatever belongs to your earthly nature: sexual immorality, impurity, lust, evil desires and greed, which is idolatry. *Because of these, the wrath of God is coming.* You used to walk in these ways, in the life you once lived. But now you must rid yourselves of all such things as these: anger, rage, malice, slander, and filthy language from your lips. Do not lie to each other, since you have taken off your old self with its practices and have put on the new self, which is being renewed in knowledge in the image of its Creator. (Colossians 3:5-10)

We must be careful, however, how we go about this. Many a person has tried to make his heart holy and failed in the attempt. *There is no way we can save ourselves from sin.* The only remedy is to turn to Christ – he is the only one who can pull us out of our sins and put us into God's Kingdom. Even then, when he saves us from the death trap that we're stuck in, we don't dare go on from there alone. The only way we can have the strength to continue in God's will, the only way we can even know what to do and how to go about it, is to rely completely on the Holy Spirit whom the Lord puts in our hearts. We will find life only by following the Spirit.

There is still time to get ready for that day. People think that the threats of destruction are just myths; they don't see God throwing lightning bolts down on the wicked, so they figure that the Bible doesn't mean what it says when it talks about a day of judgment. But those who are wise know exactly why God is holding off destruction:

> The Lord is not slow in keeping his promise, as some understand slowness. He is patient with you, not wanting anyone to perish, but everyone to come to repentance ... So then, dear friends, since you are looking forward to this, make every effort to be

found spotless, blameless and at peace with him. Bear in mind that our Lord's patience means salvation. (2 Peter 3:9, 14-15)

The reason he doesn't destroy the wicked now is because he wants to save some of them! He loves mercy; this punishment that he threatens against sinners is actually something he never wanted to inflict on man. We forced his hand, however; he has to do something about sinners because his glory of being a holy and just God is at stake. But punishment, as Isaiah calls it, is God's "strange work." (Isaiah 28:21) He would much rather we repent now and change.

There's another reason that we have to start doing our homework and become holy. There are clues in the Bible that God has greater things in mind for his people to do in Heaven. In this world they are given spiritual treasures – why? So that they can become familiar with them, and know why they're so important to their spiritual life. They are also given spiritual gifts – why? So that they can help build an eternal, spiritual Kingdom according to God's specifications. What's interesting is that the Lord seemed to make promises that these treasures and gifts aren't going to go to waste, even if we don't have much of an opportunity to use them in this life. For example, Jesus told a parable about a man who became king and returned to check on his servants whom he left in charge:

> He was made king, however, and returned home. Then he sent for the servants to whom he had given the money, in order to find out what they had gained with it. The first one came and said, 'Sir, your mina has earned ten more.' 'Well done, my good servant!' his master replied. 'Because you have been trustworthy in a very small matter, take charge of ten cities.' (Luke 19:15-17)

Judgment Day

If we are studious and faithful here, in this world, he intends to reward us with responsibilities in the next world – responsibilities that depend on the skills that we gained here. It's an amazing idea that all our hard work for the Lord in this life won't be wasted! We don't know what we will end up doing in Heaven, but we do have a few glimpses: ruling over cities, ruling over the angels (1 Corinthians 6:3), sitting on the throne with Christ, wearing crowns. And we will draw on the experiences, growth, and knowledge that we got here in this world – it's an exciting future.

But only those who work hard and skillfully here can have any hopes of being part of that future. There will also be people who relied on the name "Christian" to get along in the church without doing anything to prepare for the next life. Unfortunately their works will be judged as worthless:

> If any man builds on this foundation using gold, silver, costly stones, wood, hay or straw, his work will be shown for what it is, because the Day will bring it to light. It will be revealed with fire, and the fire will test the quality of each man's work. If what he has built survives, he will receive his reward. If it is burned up, he will suffer loss; he himself will be saved, but only as one escaping through the flames. (1 Corinthians 3:12-15)

Let's hope, however, that we are among those who prove themselves to be faithful and wise servants who are preparing for his coming.

> Even though we speak like this, dear friends, we are confident of better things in your case — things that accompany salvation. God is not unjust; he will not forget your work and the love you have shown him as you have helped his people and continue to help them. We want each of you

to show this same diligence to the very end, in order to make your hope sure. We do not want you to become lazy, but to imitate those who through faith and patience inherit what has been promised. (Hebrews 6:9-13)

Conclusion

The best way for a new Christian to grow in grace is to start out on the right foot: he must start with the basics of the faith and learn them well.

> Like newborn babies, crave pure spiritual milk, so that by it you may grow up in your salvation, now that you have tasted that the Lord is good. (1 Peter 2:2-3)

A baby who gets the right start in life will grow up healthy and strong. A new Christian who opens the Bible and learns the basics of his faith from God will go on to be a useful and profitable servant, a courageous and clever warrior, and an honor to his God.

One of the biggest reasons that so many Christians fail in their lives is that they failed to lay a good foundation at the beginning of their walk of faith. Like trying to cross a bridge that has gaping holes in it, we run the risk of falling through the rotten planks of false doctrines and opinions and traditions that we often trust in. Our lives will dishonor God as a result.

We have tried to pursue what the writer of Hebrews considers "elementary teachings." (Hebrews 6:1) If some of this material looked new, it may be because we weren't careful to fully explore these issues after our conversion. At any rate, this is the minimum that every Christian should know about God, the Bible, God's Kingdom, the world, and himself. Armed with this

Conclusion

knowledge, we are ready to move "on to maturity" (Hebrews 6:1) and tackle bigger issues. We have a Kingdom to help build, Heaven to get ready for, the Enemy to defeat, and God to glorify. So it's time for those who are mature to get started.

www.ingramcontent.com/pod-product-compliance
Lightning Source LLC
Chambersburg PA
CBHW022048160426
43198CB00008B/162